PRAISE FOR
Ellen Evert Hopman

PRIESTESS OF THE FOREST

A fascinating and romantic historical novel rooted in the author's deep knowledge of Celtic Druidism.
> —Isaac Bonewits, Archdruid emeritus of *Ár nDraíocht Féin*
> (A Druid Fellowship) and author of *Neopagan Rites*

From the very beginning I was drawn into this story and found myself mesmerized by it. It is a tale which rings with sincerity, warmth, color, and depth.
> —Philip Carr-Gomm, Chosen Chief of the Order of Bards,
> Ovates and Druids

A lively tale … While set in a richly imagined ancient Ireland, *Priestess of the Forest* offers an intriguing vision of a Druid path with lessons to teach the modern world.
> —John Michael Greer, Grand ArchDruid, Ancient Order of Druids
> in America and author of *Encyclopedia of Natural Magic*

An authentically human tale of love, hope, and survival. I was held captive until the very last page.
> —Christopher A. LaFond, Druid harper and
> professor of languages, Boston College

A beautiful glance back at Pagan culture, Druidic practices and rituals, and daily Celtic life.
> —*Historical Novels Review*

A fast-moving story that quickly drew me [into] the world of Druidic Ireland.
> —*ACTION*, newsletter for the Alternate Religions
> Educational Network

Hopman's ability to incorporate moving and beautiful examples of ritual into the narrative without too much disruption demonstrates a nascent talent for blending historical scholarship, modern practice, and individual inspiration into effective storytelling.

—*Bond of Druids: A Druid Journal*

[A] beautiful expression of [Ethne's] life drenched in the smells and songs of the herbs that are important to her craft.

—The Druid Network, druidnetwork.org

Characters are well developed and genuine ... I highly recommend this book equally to readers who are new to the Celtic tradition as well as those who practice Druidism or related earth-based spirituality.

—*Inner Tapestry Holistic Journal*

A masterfully crafted tale that teaches as well as entertains.

—Magicware Pagan Book Review, magickware.wordpress.com

An edu-tainment treasure that I recommend for any Druid library.

—Mike Gleason, Reformed Druids of North America

Hopman exudes throughout a sense of deep passion and true heart, with an earnest wish to rekindle the once great honour we had for our lands and each other.

—Druidic Dawn, druidicdawn.org

The Druid Isle

While Hopman's research and careful descriptions of Druid rituals, beliefs, and philosophy will be invaluable to those seeking the Druid path, she has succeeded in writing alive, compelling novels that will keep any reader turning page after page, far into the night.

> —Patricia Lee Lewis, founder of
> Patchwork Farm Writing & Yoga Retreats

[A] daring sequel … *The Druid Isle* is a must-have for any serious Druidic library.

> —Michael Scharding, archivist of the Reformed Druids of North America and publisher of *The Druid Inquirer*

A wonderful sequel. The book grabs you right from the start … One of the best features is the small bits of old lore from the Druids scattered throughout. I would definitely recommend this book for anyone's library!

> —Rev. Skip Ellison, Archdruid of Ár nDraíocht Féin (ADF) and author of *Ogham: The Secret Language of the Druids* and *The Solitary Druid: A Practitioner's Guide*

As I read, I realized that I wanted to learn more about this ancient philosophy and about the emergence of modern Druidry.

> —*CIRCLE Magazine*

Priestess of the Fire Temple

Through intriguing characters we encounter sagas of war, love, life, and death, and are expertly introduced to herb lore along with other insights into Druidic knowledge that will whet the appetite for more. Riveting.

> —Carmel Diviney, Bandruí agus Filidh, heritage activist with SaveTara.com and Tara Skryne Preservation Group in Dublin, Ireland

This tale of the spiritual awakening of a young woman, breaking free of the expectations that her ancient society imposes, is a master class in storytelling.

> —Raymond MacSuibhne, Pagan Federation Ireland National Coordinator and lifelong resident of County Cill Dara (Cell Daro), Ireland

Herbal lore, ancient Celtic ways, Druidic secrets, magical workings, and much more are woven into a tale that will touch your heart and grace your life.

> —Susun S. Weed, wise woman, herbalist, and author of *Wise Woman Herbal for the Childbearing Year*

A captivating and fast-paced story that sweeps the reader up in the mystery and turmoil of fifth-century Ireland … The best in the series so far. Definitely a must-read!

> —Morgan Daimler, author of *By Land, Sea, and Sky: A Selection of Re-Paganized Prayers and Charms from the Carmina Gadelica*

Romance, royalty, cattle raids, herbalism, some wonderful poetry...
I felt as if I were living at that time. Thumping good plot, as well as a
"teaching" book. Couldn't put it down!
>   —Jane T. Sibley, Ph.D., author of *The Hammer of the Smith* and
>   *The Divine Thunderbolt: Missile of the Gods*

A treasure-trove of fascinating herbal lore and prayers of old, sure to
delight anyone interested in the old Celtic ways.
>   —Andrew Theitic, editor, The Witches' Almanac, Ltd.

About the Author

Ellen Evert Hopman is a master herbalist and lay homeopath who holds a master's degree in mental health counseling. She is also a certified writing instructor. She was vice president of the Henge of Keltria, an international Druid fellowship, for nine years. She is the founder of the Whiteoak Internet mailing list (an online Druid ethics study group) and is a co-founder and former co-chief of the Order of the Whiteoak (*Ord Na Darach Gile*).

ELLEN EVERT HOPMAN

PRIESTESS OF THE FIRE TEMPLE
A DRUID'S TALE

LLEWELLYN PUBLICATIONS
Woodbury, Minnesota

FIRST EDITION
First Printing, 2012

Cover design by Ellen Lawson
Cover images: leaves, PhotoDisc; Woman, Image Source / PunchStock;
Fire Flower, iStockphoto.com / -M-I-S-H-A-
Map on pages xx–xxi by Jared Blando
Llewellyn is a registered trademark of Llewellyn Worldwide Ltd.

*Cover model used for illustrative purposes only
and may not endorse or represent the book's subject matter.*

*This is a work of fiction. Names, characters, places, and incidents are either the product
of the author's imagination or are used fictitiously, and any resemblance to actual persons
living or dead, events, or locales is entirely coincidental.*

Library of Congress Cataloging-in-Publication Data
Hopman, Ellen Evert.
  Priestess of the fire temple: a Druid's tale / Ellen Evert Hopman.—1st ed.
    p. cm.
  Includes bibliographical references.
  ISBN 978-0-7387-2925-1
  1. Druids and Druidism—Fiction. I. Title.
  PS3608.O6585P75 2012
  813′.6—dc23

                                                                                2011044291

Llewellyn Publications
A Division of Llewellyn Worldwide Ltd.
2143 Wooddale Drive
Woodbury, MN 55125-2989
www.llewellyn.com

Printed in the United States of America

OTHER BOOKS BY
Ellen Evert Hopman

Tree Medicine, Tree Magic
(Phoenix Publishers)

A Druid's Herbal for the Sacred Earth Year
(Inner Traditions / Destiny Books)

Being a Pagan, with Lawrence Bond
(Inner Traditions / Destiny Books)

Walking the World in Wonder: A Children's Herbal
(Healing Arts Press)

Grimoire for the Apprentice Wizard
co-author with Oberon Zell Ravenheart
(New Page Books)

A Druid's Herbal of Sacred Tree Medicine
(Destiny Books)

Priestess of the Forest: A Druid Journey
(Llewellyn)

Scottish Herbs and Fairy Lore
(Pendraig Publishing)

The Druid Isle
(Llewellyn)

CONTENTS

Acknowledgments   xii

Glossary and Pronunciation Guide   xiii

The Characters   xix

Map   xxii

Invocation of the Goddess Brighid   xxv

Prologue   1

part one: A Spark of Flame   5

part two: A Candle in the Wind   73

part three: The Rising Sun   123

part four: Tending the Flame   155

part five: The Goddess's Fiery Eye   185

Epilogue   235

Historical Note   237

Notes   239

Bibliography and Sources   243

Appendix: The Evidence for Female Druids   245

ACKNOWLEDGMENTS

I wish to thank Joyce Sweeney for her constant help, Alexei Kondratiev for his language assistance, and Patricia Lee Lewis for being my chief reader.

Many thanks to the spirits and voices who guide me. May their promptings be of value to the Druids of today.

GLOSSARY
AND
PRONUNCIATION GUIDE

Áine Clí (aw-nyuh KLEE): "ray of brightness"; the goddess in the sun

airslocud noíbu (ers-LOG-uth NWEE-unh): the sacred opening

Albu (Old Irish; AL-uh-buh): Britain

ametis (Old Irish; AH-me-tish): amethyst

ánruth (awn-rooth): a fili who possesses half of the poetic art

ard-ban-Drui (ahrd-vahn-dree): archdruidess

ard-ri (ahrd-ree): high king

ard-rígain (ahrd-ree-ghan): high queen

Armorica (ar-MOH-ree-kah): Brittany

Audacht Morainn: Old Irish law text of advice to kings

báirín breac (BAW-reen brack): yeasted bread speckled with raisins or currants, traditionally served at Samhain with small divinatory tokens inside

ban-Drui, pl. ban-Druid (BAHN-dree): a female Druid

ban-fili (BAHN-FILL-uh): a female poet

ban-liaig (BAHN LEE-igh): a Druid healer specializing in herbal and magical healing and surgery

Beltaine (Bee-Ahl-TIN-Ah): May Day, the first day of summer

bell branch: a Druidic ritual tool made of a branch with nine bells strung upon it; depending on their rank, a Druid carried one of gold, silver, or bronze

béoir (BYEH-wir): beer

bíle (BILL-uh): a sacred tree or a pole symbolizing a tree

Brighid (BREE-ghij): the Triple Goddess of healing and smithcraft, patroness of the Druids and bards, the summer face of nature

Cell Daro (KYELL DAH-ruh): the Church of the Oak

Ceol Side (KYAUL shee-thuh): the song of the goddess Áine that comforts the dying

Cailleach (KAL-yukh): "old woman" and "ancient veiled one," the winter face of nature; goddess of creation, storms, and winter snows; also the last sheaf of the harvest

Caledonia (kah-leh-DO-nee-ah): Scotland

carnyx (car-nix): a wind instrument of the Iron Age Celts, a bronze trumpet

Clíodna (KLEETH-nuh): goddess of the sea, of the Otherworld, and of beauty, who sometimes shapeshifts into a bird

Cristaide, pl. Cristaidi (KREES-tih-thuh): a Christian

cristall glain (Old Irish; modern reconstruction) (KRIS-tul GLAHN): clear crystal

Cú Chulainn (coo-KHULL-in): literally the Hound of Chulainn, also called the Hound of Ulster, the greatest warrior of Northern Ireland

Cuimhnichibh air na daoine bho'n d'thainig sib (Cwiv-knee-cheev air na dheenah vone dawnig shiv): "Remember the people whom you come from" (Old Gaelic saying)

cuirm (KWIR-rum): barley ale

Daoine Sidhe (DEE-nyh SHEE-thuh): people of the Sidhe, people of the fairy mounds

dessel (DYESH-ul): sunwise, in a righthand or clockwise spiral

Drui, pl. Druid (dree or drwee): a Druid

dun (doon): a fort or fortress

Éire (AIR-uh): the island of Ireland, including all five original provinces

Ériu (AIR-yuh): Ireland (Éire in modern Irish)

escra (ASK-ruh): a copper or silver drinking goblet

Emain Ablach (EH-win OW-lukh): the apple isle

Emain Macha (EH-win MAH-kah): the fort of Macha, now known as Navan Fort

fidchell (FEETH-hyell): a chesslike game

fili, pl. filid (FILL-uh): a sacred poet and diviner

filidecht (FILL-ee-thekht): the craft of sacred poet and diviner

fiana (fin-ah): roving bands of warrior-poets

fion (fee-ohn): wine

flaith (flay-v): nobles

Fomorian (fo-more-ian): an uncouth giant from under the sea (Irish mythology) or forces of chaos and blight

Gallia (Latin; GAHL-lea-ah): Gaul

geis, pl. geasa (jesh): a strict obligation or taboo placed on a person

grianan (GREE-uh-nawn): the sunniest place in a building, usually reserved for the women

imbas (Old Irish; IM-mus): poetic inspiration, prophetic vision

In Medon (en-meh-don): the Central Kingdom

Innis nam Druidneach (In-ish nun DRWITH-nyukh): the Druid Isle

Inisfail (in-nish FAHL): an old name for Ireland

Irardacht (ehr-ard-akt): Kingdom of the Eagle, the Northern Kingdom

Ísu (ees-uh): Jesus

lamdia (LAWV-thee-uh): a portable idol

léine (LYEY-nyuh): a type of long shirt worn under a tunic by both men and women

Letha (LYETH-uh): Gaul

liaig (LEE-igh): a Druid healer who specializes in herbal healing, surgery, and magic

Lugnasad (LOO-nuss-uth): the pre-harvest festival of "first fruits" celebrated from the end of July to the second week of August, depending on when the grain is ripe

lúth legha (LOOTH lyegh-uh): reed, aka the physician's strength

Muire, Mwirreh (Moyrah or Mwih-reh): Mary, mother of Ísu

Manannán Mac Lir (man-ah-nan mok-leer): god of the sea; he who opens the gateways between the worlds

Meán Geimhridh (myawn gev-ree): midwinter, winter solstice

mid (meeth): mead

mog, pl. mogae (mohg, mohg-ay): slaves

mo muirne (muh VOOR-nyuh): my beloved

Morrigu (mor-ree-guh): Great Queen, Triple Goddess of battle

Chrissie a.k.a Morgana

Murthracht (muhr-hrakt): the Western Kingdom, the people of the sea

Nechtan Scéne (NYEKH-tawn SKEY-nyuh): the mother of three warriors named Fannell, Foill, and Tuchell

neimheadh (NYEH-veth): a hidden or secret sanctuary, a ritual calendar acted out in the landscape

nemed (neh-med): a sacred enclosure

Nemed (neh-med): sacred class, the highest caste of Celtic society

oenach (EY-nukh): a gathering, a fair, an assembly

Ogum (OH-gum): the pre-Christian Celtic alphabet and sign language

Oirthir (ohr-hehr): the Eastern Kingdom, the people of the sunrise, the people of gold

ollamh (OL-luv): learned professional man such as a lawyer, doctor, judge, etc.

orans (Latin; OH-rans): praying with palms raised

Paganus, pl. Pagani (Latin; pah-GAH-nee): Pagans, non-Christians, literally "country dwellers," ones who worship the Old Gods

púca (POO-kuh): a supernatural horse (sometimes a man or a black dog)

rath (rahv): a ring-fort

reeving: cattle raiding

rígain (REE-ghun): queen

Roma (ro-mah): Rome

Romani (ro-MAH-nee): Romans

Samhain (SAH-vin): festival of the dead and the start of the dark half of the year, known today as Halloween or All Hallows

scathán (skahan): a polished metal mirror

sét (shade): a unit of currency, each coin worth approximately the value of half a cow

shanachie (shan-ah-hee): a historian and storyteller

siabainn (she-bahn): soap

sidhe (SHEE-thuh): a fairy mound

silentum facite (Latin; sil-LEN-tyoom FAH-kee-the): keep quiet (literally "make silence")

slan-lus (SLAWN-luss): plantain

Tempul Daro (TYEM-pul DAH-ruh): Temple of the Oak

torque (tork): a neck ring symbolic of noble status

Torcrad (tor-krahd): the kingdom of the South, the people of the boar

triskell (tris-kell): a triple spiral design worn by Druids, symbolic of the three worlds of land, sea, and sky

tuath (too-uth): country district or tribal area

uisge beatha (iske-baha): sacred water, the Waters of Life, whiskey

the characters

Aífe (aee-fah): former ard-rígain of In Medon

Aislinn (AHSH-linye): from *Aisling*, a supernatural dream or vision, a ban-Drui and the narrator of this tale

Alda (AHL-thuh): a Drui from Murthracht, spouse of Cainleog

Alvinn (AHL- vin): a warrior in Aislinn's retinue

Amlaim (OW-leev): a Drui from Irardacht

Ana (AH-nuh): Aislinn's birth mother

Aoibhgreíne (EEV-grey-nyuh): "ray of sunshine"; a nickname given to Aislinn by her teachers

Artrach O'Ruadán (ARD-rukh oh ROO-uh-thawn): a Drui from the Forest School of In Medon

Bárid (BAW-rith): a Drui from Irardacht

Barra Mac Mel (BAR-ruh MAHK MYEL): father of Aislinn, ard-ri of In Medon

Birog (BIH-rog): a healer from the tuath near the Fire Temple

Bláth (blawth): "flower"; Aislinn's white mare

Bláthnait (BLAWTH-nij): a female Drui from Torcrad

Breachnat (BREKH-nud): concubine of Íobar

Brig Ambue (BREEGH um-MOO-uh): a teacher of law at Cell Daro

Brig Brigu (BREEGH BREE-ghuh): senior ban-Drui of Cell Daro

Cainleog (KAN-lyog): a Drui from Murthracht, spouse of Alda

Canair (KAHN-ir): a female Drui from Torcrad

Caoilfhionn (KWEEL-in): a student of Dálach-gaes and Niamh

Carmac (KAR-vak): a Drui from Oirthir

Caur (kowr): "warrior, hero"; Alvinn's warhorse

Conláed (KON-leyth): the household bard of Íobar's dun

Coreven (KOR-even): a warrior in Aislinn's retinue

Crithid (KREE-thith): gatekeeper at the Fire Temple

Dálach-gaes (DAW-lukh GWEYS): fili to the court of Aislinn's father

Deaglán Mac Íobar (DYEG-lawn MAHK-EE-ver): prince of Irardacht

Deg (dyegh): a student of Dálach-gaes and Niamh

Dunlaing (DUN-ling): a Drui from Oirthir

Eógan (YO-ghun): brother of Aislinn

Ergan (ar-ghan): a child of Dálach-gaes and Niamh

Father Cassius: a Greek priest, abbot of In Medon

Father Cearbhall (KYER-wal): priest to the court of Íobar

Father Justan: a monk from Armorica, originally from Inissi Leuca
  (Gaulish, "island of light")

Fer Fí (FAER-FEE): Spirit of Yew, the goddess Áine's dwarf
  red-haired brother

Finnlug (fin-lug): a warrior, son of Canair

Garbhán (GAR-vawn): a warrior, son of Canair

Imar (IV-ar): a Drui from Irardacht

Íobar (EEV-ar): father of Deaglán, ard-ri of Irardacht

Ita (EE-duh): a female fili from Torcrad

Lasar (LAS-sar): "flame"; Coreven's red horse

Lovic (low-vick): king of a petty kingdom south of Irardacht

Lucius: former ard-ri of In Medon

Nessa (neh-sah): a ban-Drui of Cell Daro

Niamh (neev): wife of Dálach-gaes and ban-fili in the court of
  Aislinn's father

Roin (Row-in): son of Lovic

Róisín (ROSH-een): nursemaid of Aislinn

Siofra (SHEEF-ruh): fianceé of Eógan

Siobhan (shee-von): a pregnant woman from the tuath near the Fire Temple

Slaine (SLAW-nyuh): a child of Dálach-gaes and Niamh

Tuilelaith (twil-uh-lith): Aislinn's mother, wife of Barra Mac Mel

Úna (OO-nuh): a kitchen maid

N

S

Innis nan Druidneach
(Innis Ibrach)

Irardacht

Ériu

Murthracht

Temple of
Meán Geimhridh

In Medon

Oirthir

The Forest
House

The Fire
Temple

Torcrad

Albu
(Brittania)

Kernow
(Cornubia)

Ictis Insula

Inissi
Leuca

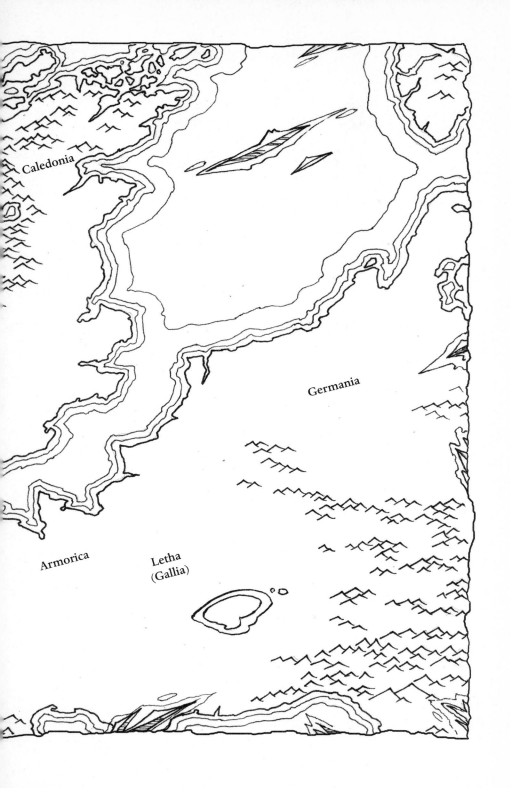

A Brigit, a ban-dé beannachtach
Tair isna huisciu noiba
A ben inna téora tented tréna
Isin cherdchai
Isin choiriu
Ocus isin chiunn
No-don-cossain
Cossain inna túatha.

O Brighid, blessed goddess
Come into the sacred waters
O woman of the three strong fires
In the forge
In the cauldron
In the head
Protect us
Protect the people.

Invocation of the Goddess Brighid
by Ellen Evert Hopman;
Old Irish translation by Alexei Kondratiev

prologue

"I hope you don't mind if I call you Sister," I said to the neophyte priestess, pulling my hand from under the worn goose-down coverlet and gesturing with a finger towards her face. My hand was as light as a newborn chick, its skin so transparent I could easily trace the bones and veins beneath.

She was two generations younger than I, and a slight shock registered on her face as I made the suggestion.

The rains of winter had set in, and a damp breeze seeped through the bare stone walls, guttering the candles and making the hearth-fire dance. My eyes were dimmer than they ever had been, but my body still thrummed with unseen energies.

"Let me tell you how it was," I declared again firmly, meaning the words as a command.

I was always teaching, ever anxious to pass along the old ways; the gods would not permit me to do otherwise. The girl was charged with my care, and we still had the long season of dark before us and not much entertainment, so it seemed a good time for a tale.

"Certainly, my lady." She leaned forward to adjust the coverlet over my frail bones as I began my story with an old saying: *"Trí ní is deacair a thuiscint: intleacht na mban, obair na mbeach, teacht agus imeacht na taoide.* Three things hardest to understand: the intellect of women, the work of the bees, the coming and going of the tide.

"That was a favorite saying of the Bríg Brigu, the one who initiated me into the teachings of the Fire Temple. What I am about to tell you now is a great mystery, and I hope that you will cherish the words…"

part one

A Spark of Flame

1

I was but fourteen years old and had not yet reached the end of my growing, and I could still wend my way around the warriors unseen if I kept my head down and minded the mud. The ladies were always too preoccupied to notice me; they were busy comparing their hairstyles, jewels, and dresses. Everyone wore their finest to the oenach, the great harvest fair on the grassy sward outside of the high king's rath.

There were a dizzying number of activities at festival time, when the usually quiet lawns outside of the dun were given over to horseracing, musical and poetry competitions, storytelling, proclamations of new laws and contracts, and a loud marketplace where vendors from all the provinces came to sell their handicrafts and produce. Since it was a royal fair, there were many imported items from the southlands; folks eagerly awaited the arrival of the new styles from Letha and Armorica, foreign kingdoms to the south from which exotic new styles and goods were brought to us by ship and then by great trains of horses and carts.

My father was everywhere, greeting visitors, joining in the fighting competitions, and awarding prizes. My mother, Tuilelaith, was also there, of course, but I hardly saw her. Her time at the oenach was spent absorbing the news of the noble families and cultivating the wives of the flaith—anything to advance my father's interests.

"The quickest way to get a man to do something is by pillow talk," she would say, for once she had convinced a noble lady of some cause of hers, the lady would take the message home and whisper the queen's desire into her husband's ear at night.

My mother was far too busy for someone as insignificant as me. Summer and winter she was preoccupied with refurbishing the round-houses of the rath. She loved to commission new furniture and woven hangings for the walls, when she wasn't knocking them down. She liked to expand her dwellings—"To let the sun in," as she would say. Everyone thought she was terribly extravagant, the way she insisted on large window openings covered with thin sheepskins that let in the light. The windows caused a terrible draft and meant that great logs had to be burned in the hearths in every season.

My father indulged her extravagance; in truth, I think he was a little afraid of her. She came from a noble family of Letha and constantly reminded my father that she was somehow superior to him. I don't know why he accepted that so readily, seeing as he was the ard-ri, but he did. He would quench his temper in cups of mid and then take it out the next morning on the warriors at practice rather than confront her. He liked a peaceful household, no matter the cost.

I think my father thought that all women were somehow superior. Or perhaps it was my mother's ankle-length hair the color of winter wheat that held him in its spell. My father's clan were dark haired, and she stood out amongst them like an exotic flower.

As for myself, I was a constant disappointment. My mother would have liked a daughter with carefully plaited hair and trimmed finger-nails and eyebrows blushing with the black juice of elderberries—a daughter she could dress in costly imported silks and furs. Instead she got me.

She did her best to ignore me, as if I were no relation of hers; I think she found me an embarrassment. But she always gave her full atten-tion to my brother, Eógan, who would likely inherit the throne. She liked to oversee his dressing and made sure he had golden earrings and circlets of gold on his arms and fingers whenever he went outside of the rath.

My mother measured out her affections carefully, calculating the potential value of each recipient.

"Only those with a great dun and many cattle are worth knowing," she would say.

Hidden behind her words was the implication that since I didn't have dun or cattle, I was not yet worthy of her esteem.

The only exceptions to her rules for affection were her cats. She kept a small tribe of them, seeing them as her true children and also as gorgeous works of art.

"See how they always choose the pillow of the exact shade to complement their beauty?" she would remark.

My brother and I hated those cats. I blush to tell you that we would swat them when she wasn't looking. Of course they would run off before we could do any real damage, and in later years I had several cats that were as children to me; some I loved even more than people.

From the time I could walk I delighted in being out of doors, collecting butterfly wings and cristall glain, the white quartz pebbles that the Druid call fairy stones. I thought that if I carried them around with me, sooner or later I would hear a voice or see a fairy. Eventually I did both, of course.

My clothes were ever smeared with dirt and the juice of wild berries. My nurse, Róisín, thought it particularly disgraceful that I ate berries from the hedgerows.

"Those belong to the fairies!" she would say with an expression of disgust.

As a child I was passionate about the subject of fairies. As you know, there are many different kinds of fairies to be felt, heard, and seen. Some of them live in trees, some in the water, and others live in great hives underground, led by their fairy queen. Some say they are creatures of fire and air. The Cristaidi say that they are "fallen angels" who tumbled to earth from the sky world called heaven and are now forced to live underground. But I can feel them everywhere.

I learned the many ways to attract the fairies; for example, by their love of shiny objects. My teachers told me to make a habit of carrying cristall glain and also ametis, the purple stone of the fairies, as a way to develop my inner sight. They said that any white stone belonged to the fairies, and I would set out such stones in a tiny circle on the forest floor to draw the fairies to me and bury them in a ring around my fairy altar.

My altar was a simple tree stump surrounded by foxglove and evening primrose flowers. I would pop the evening primrose blossoms and leaves right into my mouth in the summer and harvest the roots and seeds in the fall. The roots were simmered and eaten with butter; the seeds were sprinkled on porridge or added to bread dough. My teachers said that they were an aid to developing the Sight when eaten. But I never ate the foxglove leaves or flowers, because—as you know— that plant is a powerful medicine that will poison those who disrespect it or use it without knowledge.

It is said that the fairies gave that plant to the foxes so they would have little gloves on their feet to hunt silently.

My teachers were very insistent that the fairies and the land spirits had to be kept happy in order for the animals, crops, and tribes to prosper. I would pocket bits of bread and cheese for them at supper and bring sweets to my fairy altar on feast days. The mogae and free farmers showed respect for the good folk in their own way; every garden and field had a small corner set aside for their exclusive enjoyment, where no human would dare to tread.

I learned that the fairies love music of any kind. Often I would sit by a tree or pond and play my wooden flute for them. I had a bell branch too, nine tinkling bells affixed to an ash wand. Sometimes I would walk through the woods just shaking the branch for their pleasure.

At times I could hear them singing in a perfect three-part harmony in their own ancient language. I noticed that if I sang a song for them or if the household bard was outside singing, the fairies would quickly pick up the tune and weave it into a complicated harmony for their own enjoyment. I concluded that their singing was what caused the plants and trees to grow; it was as if they were weaving the forests, fields, and gardens into being with their songs.

I was especially thrilled when I found a fairy ring, a circle of mushrooms growing on the grass or on the forest floor. When I found one I would dance around the circle counterclockwise, because moving in that direction dissolves the barriers between the worlds. Sometimes I would step right into the ring, but I always leapt out quickly, because everyone knows that if you linger inside a fairy ring, you might be taken for seven years.

I learned that where oak and ash and hawthorn grow together is a good place to find fairies. Other such places are where two streams meet and at the edge of a pond or lake. Waterfalls and the black shore—the edge of sand between the line of seaweed and the sea—are all liminal places that are "betwixt and between" and thus likely spots for fairy sightings.

Dusk and dawn are the best times of day to encounter them, because those times are between night and daylight, neither one nor the other. I could always sense the fairies' presence because a sudden smell of flowers would envelop me. That was how I knew they were near.

My teachers gave me a holey stone, one that they had found by the sea, with a natural hole in it. They taught me to gaze through it to see the past and future and the land of the fairies. They also taught me to meditate and to focus on my third eye, the point of energy between my brows, and then slightly open my eyes. That was a great aid to seeing the fairies and other spirits.

One reason I finally learned to love my mother's cats was because I was taught to follow them around and sit where they sat. There was a stretch of lawn outside my mother's roundhouse that was surrounded by fruit trees and flowers. It seemed a very peaceful place, and Tuilelaith would often go there to sit on a wooden bench in the sun to calm herself after a trying day at court.

One time I followed a white cat out onto the lawn and noticed where she sat. When the cat got up to leave, I sat down in the exact same spot, facing the same direction the cat had faced. Much to my surprise I could feel intense activity all around me, even though there were no people or animals to be seen. When I closed my eyes and then reopened them just a bit, I clearly saw four golden pathways stretching in front, behind, and to the sides of me. I sensed that I was sitting at the crossroads of a busy fairy highway, and I could even see the evidence of tiny footsteps in the grass. Yet when I opened my eyes wide and focused on the grass, there was nothing there.

There was a whole other class of creature that lived inside of our roundhouses and barns. The dairy maids were forever weaving little wreaths of milkwort, butterwort, dandelion, or marigold, and binding them with a cord of ivy or red thread, placing them under the milk pails to prevent the milk from being stolen by the fairies or charmed away by evil spirits. And they never failed to pour a bit of each day's first milking onto the brownie stone near the barn. It was well known that the failure to make the milk offering would result in sickness for the cattle.

In the kitchens the cooks would bank and smoor the fires at night and then leave the bread dough to rise on the warm stones of the hearth. Usually the dough would have risen by morning, but if it didn't they would blame the fairies. Sometimes things in the kitchen kept disappearing and then reappearing in the most unlikely places. Then the cooks would have to make offerings at their own fairy altar, a small wooden affair hidden in a corner of the kitchen, to placate the house spirits.

I hope that I do not bore you when I tell you these things. Because they are the same things that everyone learns about the spirit realm— part of every person's basic education.

Mainly I was taught by the Druid to have great respect for the land spirits and the fairies, to develop my relationship with them and to do everything in my power to keep them happy. But I would never mention them in the presence of the Cristaidi for fear of causing offense. In Cristaidi times the fairies were not to be spoken of, as if they no longer existed. But everyone knew they were still there.

My nurse, Róisín, was short, plump, and very proper. She had no children of her own and as a result was devoted to me with a deep and abiding love. Her léine and tunic were always covered with a neat white apron that she would change if she ever got a spot on it, and she was forever handing her shoes to the mogae so they could scrape off the mud. Her hair was braided into two tight brown coils and always pinned neatly behind her ears.

She said that the wild berries I was always picking belonged to the fairies. Somehow the berries growing in the carefully tended gardens inside the rath were the only acceptable fare, and then only if handed to me on a plate.

My own red hair hung loose down my shoulders, and I almost never stopped to look at my reflection in a burnished metal scathán or I, too, might have been shamed by my looks.

Unbeknownst to me, the day of my fourteenth oenach was to be something very different. Róisín found me in the byre that was reserved for the sick cows, and I remember that a huge bullock was hanging upside down over a pit while men were doing something to its hooves. I was fascinated by the spectacle, and I am sure I was ankle-deep in straw and manure because I recall that Róisín screamed out loud when she saw me. She pulled me out of the byre and shoved me towards my sleeping house, loudly ordering a hot bath and clean clothes from the mogae.

Once she had me scrubbed, dried, and scented with lavender, she selected a léine and tunic the color of sky and sea, with a matching wool shoulder cloak that she said complemented my hair, and helped me dress. When she had my hair plaited and golden ornaments tied onto the braids (she always made tight braids that hurt—the reason I wanted to wear my hair loose), she shoved me roughly against a wall.

"You have to get married! This is no time for you to be wandering into cow sheds and around the countryside like a beggar. Your father wishes to speak with you about it this evening, before the feast!" Her fingers jabbed into my shoulder for emphasis as she uttered each word.

I recall that I was speechless. Róisín had never been that rough with me, and the whole concept was so foreign that I did not know how to frame my thoughts. I thought marriage was only for great ladies like my mother, never for the likes of me. I hadn't even begun to bleed yet. I knew I wasn't ready.

2

My father, Barra Mac Mell, had a rath of the usual sort, a large, round-walled wooden palisade surrounded by an earthen bank and a ditch that was filled with water except during the driest season. Perched high on a hill, it had a commanding view of every direction.

Inside its walls were stone roundhouses with their cone-shaped thatched roofs of willow rods. My mother and father had their own sleeping houses, of course—one for each of them and their retainers—and my brother and I had our own private houses as well. There were the usual guesthouses and roundhouses for the mogae, the warriors, and the craftsfolk and farmers who served the rath.

Old Father Justan was given his own roundhouse within the dun, but he seemed to spend most of his time in a little stone cell outside of the walls. He had come to us before I was born, all the way from Inissi Leuca in Armorica. He had white hair and a toothy grin and was very humble. We all liked him. Apparently there was some kind of scandal attached to him because of his beliefs, and that was the reason he had set out on a pilgrimage to the north and eventually found us and settled in our tuath.

Father Justan was a great scholar and a follower of Pelagius, the "heretic monk" from Albu who taught that all people were sacred, created by God, and thus able to save themselves by their own free will.

Pelagius denied the idea of original sin and believed that every person had the natural capacity to live a holy life, and for that reason he was despised by the other Cristaidi. They insisted, as they still do, that we have to have a priest to absolve us from our original sin.

"If the people don't go to the priests, then the church can't collect any tithes, but any Cristaide can hear the confession of any other in the sight of God," Father Justan would say.

Everyone liked to go to Father Justan for confession. He always ended by giving you a hug or an apple or some other dried fruits that he had in store. Father Justan saw the sacred in everything: the trees, the river, the plants and animals, and in all people.

"In every person I see and in everything I experience, there is a gift from divine grace. Everything comes from God; thus, the whole world is sacred to me. It's all thread of the same cloth, woven by divine providence. My little hazel bush and my stream are all the church I need."

In that way he was very like the Druid.

Sometimes the other Cristaidi would come to his hut for a visit, and they always left angry. They could never bend Father Justan to their way of thinking.

We also had small roundhouses and a private enclosure for my teachers, our filid, Dálach-gaes and Niamh, well hidden behind a thick screen of yew. My mother felt that having houses and a nemed dedicated to the old religion within the grounds lowered our status in the eyes of guests, so she tried her best to keep them hidden from view. But Father felt differently; his views were ever the opposite of hers.

My father made a great show of hospitality towards Father Justan and the Cristaidi to keep the peace, but in his heart he still honored the old ways. I know this because shortly before he died he asked for a Pagani funeral to the shock and surprise of everyone, including me. I will tell you all about that later.

It is common knowledge that a king without a poet to praise him is a poor king, so Dálach-gaes was one of the most important figures at court in the eyes of my father. Dálach-gaes and Niamh were both tall, blond, and blue eyed, and like my mother they stood out in any gathering. It was immediately obvious that they were strangers to In Medon, the central kingdom of the island that was under the rulership and protection of my father. Some even thought they must be visitors from the Daoine Sidhe realm, with their long blond hair and regal bearing.

Besides their own house, Dálach-gaes and Niamh kept a separate hut for their children and a larger roundhouse for their students, who labored long into the night, composing their poems in the dark.

Dálach-gaes and Niamh's children studied the arts of filidecht under the guidance of their parents, alongside the other students, who came for instruction from distant tuaths. I learned to read and write my Ogum and my Greek and Latin letters at their side and also received the teachings of the fili, though I never reached the full status of an ánruth, with 175 compositions and an honor price of twenty séts. No one really expected me to make my living as a poet.

These were the only children in the rath that my father thought worthy for me to spend time with, because they came from one of the oldest families of hereditary poets. But they were such solemn and quiet creatures that we often had a hard time finding common interests. They always seemed to be tired, having been kept up late into the night memorizing genealogies and sacred stories and incubating poems.

Dálach-gaes and Niamh had a nickname for me: Aoibhgreíne. Compared to their sober offspring, I must have burst into their private enclosure like a ray of sunshine with my red hair and wild ways as I sporadically came and went from their school to attend the Druid rites and helped gather and apply the healing worts.

I first appeared at the gates of the nemed when I was just four years old. I can still remember the day because it was my father who brought me there. I remember that we walked across the open space of the dun together and that he held my hand. It was such a rare thing to have my father all to myself that it stood out in my mind as a very special day ever after. I am not sure why we went at that particular time. I think it was a kind of testing, to see if I had the wit to study the poetic arts.

When I saw the ritual space, the very first words out of my mouth were "What is a Drui?"

I remember that Dálach-gaes seemed impressed by the question. I liked him immediately because he crouched down to match my height and spoke to me seriously, as if I were his equal.

He replied, "That is a very good question, and one that will take a long time to answer. For now I will tell you this: a Drui is an oak-wise person, one who carries the oak wisdom in their head and their heart."

I had no idea what that meant. "Why is a Drui like an oak?" I asked.

Dálach-gaes smiled and answered, "On the spiritual plane, an oak is the one who attracts lightning—the attention of the gods—and lives to tell the tale. An oak-knower lives like that. She is one who is like a great tree that gives wood and shade, fruits, flowers, nuts, and medicines to the people, even when they cut off her branches. She bears rain storms, snow, and sun with equal grace. She has her roots deeply and firmly in the ground and her head high in the highest clouds.

"Each time you see an acorn, let it remind you of this truth, for a mighty oak tree is hidden inside of every acorn."

Then he reached into a leather pouch that hung from his belt, pulled out an acorn, and handed it to me.

"This is for you to keep, so that you won't forget what I have told you."

That acorn was as precious to me as any jewel, and I carried it with me for many years thereafter.

I was immediately accepted at the Druid school, and my education began within days. Niamh was the one who taught me wortcunning, which was never a formal training. She would simply announce that it was time to gather a certain root, bark, or berry, and we would be off to the fields or the forest with baskets on our arms. "You have a certain window of opportunity to gather the medicines," she would say. "If, in a certain year, we are too late for the harvest or if we somehow forget when something is ready, it could spell disaster, because it will be an entire sun cycle before the medicine is available for harvest again."

I soon learned that an important part of being a Drui was to pay attention to the cycles of the land, to be aware of everything, and to forget nothing.

There were certain herbs that we had to be sure to gather every year without fail. Comfrey was easy because it grew in the garden, and every winter we had fat bunches of the hairy leaves hanging near the hearth to dry for the poulticing of wounds and fractures. Loose-strife was another staple that we brought in without fail from the bogs. There were bunches of purple heather tips, gathered just as they came into bloom, for the cough and to help us sleep, and the inner barks of apple and oak for lung fevers. And there was always reed, the mainstay of every healer's art. We waded deep into the ponds each summer to cut the freshest roots and leaves.

Niamh was a granddaughter of Lucius and Aífe, the former ard-ri and ard-rígain of In Medon. Her mother had been among the last to receive Druid training on Innis nam Druidneach, the sacred island of the Druid off the coast of Caledonia. That was before it was taken over by the Cristaidi, of course.

The Cristaidi had their own village not far from our fort, where they lived with their families in their beehive stone huts and celebrated Mass in their little stone chapel that was shaped like an overturned coracle. They kept to themselves and only came by to pester Father Justan and try to convert him to their philosophy.

We had our own small stone chapel inside the rath where I and my family attended Mass regularly, but I never understood why we had to worship indoors. If God created the whole world and the heavens, then why not celebrate outside, in the free air under God's sun, moon, and trees?

Our chapel was built under an ancient ash tree that had once marked the sacred center of a Druid enclosure. People still left gifts under the tree, such as honey, cider, cheese, and apples, to show respect for the ancestral spirits. My mother thought the gifts were an eyesore, but father gave strict orders that the offerings were not to be disturbed. Dálach-gaes would collect them after a few days and take them to the nemed to drop them into the votive pit. He said it was very bad luck to eat food that had been left out as a gift for the spirits.

Father Justan said Mass for us, and looking back I realize that I had a most unusual education, steeped as I was in the teachings of the Pagani Druid and the Cristaidi all at once. As Niamh liked to tell me, "The best honey comes from bees that feed from different flowers."

But the pride of my father's rath was its great mead hall. It was long and narrow—so long that there were four fire pits down the center of the building, with two rows of six roof trees to either side of the hearths. There were great iron hooks on the walls so that the warriors could hang their shields on one side and the flaith could hang their shields on the other—twenty hooks on either side. My father's imposing ashwood throne presided at the far end on an elevated platform.

The walls of the hall were lavishly carved with complicated interlace patterns and strange beasts and foliage of many kinds. My mother was ever making the mogae polish the wood until it gleamed. The tops of the walls were painted in bright colors that the mogae had to wash and repaint frequently because of the constant wood smoke. It took a dozen servants just to keep the wrought-iron sconces on the roof trees oiled against the damp.

My mother arranged the menus for the feasts. There were always three kinds of meat—deer, oxen, and boar—that were cooked outside in deep pits. My father made sure that sheep, chickens, and fish were roasted separately for the free farmers and the mogae; he was ever mindful of the political value of hospitality.

From Letha, Mother would order huge casks of fion, a drink she considered more elegant than the local béoir. She must have been right, because the flaith and the warriors couldn't seem to get enough of it, and it made her a popular hostess.

The evening of the oenach feast was clear and dry, and there were bright stars and an enormous full moon. The high feast was always timed for maximum moonlight so that everyone could travel to and from it with ease. As the enticing smells of roasting meats and freshly baked breads mingled with the wood smoke from the cooking pits and torches, everyone assembled outside of the mead hall to await the carnyx that would summon us inside.

Looking up, I could see the glow of distant bonfires dotting the hills; the Pagani were celebrating in the old way on the mountaintops. I guessed that Dálach-gaes would be up there with Niamh and their children and students, and I longed to be with them, as I had been in years past.

In former years we had walked together to a nearby hill in the dark, and at dawn we circled the hill seven times sunwise. Then, bearing a large cristall glain and a sheaf of the new grain, we would climb the hill and leave those on the top as a thanks-offering to the land spirits. Then we'd spend the rest of the day playing games on the hillside and feasting on pig's feet, mutton, bannocks and honey, béoir, and the purple whortleberries that we gathered in our willow baskets.

Dálach-gaes, Niamh, and the older students would pair off and disappear into the whortleberry bushes from time to time to enjoy the sun and each other's company. I could hear them murmuring soft endearments and laughing softly. It was always a jolly time, and I missed it sorely.

Róisín watched me, following my gaze towards the hills as if she could read my thoughts.

"That's no place for you now, my lady. You are nearly a woman grown this summer, and it is time for you to take your proper part in the high feasts at the side of your brother and your parents."

I am quite sure I made a face because she gave me a look of despair, as if to say that in her opinion I would never really be up to the task.

The crowd parted as a warrior approached us from inside the mead hall.

"Lady Aislinn, the ard-ri desires to speak with you before the guests enter. He wants you to come in alone."

Then he offered his arm to help me negotiate my way through the crowd. I left Róisín to the swirl of guests outside the door.

As I stepped into the hall, I took in my mother's impressive decorations: corn dollies made from churn staffs and sheaves of new grain hung gaily from the rafters as if they were flying overhead, and large loaves made from freshly ground flour were placed in neat lines down the center of each table. There were thick bouquets of red field poppies and trailing bunches of ivy spilling from gaily painted pottery vases ranged between the bread loaves.

The last sheaf of my father's grain harvest held the place of honor, dressed in woman's clothing and propped against one side of the throne as if the Grain Goddess herself were lending strength and blessings to his reign. A pair of wolfhounds sporting wide red leather collars had been freshly washed and combed and now lolled companionably on the other side of the throne. They were huge and confident and barely looked up as I approached.

It was strange to be having a private audience with my father, who had taken so little notice of me throughout the years because he was often away on battle campaigns for months at a time, or busy conferring with his warriors. But as he fixed his gaze on me alone, his eyes looking deeply into mine, it was as if he saw me for the very first time that day.

"How is the oenach going for you this year?" he asked, leaning forward with interest.

"It goes well for me, Father," I said as I curtsied out of respect.

I didn't dare tell him that I would have preferred to be dancing around the hilltop fires with the Pagani, though knowing what I know now, I doubt he would have minded.

"You are fourteen summers old and a mostly grown woman," he said, appraising my body and form as if I were a stranger. I thought it odd that a father should know so little of his child; Dálach-gaes, Niamh, Róisín, and even Father Justan had watched me grow and knew me far better than either of my parents did.

"I have found a husband for you, a prince from Irardacht. Your union will bind our kingdoms and help us to keep the peace. Their tribesfolk are ever stealing cattle from our tuaths on the border, and we must do everything we can to stop it. This reeving has caused far too much bloodshed and loss of life. Íobar, the ard-ri of Irardacht, has agreed to this union, and the young man is here now. His name is Deaglán." He gestured towards a dark corner of the hall.

It was only then that I noticed a movement in the shadows as a tall figure stepped into a pool of torchlight. That was how I caught my first glimpse of Deaglán.

His long black hair was plaited into thick braids, and he had a blue mantle of some soft fabric thrown over one shoulder. His scarlet léine and tunic were edged in embroidery done with gold and silver thread, and his leather trousers were strapped at the ankles with silver cloth and laced up the sides with leather strings tipped in bright bronze. He had a thick golden torque to show his status, as if anyone could fail to notice. His eyes were dark and lustrous, but he seemed to see right through me—as if I wasn't really there, as if his mind were occupied by other, more important things.

I was so young and inexperienced then. I was easily taken in by all that splendor.

Three more men stepped out of the shadows. I recognized them as men who served my father—the marshal who kept order and supervised the seating, the carnyx player who would sound three times to let the guests know when to enter, and, much to my surprise, Dálach-gaes. I should have realized that he would be acting as shanachie for the gathering.

"Dálach-gaes, I need praise poems from you this evening that will impress my guests, but more than that I need them to work magic. Íobar must know what a prize he is getting by uniting his son with my daughter."

Now Deaglán finally began paying attention, looking anxious and vexed by turns. I am sure he was very disappointed to be getting such a young and inexperienced wife, someone he would be forced to spend his life with whether he desired me or not. He was, after all, an already seasoned warrior, and I was still a girl.

I was too inexperienced in the ways of love between the sexes to feel anything other than the strangeness of being the center of everyone's attention. Father instructed Deaglán and me to sit beside him at the high table that was set up before the throne. It was an honor to be seated next to the king and a huge responsibility, as I knew. Every third drinking horn had to be passed directly to him, and women were almost never seated at the high table. Even my mother was expected to sit with the ladies of the flaith.

The carnyx sounded the first blast, and the lesser kings from the surrounding tuaths, the ollamhs and their wives, began to enter. Even though they were people of rank, they all removed their shoes at the entrance. They were followed closely by their shield bearers, who presented their shields to the marshal and were then guided by the shanachie to hang the shields in order of rank, the highest ranking placed closest to the throne.

Another carnyx blast and the shield bearers of the warriors presented their shields, which were hung in order of rank after much careful deliberation between the marshal and the shanachie. Any perceived insult to a warrior could have nasty consequences, and so extreme care was given to their seating.

A final blast from the carnyx signaled the remaining guests to enter and remove their shoes. These guests were placed farthest from the high table, carefully seated a sword's-length apart, each under his own shield. No one sat opposite, and everyone sat side by side, with his back to the wall, for added security.

Father Justan, as usual, was nowhere to be found. He avoided these occasions of state as often as he could.

The light of the four hearths and of the many torches in their ironwork sconces sparkled and shone, reflected and magnified by the polished silver and bronze of the shields and the gold jewelry of the guests, and by the copper, silver, and polished wood plates and drinking goblets that filled the tables. The hall was suffused with a warm orange glow.

Once the lords, warriors, and wives were settled, Dálach-gaes stepped forward into a pool of light to deliver the praise poems, and the ripples of conversation gradually died down.

Welcome to the court of Barra Mac Mel
Who is famed for victory in battle
For protecting his borders
And for devotion to the gods of his people.
Who is famed for patronage of music
of poetry and scholarship
of games and competitions
and of fidchell.
Who is famed for chasing and bringing down
the noble boar and the deer.
A fearless defender of the faith.

I remember that Dálach-gaes did not say precisely *which* faith.

Then Dálach-gaes turned to Deaglán, made a small bow, and faced the audience once more.

Today you are also made welcome
By Prince Deaglán Mac Íobar
Son of the ard-ri of Irardacht
Famed for reddening of swords
For defending his borders
For hunting the red deer and boar
For racing of chariots
For hunting with hawks
And a patron of wizards.

It was well known that Irardacht was a mystical kingdom. For untold generations the Druid had come and gone from its shores to Innis nan Druidneach, so it seemed poetic to add the last bit about wizards. Dálach-gaes had no idea how Deaglán felt about wizards, but he knew that a poet could as easily blight a reputation as create one, so he sought to make the prince look as exceptional as possible in the eyes of everyone.

Lastly, he turned to me with a look of mingled pride and pity. That was the first inkling I had that my fate would be difficult.

You are made welcome as well
By my lady Aislinn of the red hair
And the blushing cheeks.
She who is learned and pure
Reverent and wise
Who knows her letters
Who is deft with a needle
Who has learned the healing herbs and grasses
And the birds and creatures of the forest
Both the seen and the unseen ones
And all the duties of a lady of the court.

Dálach-gaes made an especially low bow that was designed to enhance my status but only embarrassed me; I felt that my teacher had no business bowing before me like that. It must have strained his poetic imagination to heap such praise on such a young and unaccomplished child, but apparently the poem worked.

I recall that the ladies of the court strained their necks to look at me then, and Róisín, who was seated in a corner, began to sob audibly, which only added to the drama of the moment. My mother, who was seated with the other ladies, craned her neck towards me with an expression of disbelief. I am sure it came as a shock to see her incorrigible daughter being shown such honor in a public setting.

"Honored guests, today we celebrate the Lugnasad feast and an added joyful occasion. Today I pass the marriage cup to my daughter, Aislinn, and to her intended husband, Deaglán."

My father rose as he spoke, ceremoniously handing Deaglán a silver goblet. Deaglán took a swallow and then handed the goblet to me. I took a sip. It was as simple as that.

The world of my childhood melted away like the mist on a lake at sunrise.

3

The next morning my husband and lord was nowhere to be found. I had spent the night alone, waiting for him until I fell asleep. I had a vague idea that he had taken up with a newly widowed lady at the feast. I remember that she was very beautiful, and that her long dark hair was ornamented with silver combs. She wore a blood-red gown that perfectly set off her pale skin, and her eyebrows, mouth, and fingernails were stained crimson with elderberry juice, which made her all the more dazzling to behold. I felt wholly inadequate compared to such a graceful creature—small and dowdy by comparison. She was as gorgeous as a peacock while I was just a little brown quail.

My head was still swimming from too many cups of fíon, but I dimly recalled that I had swooned the night before and that someone had carried me to my bed. The next thing I knew, Róisín was pulling my very best léine over my upstretched arms, and I was being handed a mug of spring water and a bowl of hot oatmeal gruel with butter, chopped dandelion roots and leaves, and cracked hazelnuts mixed in.

"That's the best thing for your head," Róisín said, biting off each word.

At first I thought she was angry with me, but then I noticed that she was fighting back tears.

"Why so glum, Róisín?" I asked. "Aren't you happy for me?"

Her only answer was to pack more furiously, finally resorting to sitting on my carved wooden chest to close it, stuffed as it was with more than one of every possible article I might need in my new life. At last she stopped and looked me full in the face.

"Your mother should be doing this. It's a disgrace. You are too young!"

And then she walked over and gave me a hug.

By mid-morning all my possessions were packed into a small cart, and I was lifted on top like so much baggage. The cart was positioned in the middle of a long retinue of pack horses, warriors, and wagons bearing gifts for the king of Irardacht.

Dálach-gaes, Niamh, and the children pushed their way through the horses and riders to bid me goodbye.

"Remember that you are yet only half a sage," Dálach-gaes was saying, though my ears could hardly take in his words through the general din. "Don't get ahead of yourself, but don't forget our teachings either!"

Then, as if he was trying to cram one last morsel of poetic knowledge into my head, he began to recite from the law of poets.

"Excellence is more venerable than age, youth takes precedence over the dotage of old age, spring is more sheltering than a tempest… Stay calm, and never doubt yourself or your abilities!"

Father Justan elbowed past the warriors to thrust a tiny carved crucifix into my hands. Hanging from a leather thong, it was a Cristaide cross imposed upon the round sun symbol of the Druid.

"Bless the land where you now go, bless the things that you shall see, bless the journey you undertake, bless the earth whereon your feet tread. The King of Glory blesses you."

There were tears in his eyes as he uttered those words, and his hand shook as he raised his three fingers to make the blessing over me.

"*Cuimhnichibh air na daoine bho'n d'thainig sib*. Remember the people from whom you come," Niamh added, handing me a cloth-wrapped bundle of cracked hazelnuts and dried apple slices for the journey. I could feel the love she had put into the gesture; she must have been up long into the night picking out the sweet kernels for my enjoyment.

My years of study rushed in on me as I surveyed them, my teachers, the people I loved. What exactly had it all been for? Why the endless hours of practice within the nemed, struggling to attain the level of a "flame" and then a "splendid flame"? Of what possible use were these labors to me now, bound as I was to a new husband and foreign tribe?

And what of Father Justan's teachings? Many were the days I had sat with him on the grass before his tiny stone roundhouse asking about the new god called Ísu. I never completely understood his dedication to just one god, nor his unwillingness to honor goddesses, though he did seem to feel a special reverence for the mother of God, whom he called Muire.

"If God has a mother, then shouldn't she be the one we pray to?" I had asked, thinking that the elder goddess deserved more respect than her young son.

"We love him best because he loved us first" he replied.

Deaglán finally appeared with the lady in red still clinging to his arm. He kissed her full on the lips in the sight of everyone and then mounted his nervously prancing white horse that was being steadied by a retainer. And then we were off.

They say that men who leave home to seek adventures are special heroes. But every woman who has ever left the familiar home of her birth to join the unknown clan of a husband is a heroine just as well.

As the caravan lurched forward, I wondered what I was supposed to do. Was I to ignore Deaglán as haughtily as he was ignoring me? Or should I fawn before him and try to win his attention? There was no one in the train of horses and carts to whom I could appeal; I had neither a nurse nor a Drui nor even Father Justan to consult with. I was utterly alone, set adrift like a leaf on the autumn wind.

I fingered the little wooden cross that Father Justan had bestowed on me, hoping to derive some counsel from it. The smoothness of the wood reminded me of his gentle and reassuring presence, and his words of comfort did come back to me: *Remember your centering prayer. Concentrate on the word Abba—Father—and drive all other thoughts from your mind. All will be well.*

"Abba, Abba, Abba," I recited silently for a while, and for a space I did feel a measure of peace, and my tumbling thoughts were for a moment stilled.

That night when the entire camp was arranged around a roaring fire after supper, it was no longer possible for Deaglán to avoid me. The mogae had prepared a single pavilion for the two of us to share, and I put on the pale green silk nightgown that my mother had given me as a marriage gift. I waited under the linen sheets and furs for Deaglán to appear. When he finally did, he was drunk.

"I did not want this marriage," he said, mushing his words and crawling under the sheets as far away from me as he was able while still remaining covered.

"I wanted to travel, to go to Greece. The last thing I wanted was to be tied down—to *you*."

He added the last bit sharply, for cruel emphasis, as if all of this were my fault.

I did not know what to say. Róisín had tried to hastily impart the womanly arts to me as we were finishing the packing. She told me to be quiet and demure and to always submit to my lord and husband, no matter what he said or did.

"It's the only way to keep the peace," she explained.

But it just wasn't in my nature to stay quiet. I reached out to my husband and moved closer to his side of the pallet. That was a mistake; he pulled away angrily and huddled miserably on his own side of the bed. We did not speak again that night or for the rest of the journey, which took several weeks to complete.

I recall that the men in the retinue started the first day with ribald jokes and well wishes for our marriage night, but by the second day they were already wondering what was amiss. We were a morose and silent group by the time we reached the dun of Íobar.

Íobar's fort was very different from my father's. Instead of a wooden palisade, it had a high circular wall of smooth stones and one easily defensible narrow gate. The stone wall was an effective shield against the sea winds and also against any would-be attackers. It was pocked here and there with tiny windows that afforded a lookout in every direction and just enough space to shoot an arrow or hurl a spear.

There were three rows of "dragon's teeth" around the dun—concentric rings of black rock spikes that jutted outwards at an angle, designed to impale any onrush of warriors or to slow them down so they might be easily picked off with arrows or spears.

From the outside, the fort seemed cold, fierce, lofty, and forbidding, but once inside the gate I could see that there were graceful stone stairs curving up the wall at regular intervals, and I soon learned that there was an awe-inspiring vista from any point on top of the wall: the ocean on one side, and houses, fields, and forests on the other.

The top of the wall was a popular spot for the young folk, who would dangle their legs over the side and help the warriors by keeping watch for cattle thieves. It was also a favorite spot for lovers, who would meet there to kiss under the moon.

There was the usual collection of stone roundhouses, barns, work houses, and storage sheds within the looming outer wall. They all had the familiar conical roofs of willow that I knew from my childhood. There was a large grassy sward in the center of the fort that was large enough to accommodate the king's cattle when they were brought down from their summer pastures at Samhain, and there were three deep wells within the walls from which the mogae drew water day and night. The fort was well built to withstand a siege.

The Cristaidi were just putting the finishing touches on their square stone chapel that was being built right outside the wall when we arrived. The little building was nestled in a deep earthen pit on the seaward side of the fort, because the monks wanted to be as near the dun as possible yet as far away from lay folk as they could manage. The deep pit protected them from ocean winds and chill and preserved their silence, but it meant that they were almost always in the dark.

Why they wanted to be walled off from all that is, I would never understand. Íobar had to provide them with a constant supply of beeswax candles and whale oil for their lamps at fantastic expense.

Íobar's Druid had their own sacred precinct outside of the walls. It consisted of three ancient standing stones perched on a rise surrounded by ocean on three sides. Below the hill was a large communal roundhouse that all the Druid shared.

Like the fort, the Druid's nemed looked sparse and forbidding to my eyes. I was used to the thick yews and greenery of the nemed in my father's court, but I soon learned that their sacred space had its own unique beauty. The land on which the stones were perched was thick with purple heather and covered by the glorious vault of the ever-shifting clouds and sky.

Íobar, the king, had a leather-brown face—the result of much campaigning—that was deeply lined with worry. But his eyes were calm and grey. He saw me the instant I appeared in his great hall. He looked up the moment I entered and then greeted me and met my eyes as if I were a fully grown woman of Nemed rank. I could sense that I mattered to him in a way that I never had at my father's court. Perhaps it was due to my newly married status, or maybe it was the hope of peace that I symbolized.

Íobar was kind enough as a father-in-law. His marriage gifts to me were several stylish capes and jackets made of seal, otter, badger, and fox furs—"To protect you from our cold northern winds," as he put it.

Outwardly, at least, I was an ideal princess. I had a golden torque from my father and red leather slippers and gloves from my mother that were embroidered with golden thread. I am sure that when I stepped into the sunlight my red hair was dazzling.

Deaglán's mother had died of a fever some years before, and by then his father had three concubines for companionship. One of them took a motherly interest in me. Breachnat was short and round, with white skin and thick black curls that exploded around her face, even when she plaited them into braids or stuffed them under her shawl. Her eyes were wide-set and blue, and her expression was kind.

"It must be exciting to be a newly married wife. Does your new husband please you?" she would ask. An embarrassed silence was my only reply.

"Soon you will have a baby, no doubt," she would opine hopefully, digging for a response.

How could I explain that my husband hadn't touched me since we met? I felt a complete failure. I did not reveal the painful truth, because I was too ashamed. As a result of Deaglán's and my silence, everyone assumed we were doing fine. Even if we spent our days apart, at night we still went dutifully to the same chamber in the same roundhouse.

Everywhere I went, the dun's inhabitants would stare at my belly before raising their eyes to my face. Everyone wanted to be the first with the news if I was at last with child. But I had still not bled in the way that women do when their belly is ready to hold a new life.

Deaglán kept to his side of the huge heather mattress we shared. Our togetherness was a fiction that we kept up for many months, until I could take it no longer.

"We can't go on this way!" I wailed one evening as a bright moon shone through the skins that covered our small windows. "Take me now! Please! You *have* to."

"Anything to keep you quiet," he finally said.

And at last Deaglán did the deed. He did not kiss me or gentle me in preparation for the act; he was simply rough, quick, and brutal. There was one brief moment of piercing pain, and then nothing; I was numb.

As I lay alone once more on my own side of the linens and wept silent tears, blood and male fluids oozed from my private parts. I wondered what all the fuss was about, why women and men wanted this thing so badly.

Maybe I will have a baby now, I thought. *Then everyone will be happy.*

For many moon-tides after that, it was the same. I would not see Deaglán all day, but at night he would come into our house, as often as not reeking of fíon or béoir. He would crawl over to me, grab my breasts and pull at them roughly a few times, insert his fingers into my private parts, and finally push his male member into me, making a few grunting strokes until his milky white juices were deposited and then rolling over again onto his side of the furs.

Soon he would be snoring noisily beside me, oblivious.

Things went on like that for almost a full sun cycle. Íobar would eye my belly from time to time, and I would overhear Breachnat providing him with regular reports about me and my "health."

Still I was not pregnant. I knew this was probably because I had not yet begun my courses of the moon. Or maybe it was simply because the gods had other plans.

In the way of couples, our sad relationship gradually drifted into a routine. By day Deaglán would practice his swordplay and flirt with any available widow or wench; at night he would part my legs and strive to plant his seed. We expected and even derived some vague comfort from the familiar warmth of each other's bodies in the cold dark until we were gradually resigned to our fate; there could be no escape from our pledge of troth, so why fight it?

As a princess, I was expected to keep up appearances; the days when I could wear my hair loose and go wandering in the forest were far behind me. But inwardly I had not changed; I still hungered for the Druid teachings that I had received so generously in the school of Dálach-gaes and Niamh.

Yet I was not a full Drui, nor was I officially an initiate. The Druid of Íobar's court simply ignored me, thinking I was but another young, uninteresting, and unlettered member of the flaith.

The Cristaidi had even less use for me. As a woman, I was banned from their church unless it was time for Mass. When we went inside the dark chapel, only the king sat; the rest of us were expected to stand and keep our heads down, and we women had to have our heads covered.

No matter who was in the congregation, Father Cearbhall would most often focus his sermons on the subject of women. He would remind us of how Pagani women were forced to fight in battles and insisted that it was our duty to urge all women to abandon Pagani warrior ways. It was not that he was against wars; rather, he was against women taking any part in them. Perhaps he didn't know that women warriors were as fierce and took as much pride in their work as male warriors did.

His view on marriage was that it was just a necessity, an inferior form of evil. He said that "sex dulls the senses and repels the Holy Spirit" and "lust is caused by women who go about with their hair loose; if a woman is not veiled, she will cause lust even in the angels."

He would remind us of the angels of the holy scriptures, who mated with the daughters of men and thus brought the calamity of the flood upon all creation. He said those angels brought weapons and war to humanity and debauched women with perfume, jewels, makeup, and fine cloth, and that they introduced evils into the world such as idolatry, astrology, and other occult arts. He said that all the daughters of Eve should wear plain garb and always keep our heads covered as a mark of our shame because we had fallen so low.

But he never asked the men to give up their concubines.

It was strange to emerge from that dark chapel into the sunlight wearing my red kid gloves and shoes. I could feel Father Cearbhall's eyes on me, his disapproval of my red hair and my fox-fur cape. It seemed that the only message he brought was shame—so different from Father Justan's message of love for all creation.

And then a very strange thing began to happen: I began to grow. As I had just turned fifteen summers, it was perhaps natural in my family. I hardly noticed it myself until one day I happened to be standing next to Deaglán as we waited to enter the mead hall and he was staring at me, eye to eye.

"Don't ever wear shoes with heels again. I forbid it. You are becoming large, a giantess. In those boots you look like a Fomorian she-devil."

I believe he said those things because his own mother had been dark-haired and tiny, and so he favored women who were raven-haired and small of stature. But what could I have possibly done about it? I began to bow my head and hunch my shoulders when I was near him.

"You are like a cuckoo in a wren's nest," Breachnat said, shaking her head.

The native people of Irardacht were mostly small and dark, and it was very obvious that I was a stranger in that kingdom.

4

It was once again the time of high summer, yet the spring rains had never ceased. I knew that the climate in the north of Ériu was usually dreary, but this was something different. Nearly every day brought a storm with lightning and hail, and the skies were dark grey six days out of seven.

When I went out on walks I was always accompanied by a mog, because I was not allowed to go anywhere alone. I noticed deep pools of water collecting in the ruts of the fields of cabbages and carrots—water that could easily lead to rot.

Earlier that spring the blossoms had been knocked off of the apple and plum trees by wild wind storms. Worse yet were the grain fields; the stalks of oats and barley were laid flat by the constant wind and hail. There would be a terrible harvest that year. As a king's daughter, I was used to thinking about the people. How would they survive? What would they eat? I could see sickness and starvation looming.

I accosted Breachnat one morning as she was supervising the mogae who were replacing the damp floor rushes in the mead hall. Her dark curls were modestly stuffed into a linen kerchief, and her blue léine and tunic were topped with a stained grey apron that reached to her ankles.

"What is the king saying about this weather? I was taught by the Druid that the king and the land are one. What has he done to bring this about? What will he do to try and reverse it?" I asked in my usually brusque and straightforward manner.

I could see that Breachnat was shocked by my tone. Niamh and Róisín had warned me to be careful about keeping my mouth and my inner thoughts in check, but I just couldn't seem to do it.

"You are implying that the king is at fault for the terrible weather?" Breachnat asked, striving to keep her voice even.

"Well, the Druid of In Medon say that the state of the crops and the land are a direct result of the actions of the king. If the land is suffering, then the king has to do something differently!

"The *Audacht Morainn* states that it is through the justice of the ruler that there is abundance of every high, tall corn. It is through the justice of the ruler that abundances of great tree-fruit of the wood are tasted, fair children are well begotten, milk-yields of great cattle are maintained, abundance of fish swim in the streams, plagues and lightning are kept from the people…"[1]

I ticked off on my fingers the benefits of just and competent rulership as they had been enumerated in the ancient king-making rite. It all seemed so logical and obvious to my mind. The king's justice had been faulty, and now the land and the people were suffering.

Breachnat's eyes grew wider with each word. "Hush now, child, you are not to speak of things that do not concern you—that are beyond your understanding. Your only job is to bear an heir for the prince; there is nothing more that is expected of you. But if you like, you can watch me as I supervise the mogae. It may fall to you to change the rushes yourself one day," she said, as if it were a lofty privilege anyone would be proud to aspire to.

I swallowed my concerns for the weather and the crops and stayed by Breachnat the rest of the afternoon, taking careful note of how she ordered the mogae in their jobs and learning where the best rushes were to be found for cutting, and where and how to hang them to be dried. I, who knew Latin and Greek and the Ogum letters, tried to see this as yet another kind of school, a further mystery to be penetrated: the mystery of housekeeping.

Always a diligent student, for the next few weeks I set myself the task of learning the secrets of the kitchens and the storerooms. I studied all their locations and the contents of their chests, urns, and barrels. Druid-trained, I was able to memorize everything quickly, down to the smallest detail.

"Would you like me to write out a list of the produce and spices you will need for the next market day? It will make it so much easier for you to remember what needs to be bartered for or purchased," I innocently asked the chief cooks, a plump couple from Letha who had been imported to provide exotic dishes for the king's table. I had forgotten how rare it was to have learned the arts of reading and writing.

The cooks froze for a moment, gaping in their stained aprons, their hands completely hidden in the midst of two enormous piles of wet dough, staring at me as if I had suddenly grown two heads. No one had ever suggested writing down a list of such things before. As far as they knew, writing was a sacred and arcane art known only to Druid and Cristaidi clergy. Seeing their expressions, I was ashamed; I had not meant to make them feel ignorant.

Breachnat's form suddenly filled the doorway as she beckoned me to come back outside. She had been watching my movements all morning from a distance.

"The kitchen is no place for you to be holding conversations; your only role with these people is to order a meal or plan a feast. What do you think you are doing? It is far beneath your station to be spending so much time consorting with servants. Why don't we go to the grianan, and I will teach you how to work the loom."

Yet again I was left feeling useless, out of place, a failure.

One day I screwed up my courage, put on my plainest gown and cloak so as not to be noticed, and went to visit the Druid. I hoped that I might find some solace or conversation with them, if only they would get to know me.

By keeping my head down and my hair well covered, I was able to escape the fort, and for the first time in many moons I was outside the gate, alone. Blessed freedom! I raised my head to the sky and took in deep breaths of wild air.

As I climbed the heather-crowned hill I exulted in the soft, springy feel of the plant life beneath my feet. Above me sea gulls glinted white against the sky. Then I noticed moving forms. In the distance was a group of male Druid crouching around a small Fire Altar. The fire seemed tiny—pitiful even. I approached them slowly; dressed as I was in a cloak of muted browns, I blended into the hillside, and they did not even see me coming.

"There are many ways of killing a pig," I could hear one of them say. He was the tallest, a thin man with long auburn hair and crinkled blue eyes. It was obvious that the Druid were not eating well; the man's white wool robe was patched, and he had only a plaited rope for a belt. His waist was wasplike.

"I say we approach the king directly," said another Drui, a shorter man with long grey hair and brown eyes, dressed in a faded, patched blue cloak and tunic. "Surely he must appreciate the gravity of the situation."

"If we do that, we will just be attacked. Don't forget that in the new version of the laws, we have been debased to mere magicians," said the third Drui, who was dressed in a simple brown wool léine and tunic. "And they hate magicians; they say magic goes against their sacred book, the Bible."

The man speaking was blond and grey eyed and, like the other two, his head was shaved in the familiar Druid tonsure: across the forehead, signifying a radiant brow filled with wisdom.

"I think we have to be more subtle, perhaps by bargaining with one of the petty kingdoms. You know that the ard-ri favors the Cristaidi. He would never allow us to do it properly—" the man in brown stopped in mid-sentence. He had finally noticed me from the corner of his eye.

Suddenly there was a flurry of hand motions and sign signals. Furious, silent speech and gestures flew from one Drui to the next. It was palm Ogum! I recognized it immediately. Palm and shin and nose

Ogum were the familiar sign language of the Druid that I had learned at Dálach-gae and Niamh's knees as a baby. By the age of four I was proficient in all forms of Ogum. I could draw the letters, recite the tree alphabet, and form the letters with my fingers against my nose, shin, or hand.

I could see that they thought their speech was private. They assumed I was just an ignorant onlooker, a servant out collecting wild herbs or on some other errand.

"Keep silent. We are being watched by that girl," said one with his fingers.

"Let's continue our discussion," signaled another impatiently.

I bent down and innocently plucked a few stalks of heather, as if I were gathering them for a medicinal brew.

"This is a task that requires a large white bull. If we dedicate the eyes to the sun, the blood to the rivers, the breath to the winds, and the flesh and bones to the earth, it should strengthen the land to withstand the storms," signaled the Drui in the blue robes. "And afterwards everyone can eat. That will be a great comfort to those who are hungry."

"I'd say it requires two bulls," signaled the Drui in brown. He wore a serious expression and seemed to be speaking from experience.

"Yes, but how do we do it? We haven't access to anything as valuable as white bulls for a sacrifice," the blue-robed Drui signaled back with an unhappy face.

"We need to find a friend inside the king's dun," said the fingers of the man with auburn hair, "because if we don't do this, the people will surely starve."

"Agreed," gestured the man in blue. Then they went silent for a while, collecting their thoughts.

I understood everything they were saying; it was obvious that they were seeking to change the weather, to find a way to perform a sacrifice so that the people would be able to eat. It was supremely logical and exactly the right thing to do. Finally I had encountered people in the kingdom who made sense—whose minds I could understand!

I raised my head and walked towards the men with complete confidence, something I had not felt since I left my father's dun in In Medon. Without giving it another thought, I began to sign to the men in palm Ogum, using my fingers against the fleshy side of my hand to quickly spell out the words.

"I understand what you are trying to do! I fully agree and approve. Something has to be done to turn the weather or the kingdom will fall. It will be a disaster!"

My fingers flew. I waited expectantly for their response. But only shock registered on their faces, and they looked as if they wanted to run away.

"Please don't be afraid of me!" I gestured. "I am the daughter-in-law of the ard-ri. I can help you!"

"Who are you?" cried the man with auburn hair out loud. "How is it possible you can understand us? Only a trained Drui could possibly know the secret language of the poets!"

"Not hard to answer," I responded, using the formulaic response familiar to every Druid school. "I was a student of the filid Dálachgaes and Niamh in my father's court. I would have happily remained there studying the Druid mysteries, but my father thought it best that I marry the prince of Irardacht to keep the peace between the kingdoms. Our union was designed to stop the cattle raids and the bloodshed on the borders."

I felt sure that they would accept me as a friend, as an equal, now that they knew my true identity.

"No, it's just not possible," said the man in brown. "You must be a fairy or a spirit. No daughter of a king would ever be shown the Druidic mysteries, especially not in these times!"

"In any case, we cannot speak with you if you are a member of the royal dun, as you claim," said the Drui in blue. "It's too dangerous for us."

Then, to my shock and horror, the three men wheeled away from me, flocking down the hillside as if chased by a phantom.

I fell to my knees and began to cry. I had understood exactly what they were trying to do. Why couldn't they accept me? All I wanted to do was to help them, and now I was completely lost. There was no place in the three worlds left for me; I was nothing under land, sea, or sky. I was insignificant, loved by no one. I was nobody. My mind was desperate for something valuable to do, someone to serve, someone to love. But who? And how?

Above me was the dark sky, lowering and threatening; at my feet was the soggy land, as barren and fruitless as my own body. There was no comfort, beauty, or joy anywhere to be found. I had lost everything.

I flung myself onto the heather and wailed my misery to the Mother Goddess in the earth, giving vent at last to the torrent of tears that I had held back for so long, moaning and crying until I could weep no more, pounding the moist sod of the mother with my fists in a helpless rage. When I reached the end of my weeping, my spirit was left as flat and as grey as the vast, empty sky that pressed upon my shoulders.

5

Though I escaped outside to the open air outside the dun as often as I could, at times I felt I was dying. Once in each moontide a fever would come on me and then my lungs would burn. A Drui could have told me that my lungs were speaking, trying to push out the words that my mouth dared not utter. I would cough so loudly in the night that Deaglán was finally forced to move to another roundhouse. He soon found a plump, black-haired concubine to warm his furs.

Now the cough settled on me so deep within my body and spirit that I could hardly move. I was suffused with a kind of fire, and my lungs felt as if live coals burned within them. I took to my bed.

At the beginning I was grateful for my time spent under the linen sheets and furs. It gave me space to dream and a kind of privacy I had not known for a long time. I was like a wounded animal hiding deep in my lair. Some days I wouldn't even bother to light the candles or the brazier; I would just sleep, burrowing deeper and deeper into my inner landscapes. The mogae were not happy with this; they tripped over the hearth stones when they came in to bring me a tray of soup or an herbal brew from the kitchens.

When Breachnat came to visit, she would throw open the door and force me out of bed so she could change the sheets and bring me a fresh nightgown. "It smells like a barn in here!" she would say as she lit the beeswax candles and built up the peat fire on the hearth to clear the air.

After a few days I became restless, and I could feel the fires of life rekindling in my belly, chest, and head, and I began to wonder what was happening outside my walls.

Father Cearbhall came to visit and to sprinkle holy water upon me and all around the house.

"Good morning, Father, what news have you of Deaglán, of Íobar, and of the court? What's happening outside my door?" I asked as if he were a friend. I was suddenly delighted to have any visitor to divert attention from my own bare stone walls.

"*Silentum facite!*" he responded, willing me into silence with his beetling eyes and rough voice. I had forgotten how hard this man tried to keep away from women. It must have been a trial for him to see me like that, in my nightgown and with my hair undone.

"Sickness is visited upon us to test our faith. Your soul is in the bondage of Satan, but hidden within it are still the seeds of good. Awaken those seeds by turning to the one god, who made the world out of nothing. I know well that you are a Paganus at heart—and that you take every opportunity to roam the hills alone, with your hair wild and uncovered.

"Mend your ways, turn to the true faith, and you will be healed. Repeat after me: *Crist issum* (Christ below me), *Crist usasam* (Christ above me), *Crist im degaid* (Christ behind me), *Crist reum* (Christ before me), *Crist dessum* (Christ at my right), *Crist tuathum* (Christ at my left)."[2]

I dutifully recited the words, but it didn't stop my coughing.

One day Breachnat asked the household bard to sing and play his harp for me. The Druid teach that music can heal the body and mind and lighten the burdens of the world. She had seen with her own eyes the way the bard could soothe the dying with his harp, even if he was an unrepentant Paganus and thus likely doomed to hell.

Conláed was a skinny young fellow with a beautiful voice who had begun his training as a Drui but had been unable to master the dry memorization of poems, alphabets, and languages that were needed to attain the high rank of fili. He was graduated with honors as a bard and finally let go.

He sang to me of the goddess Clíodna with her three bright birds that ease all sorrow and lull you to sleep with their song, and of Emain Ablach, the immortal land of apples, where endless feasting, sport, and merrymaking are found and where there is no death, evil, disease, decay, or aging—the place where the trees bear flowers and fruit in every season. He strove to bring harmony to my spirit with his harp.

But each night I had the same dream. I would sleep peacefully for a while, and then the sharp talons of a huge black bird would dig into my forehead. I could hear it screaming in raven tongue; somehow I understood the words: "You must come with me. *You must come with me!*"

And then the talons would pull on my scalp, up and up and up, until it seemed the bird was lifting the top of my skull. And then the world would turn red as blood, red as fire, and I would be floating over the dun, seeing everything through a crimson haze. The bird was pulling me away to somewhere unknown, someplace distant from where I was sleeping.

And then I would wake sweating and terrified in my bed, light my candle in the glowing brazier, and check my face for blood. I could still feel it streaming into my eyes from the force of the talons, but there was no blood on my face or on my pillows. Then I would fall back into a troubled sleep and rise again coughing in the morning.

At dawn I'd rise and dress in my warmest cloak and climb the outer stone wall before I broke my fast. On the top I would sing a prayer to Áine Clí, goddess of love and the sun:

Mother of the stars
Eye of the gods
Queen of the heavens
Sister of the moon
You who rise up and lie down

In the terrible ocean
Without fear
You who abide forever
Coming and going
Shining equally on all that is
Help me!

At dusk I would repeat my ritual, watching until she lowered her glowing form into the dark, distant waves.

I derived some comfort from this, as she was the only soul friend I could still count on. The sentries watched my movements but never made a move to stop me.

In those days I was careful to leave a small portion of every meal I was brought on my windowsill or on a rock outside the door as a gift for the Daoine Sidhe. I meant it as a signal that my house, at least, was prepared to be generous. Hopefully the Good Folk would be generous in return.

It had been drilled into me from childhood that the relationship with the spirits of place was of supreme importance—that they must be treated as honored relations in order that the people and the animals remain healthy. I was filled with concern for the land and the tribes, and there was little else I could offer in the way of Druid magic.

My offerings were paltry, I knew. They were hardly a fair recompense for the labors of the land spirits who grew the crops and fed the kingdom, but there was little more that I could do.

The folk of the tuaths still appeared at the gate with their carts full of the obligatory butter, milk, cheeses, berries, plums, apples, lambs, smoked hams, venison, and fish. They brought us their nettles and watercresses, cabbages, carrots, and onions, and the storerooms of the dun were filled with spelt, barley, and oats. Somehow there was always ample béoir for the warriors and honey for Íobar's table, but I knew without being told that the people outside the walls were suffering, even as they brought their best food to the king.

As the moontides wore on and I had no relations with Deaglán, my status in court diminished until even Íobar no longer asked for me.

"My lady, I bring news," Conláed the bard said to me one morning as he ducked through the doorway of my roundhouse clutching his harp. "Deaglán's concubine is with child. And the tribes have begun raiding on the borders of In Medon once again!"

I knew that according to the laws, any child born to a concubine had the exact same rights as a child born of a chief wife. Deaglán's concubine could easily be the mother of the future king. With the peace broken, my only function in the court had been usurped and the reason for my marriage obliterated. Now I understood why I had become invisible. I was no longer of interest to Deaglán, Íobar, or the court.

It was an unexpectedly warm morning, and the young priestess took me outside to sit on a little bench on the sunny side of the roundhouse. She tucked thick woolen blankets around my legs and shoulders and began to comb and braid my hair.

"Have I told you about the Beltaine Druid Council in that fateful year?" I asked her.

"No, my lady," she replied.

It felt good to have my hair freshly combed and plaited, and I was grateful that the braids were loose and didn't pull my scalp.

"Well, then, I had a full account from those who were there. Let me tell you about it…"

The Druid Council was an event that was rotated yearly from district to district, in a sunwise spiral from kingdom to kingdom. Representatives were sent to the gathering from each province of the island, who would in turn report back to the Druid of their own kingdoms so that every Drui was kept current with the local politics of Ériu.

The Druid were able to travel across the borders because at that time they were still allowed the privilege of free movement across kingdoms, a remnant of the ancient respect once accorded their ranks. By tradition, the council always took place on the nearest full moon after the Beltaine festival, the time of green shoots, rising sap, and new growth—"The time of optimism and change, when the green sap causes new leaves to unfurl," as Niamh put it.

That year it was Niamh and Dálach-gaes's turn to host the council. Their students helped them prepare for the event by gathering huge piles of firewood from trees outside of the rath and by cutting peat bricks from the nearby bogs, which they stacked neatly within the Druid enclosure, covered with straw and rushes against the rain. They also made soft beds of heather and straw, covered over with furs and woolen blankets borrowed from the stores of Barra Mac Mel, king of In Medon.

Dálach-gaes, Niamh, and their students and children moved into one house, giving over the children's house to the expected female guests. The schoolhouse was filled to bursting with extra beds and provisions for the men.

Ever conscious of the political value of hospitality, Barra Mac Mel was generous with his gifts of food and drink for the council. He donated a pair of mogae to carry hot water for baths and to shuttle daily cauldrons of stew, roasted meats, and platters of bread, butter, and cheese from the kitchens of the royal house. In anticipation of the event, Niamh had been hoarding honey, dried apples, plums, and hazelnuts since fall.

The meeting would take place in the nemed's outdoor ritual enclosure unless it rained, in which case it would have to move indoors.

The nemed of In Medon's Druid was far smaller than the nemed of former years. The elaborate Fire Altar was no more; that structure had been subsumed by the stone chapel of the Cristaidi, and the herb garden that had once surrounded the Fire Altar had become a graveyard. The sacred ash still stood, but it was right next to the stone church, so there was little chance of performing a sacred Druid rite under its sheltering branches.

But hidden behind the thick screen of yew was a round enclosure of soft, mossy earth that was covered with several inches of freshly cut grass when a ceremony was to be performed. In the north of the circle stood a tall carved wooden pole, the bíle, or world tree, emblem of the three realms of land, sea, and sky because it was buried deep in the ground, stood at ground level, and reached for the heavens.

The bíle was carved with intricate interlace patterns that symbolized the interconnectedness of all creation, and long white feathers hung by threads from the top. By watching the movement of the feathers, the Druid could read from which direction the wind was blowing—an all-important divination aid.

"The bíle is placed in the north because all magic comes from the north. It is easiest to read the currents of magic from that direction," Dálach-gaes explained to the children, who were entranced by the feathers dancing in the breeze.

At the center of the space stood a simple stone altar: three rocks upon which lay a flat slab of stone. The altar was hallowed by a grave. Daire, a former prince of In Medon who had achieved initiation as a Drui, had asked to be buried there after he crossed over, to bless and guard the nemed in death as he had sought to defend it in life. In honor of the council, the altar was now covered with a white linen cloth, its edges embroidered with green and silver knotwork designs.

On the eastern side of the stone altar, in the direction of the sunrise, was a small Fire Altar that was a hole dug into the earth. It was square and lined with stone. On the western side, in the direction of the sunset, was a deep votive shaft into which offerings could be made to the underworld Sidhe realms.

Thick oiled-wool blankets were neatly folded and placed on the freshly cut grass for the guests to sit upon or to wrap around their shoulders in case of cold and damp.

Dálach-gaes studied the fluttering feathers at the top of the bíle for a few moments.

"The wind is blowing from the north just now, the direction of battle. Either there is important news coming from Irardacht or a conflict is already brewing there," he mused out loud. "In any case, the spirits want our attention to go to battles and to the north for some reason—to the kingdom of the eagles."

Everyone within hearing had a sick feeling; winds from the north always presaged some kind of deadly conflict, and they steeled themselves to receive bad news.

Dunlaing and Carmac from Oirthir were the first to arrive at the Council. As was usual for Druid of the Eastern Kingdom, the Oirthiri looked sleek, well dressed, and prosperous. Carmac was the shorter of the two; his dark hair was carefully braided and decorated with golden ornaments. Dunlaing was taller, with blond braids and bright gold glistening from the interlaced designs on his belt. Both wore golden torques and immaculately clean white fleece robes into which they had changed just before entering the dun.

Dunlaing presented Dálach-gaes with a gift for the school, a large bronze bell that he had carried with great effort in his backpack. Carmac had carried his personal lamdia, a portable bronze idol of a goddess with antlers that were removable from their sockets. The antlers were to be taken out in the dark half of the year, when the sun was on the wane, and put back in at Beltaine, at the start of summer.

On arrival, the very first thing Carmac did was to set up the lamdia in a place of honor under the yews. He reverently unwound the deerskin coverings and laid a silver plate and cup before the little statue so that everyone could make offerings to her each day of the gathering.

"He never goes anywhere without that statue. He is under a geis," said Dunlaing stoically. He had been forced to "feed" the statue every day of their journey, at dawn and at dusk, or risk Carmac's displeasure. Carmac was a special devotee of the sun goddess in her deer form, and he always made sure that there were fresh flowers and food offerings at the feet of her statue at daybreak and again at twilight.

As soon as the statue was settled into a place of honor, he welcomed her with a song:

> *Beloved Goddess*
> *Queen of the Sky*
> *White deer of purity*
> *You who guide the seekers*

You who welcome the departed spirits
To your shining realm
Of immortality
We welcome you into this place
Be with us now!

Making a deep bow, he ceremoniously unwrapped the final silk coverings that covered the little goddess and began to dance in ecstasy before her as the others watched and smiled, clapping their hands to provide accompaniment.

When Carmac at last settled down, Dálach-gaes approached the two arrivals with brimming cups of mid to formally welcome them to the gathering.

"A cup of joy to welcome you to our tuath," he said, beaming.

The next guests to appear were three ban-Druid from Torcrad. Bláthnait was a tall, willowy woman wearing green robes who carried a small harp packed into a sheepskin bag, with the wool side inward to protect the wood and strings.

Canair was a dark-haired, dark-eyed ban-liaig who wore practical brown robes "because they don't show the dirt," as she would often say. Her daily forays into the fields looking for edible greens and medicinal herbs invariably left the hems of her robes stained and muddy.

Ita was the eldest of the three, a ban-fili in grey robes whose red hair was rapidly fading to white. All three wore thick bronze torques to advertise their rank, and Ita also wore a knob of polished amber on a string around her neck. Embedded within the amber was a dragonfly, the symbol of transformation.

"Dragonflies are dedicated warriors who will devour any obstacle in their path. Don't let their beauty fool you!" she told the children as they stared up at the magnificent necklace. Though Ita was small of stature and thin, she was as fierce as a feral cat when challenged.

Canair's sons, Finnlug and Garbhán, were warriors who accompanied the three ban-Druid as guides and protectors. They were both clean shaven save for their moustaches and their dark hair, which was neatly plaited into thick braids. They had deerskin trousers and tunics under their woolen capes, and each carried a sword on their belt and a shield on their back. Being sons of a ban-Drui, they were entitled to wear bronze torques.

The five were each handed a frothy cup of joy upon their arrival.

"Finnlug and Garbhán, you two will guard the perimeter of the nemed to prevent eavesdropping by curious folk of the rath," Dálach-gaes announced. The yearly convocation of Druid was no place for warriors.

The brothers loped off willingly; they had become tired of listening to women day and night. The sights and sounds of the dun would be a welcome diversion.

Next to arrive from Murthracht were Cainleog and Alda, a newly handfasted pair who were clearly excited to be journeying so far together. Both had long black hair, blue eyes, and matching blue robes, and both of them were shanachies. They brought a small barrel of mid as a gift for the gathering.

"Left over from our honeymoon," they said in unison as they handed it to Dálach-gaes.

"A couple!" exclaimed Niamh. "Where shall we put them to sleep?"

"We are happy to sleep outside, so long as we are together," said Alda, giving his new wife a squeeze and a moist, tender look, a look that she returned with equal intensity and a deep blush.

"They are like a matched pair of fine horses," Niamh later confided to Dálach-gaes in private.

Cainleog and Alda sipped their cups of joy side by side, seemingly more interested in each other than in the gathered Druid.

The last to arrive were three harried-looking Druid from Irardacht. Bárid was tall and thin, with auburn hair; Amlaim was shorter, with long grey hair; while Imar was tall and blond. All three wore patched and faded robes. They were painfully thin.

Seeing their condition and knowing that they had come from the north, Dálach-gaes determined to make their plight the first order of official business.

When everyone had chosen their beds and dropped their packs and anything else they were carrying, they washed in warm water to remove the dust of the road. Niamh had ordered the mogae to put chamomile and lavender oils into the wooden tubs of bathing water because their scents soothed the senses and removed the tensions of travel.

Everyone changed into comfortable deerskin slippers and clean robes and padded softly out to the grass-covered nemed.

"There will be a feast this evening," said Dálach-gaes. "But first we must begin our council in the proper way. Just as the first task of every day is to light the hearth with a prayer of awakening, so must we light the Fire Altar to begin our work."

The Fire Altar had been prepared beforehand with a mound of dry birch bark over which three bricks of peat, symbolic of the three worlds, were laid in a pyramid. To ensure a successful outcome at the fire lighting even if the weather turned damp, Niamh had taken the precaution of sprinkling melted tallow and beeswax over the peat logs. It wouldn't do to have the fire go out; that would be seen as a terrible omen for the meeting.

To one side of the fire pit was a small pile of nine sacred woods: willow, hazel, alder, birch, ash, yew, elm, oak, and pine. Each of these woods had its own unique energy to lend to the proceedings, and nine was a sacred number.

"Let each of you take one stick of a sacred wood and lay it on the fire while uttering a prayer of intent for this council," Dálach-gaes announced.

One by one, the Druid approached the little Fire Altar and laid their sticks with respectful purpose upon the stack of peat. As they did so, each of them invoked the gods of their people and asked for a blessing on the work ahead. At the same time a student fed tufts of wool onto a fire drill as another briskly rubbed two pieces of oak to start a new fire by friction. A waft of smoke finally puffed from the drill and then, suddenly, a small spark of flame, which was carefully nurtured with straw. Gradually an entire sheaf of dried straw was set ablaze, then pushed under the birch bark until the pyramid of woods and peat ignited.

"May the Fire Altar bring warmth, light, and sanctification to our work in these next days; may our hearts be warmed to each other. May the warmth, light, and promise of our meeting radiate out to all the kingdoms and to every life on Ériu. May the gods watch over us and inspire us. May what we do here be a blessing for the people."

Dálach-gaes bent over the stone altar, picking up a small silver escra, and held it aloft for a moment so that orange firelight glinted off its polished silver surface. Then he slowly poured a stream of uisge beatha from the cup onto the flames.

"A gift for the fire. May the fragrant essence of this liquid find its way to the sky gods above."

As the smoke and flames reached cheerily for the sky, the next ritual act was to honor the Daoine Sidhe. Niamh bent to pick up a sky-blue clay pitcher from the stone altar.

"In this pitcher is fresh milk mixed with honey and uisge beatha, the sacred liquid that the Liaig use to heal. May our offering bring peace to the Daoine Sidhe as it brings peace and health to our human bodies and spirits."

Niamh walked to the votive pit and carefully poured out the liquid, thinking of her own honored ancestors—those of her blood kin, those who had died to protect the Druid, the kingdoms, and the land, and those who had been her teachers and spiritual guides in this life and in former lives.

Each Drui in the circle reflected on the ancestors of their bloodline and their spirit as they watched the familiar rite.

Deg, one of the students, took up a wooden plate with slices of buttered bannock and cheese and walked to the perimeter of the nemed, reverently laying the plate on the ground just outside of the ritual circle, saying, "A gift for the land spirits—that they may feed upon it and feel welcome."

Caoilfhionn, another student, took a small bowl of cooked oatmeal and cracked hazelnuts with a gob of melted butter on top and carried it away from the circle altogether. Placing it respectfully on the ground, she spoke in a firm voice: "Fomorians, outlyers, forces of chaos and disruption, here is your due! Trouble not our meeting!"

Deg and Caoilfhionn stepped back into the circle together and led the group in a hymn to Manannán Mac Lir:

O Manannán of the white waves
Come on your grey horse
To part the veil
That the gods may cross
From their realm to ours
And back again
May all evil be kept out
And only the good pass through!

Then each dropped a thick slice of cheese and a knob of butter into the fire as a gift for Manannán.

Dálach-gaes removed a golden bell branch from his belt and walked around the ritual circle three times, shaking it forcefully. "Let the Daoine Sidhe and all the fairy realms know that they are welcome here! May all with ill intent be banished and only helpful spirits remain!"

Niamh took up her carved staff, which had been lying across the stone altar, and struck the butt end onto the sod three times, saying, "I declare this meeting open!"

At that exact moment the two mogae appeared, each of them holding one end of a plank upon which were huge oaken bowls of boiled cabbage flavored with a delicate sauce of wild garlic, leeks, and onions in butter, bowls of braised parsnips and carrots, and an entire honey-roasted yearling pig that Barra Mac Mel had generously donated. A cheer went up from the crowd, and Bláthnait hurried back to the children's house to get her harp.

The Druid arranged themselves in a comfortable circle around the fire, with Dálach-gaes and Niamh near the center as the honored hosts, and the bowls of food and a large two-handled beechwood cup filled with cuirm were passed from guest to guest. It was Deg's job to make sure the cup stayed full and that it was kept in constant circulation.

Everyone ate with their two hands, and from time to time the mogae would present a fresh, fragrant, and warm linen towel so that the guests could wipe their fingers and faces.

Bláthnait played ale-music until the growling of her stomach made her at last put down the harp. By then everyone was comfortably full, sucking on bones and enjoying the warmth of the fire and the stars above. Even the two warriors Finnlug and Garbhán had eaten their fill; Deg had carried heaping plates of food to them at their posts outside the nemed. Now Bláthnait and Deg could finally help themselves to the remnants of the roasted pig and the buttery dregs of cabbage and carrots.

The gathered Druid were half asleep from the exertions of travel and the fine meal when Finnlug burst through the yew hedge.

"There is yet another Drui who asks admittance to the council. His name is Artrach, and he says he was sent here by the Druid of the Forest School of In Medon!"

"Let him enter and be welcome," said Niamh, already rising to prepare a fresh plate of food for the stranger. No one would ever go hungry in her house, even if she herself had to go without.

"Deg, go to the children's house and fetch me a large loaf of barley bread. Our guest can at least sop up the juices and butter from our meal!"

Dálach-gaes rose to fill a cup of joy to welcome the stranger, and the others sat up expectantly, prepared to welcome yet another arrival.

When the man at last appeared he wore a pleasant smile, and even in the dark they could see that he was comely and graceful. His bright red hair hung down past his shoulders, and his grey hooded cloak was practical and well made. He had a beautifully carved walking staff, tall leather boots, and a stout leather pack. He looked intelligent, competent, and strong, a young man who would navigate the forests and mountains with ease.

Seeing their curious looks, Artrach introduced himself formally.

"I am Artrach O'Ruadán, great-grandson of Queen Ethne and Ruad of the fiana. My parents sent me to the Forest School for training."

"Then we are kin!" Niamh exclaimed, delighted. "How are things at the school these days?"

"Everyone is well, thank you. The school is flourishing; in these times, we have mostly taken to training the young ones to be bards rather than Druid. We find that we can best keep the old stories and wisdom alive by weaving them into poetry and song. That way we can pass down our traditions right under the noses of the Cristaidi."

"That is a good solution," said Bárid, "because it keeps the peace."

His face suffused with gloom as he said the words; he was visualizing the thin women and children with hungry eyes who roamed the roads of the north, hoping for charity.

They let Artrach eat in silence because it would have been rude to pelt him with further questions when he had just come in from the road. When he had finally sopped up the last bit of butter sauce with a thick slice of bread, everyone said their goodnights and padded off to their pallets. Deg led Artrach to the men's house to help him make up a bed near the hearth.

Niamh stayed behind to cover the fire, singing a prayer as she banked the embers to keep them alive until dawn:

I smoor as Brighid would
The banked coals this night
May the Three protect this space
May the Three protect our home
May the Three protect the kingdoms
May the Triple Goddess protect us
Land, Sea, and Sky
Be our strength through this night.

She glanced skyward towards the full moon and murmured a further blessing:

Hail to thee
Jewel of the night
Sister of the sun
Mother of the stars
Thank you for your light!

Then at last she too found her way to the warmth of her husband and family.

The next morning at sunrise, bright fingers of yellow light pierced the yew hedge and a chorus of bird song signaled that the new day had begun. Once again Niamh tended to the fire, softly brushing and blowing away the ashes from the banked embers while adding fresh sticks of dried peat. As she did so, she sang her morning kindling song:

I kindle as Brighid would
Three flames of her cauldron
Flames of the forge
Flames of the cooking pot
Flames of truth and knowledge
I give thanks for the white morning flame.

Alda and Cainleog were still snoring under their oiled-wool blankets on the grass of the nemed as Niamh prodded them gently, proffering steaming cups of elderberry brew to lure them from their warm nest.

The others emerged sleepily from their respective houses, still stretching and yawning and brushing their teeth and gums with fragrant birch twigs. Deg and Dálach-gaes fed the embers of the little fire with more peat and wood, coaxing it back to life.

After Carmac had danced before his goddess and everyone had given her a food offering or a drink, Dálach-gaes and Niamh made fresh offerings to all the gods at the Fire Altar and to the Daoine Sidhe at the votive pit. Then everyone settled themselves in a circle to eat the fried eggs, sausages, and mushrooms brought by the mogae and to begin their discussions in earnest.

"It appears that the major problems this sun cycle are in the north of Ériu. Perhaps one of the Irardachti Druid can fill us in with the details," Dálach-gaes said, efficiently steering the conversation towards the most pressing issue before them.

Amlaim was the oldest and the first to speak.

"The northern province is suffering under terrible weather; the crops are rotting in the fields, the trees have lost their blossoms in the storms and bear little or no fruit. There is mold on the grain, and even the little bit that is stored has been spoiled by the damp.

"As you know, the Druid have lately been debased in the laws to the status of mere magicians—these days we can't even gain access to the court unless we go in as bards or jesters. We know exactly what we need to do, but we are just too poor to do it properly."

Amlaim stared bleakly into the fire, seeing with his inner eye the blackened fields and the plight of his people.

Bárid touched his shoulder by way of comfort and added his own thoughts. "Before the Cristaidi came, we would have had the ears of the ard-ri. We could have asked him for two white oxen, which we would have sacrificed in the old way, painlessly and with honor, not like the butchers do these days. We would have dedicated every part of the animal to a power of the land, to strengthen the forces that grow the crops and nourish the people. Instead we are helpless. All we can do is lay a few pitiful offerings upon our tiny Fire Altar and hope that the gods will notice our plight. So far they haven't."

"But you do have the ears of at least one of the royal household," interjected Niamh hopefully.

Imar, Amlaim, and Bárid gave her a blank questioning look and then glanced at each other. They had no idea to whom she might be referring.

"We sent her to you almost two sun cycles ago! She is a student of our school and the wife of Deaglán Mac Íobar, prince of Irardacht."

"What does she look like?" asked Imar, confused.

"Princess Aislinn has red hair and a fine figure. She is sprightly and bold in her manner, knows her sign languages and alphabets, and is half trained to be a fili! Is it possible that you do not know her?" exclaimed Niamh.

The three Druid looked at each other again as comprehension slowly dawned. Surely Niamh must be speaking of that strange red-headed girl who was so fluent in palm Ogum.

The realization of who I was, of how I had come to them on a heather-topped hill by the sea, came flooding back to them.

"Ye gods, we had no idea. She was there all along, and we thought she was just a madwoman!" said Bárid, feeling desolate about the opportunity that had escaped them.

"My best advice is that you find her and explain your dilemma. Surely she can obtain the needed bulls for the sacrifice. Tell her to advise the king on this matter. Afterwards he can distribute the meat to the poor, and if they are as bad off as you say, it will be a popular gesture and good politics," said Dálach-gaes, who was no stranger to the machinations of kingship.

"May I go with you when you travel back to the north?" asked Artrach. "My teachers have told me that they want me to see the world and learn of the kingdoms. If I am to make a sun circuit of Ériu, I might as well start at Irardacht."

And so it was agreed. That day and the next were spent sharing the news of each province. Kingdom by kingdom, all the important marriages, alliances, betrayals, elopements, deaths, births, thefts, and contracts were enumerated and memorized around the ritual fire.

One night Dálach-gaes met privately with Barra Mac Mel, and together they composed a letter advising Íobar to heed the words of Princess Aislinn regarding a matter of royal hospitality towards the poor. The four Drui would carry the letter to the north the very next day.

7

In Irardacht, the season of summer began, and I was still coughing.

"Conláed, will you pick me some fresh rowan berries from that tree just outside of the dun? They are still green, but perhaps you can find some with a blush of red on them or dried ones from last winter that are still on the branch." I addressed the household bard as he ducked through the doorway on his daily visit, as always clutching his harp.

"I have been lying here sick for months, dutifully following the instructions of Father Cearbhall in order not to cause offense. Clearly his methods are not working; I pray and pray to the god Ísu and faithfully enumerate my shortcomings, for which I am heartily sorry, but it still hasn't helped my cough."

"I was wondering when you would stiffen your spine and look to your own training to heal yourself. This is welcome news indeed!" Conláed said with a smile, striking a joyful chord on his harp for emphasis. Druid trained, he had long felt that my sickness was as much a matter of my mind and spirit as my body.

That evening I prepared a thick syrup of sliced green apples, rowan berries, and honey, to which I added the chopped roots of reeds from the bog outside the dun. I cooked it gently all night in the small cauldron that hung over the embers of my hearth fire and then took spoonfuls throughout the day, every day, for half a moontide.

My coughing finally stopped. Father Cearbhall told me it was because of the Masses that were being said in my honor, but I knew better. The Druid teach that there is magic in the berries of the rowan tree and in the reeds of the bog, and even old Father Justan said that his God is everywhere and in all things, so I knew that there was a divine presence in those roots and rowan berries and that that was what had finally cured me.

Once I had my strength back, I began to consider my options. The stone walls of Irardacht were nothing more than a prison for me now; within their confines I could not exercise my learning or my gifts. There was no one other than Conláed with whom I could share my true thoughts, and he was often busy by day, and at night he was always working, playing his harp and telling stories in Íobar's mead hall.

I never went there because I knew I would have to see Deaglán with his concubine, and I would be shamed before everyone. By law I could have scratched her eyes and beaten her for three days and been exempt from liability, but I just didn't have the heart for it. I knew that even if I gave her two black eyes, he would still favor her over me, and then I would be right back where I started.

8

I emerged from my house one morning fully healed. I knew it because I had not coughed for days and I had a ravenous appetite. I could not seem to get enough of the buttered bannocks, honey, and milk that Breachnat ordered the mogae to bring me.

I emerged from the darkness of my fevered solitude into the bright sun of day, and it was as if a veil had been lifted from my eyes. When I looked into the faces of those I met, I saw suffering there. All of them—from the powerful and richly adorned to the meanest mog working in the pig enclosure—seemed to wear a mask of sadness. Why hadn't I noticed this before? Had I been so preoccupied with my own troubles that I had not looked deeply into anyone's eyes until now? What had happened to their spirits to cause this pain? What had happened to their inner fires? I began to dwell on these things.

I sorely missed Niamh and Dálach-gaes and even old Father Justan at that time, for they could have given me an answer from their philosophy.

The only thing I knew for certain was that the trees and grasses had healed me. The Cristaidi discourage the use of plant medicines because they feel these are a distraction from their own healing methods, which involve relics, prayer, and repentance. I concluded that I must be a heretic like old Father Justan. There was some comfort in the label, because at least now I had an identity, and I wore it secretly like a badge of distinction. *Heretic.*

It was then that I first began to make my plans to escape. I knew it was a mad idea, but my nurse Róisín had always said that I was a wild, untamed creature of the fields and forests. In a strange way, I felt more comfortable with the animals and the trees than I ever did with humans, with rare exceptions.

Old Father Justan was just like me. We would sit under his little hazel tree for hours just watching the bees, moths, and butterflies as they made their rounds of the wildflowers. Sometimes we were so still that dragonflies would land on us, and we became a lookout perch for their hunting. We both felt honored to be used in that way.

Dangerous as it might be, the freedom of the open road seemed far preferable to the miserable existence to which I was bound. I began to casually visit the kitchens, storehouses, and even the barns, secretly collecting what I thought I might need—a pack, some oiled-wool blankets, a stout staff, a hooded cape, flasks for well water and the Waters of Life, dried apples, flour, and wax-covered wheels of cheese.

I had finally stopped growing, but being taller than most women of the dun, my feet were large. I pilfered a pair of sturdy men's boots from the riding stable that fit me well.

I rose one morning thinking of what I could do as a parting gesture, something to help the tuath I was leaving so that my name would be more than just a shameful memory after I was gone. I sought out an intelligent kitchen girl named Úna who I had met outside the rath when walking one day and finally found her in the bog outside the gate, gathering heather tops with a small bronze sickle and stowing them in an old willow basket.

She was small and dark haired, tanned by work outside, and dressed in a simple dun-colored dress, a typical tribeswoman of the area. She had a blue triple spiral tattoo on one cheek, marking her as a healer or the daughter of one.

"What are you planning to do with those?" I asked innocently.

The girl startled at the sound of my voice. Gathering simples such as these could be dangerous in Cristaidi times. One could easily be labeled by the priests as an evil sorceress or a witch.

"One of the mogae is ailing, my lady. He has a bad flux from his bowels and a sore belly. My mam used to keep heather in the house for all sorts of ailments. I hope you don't mind?" She stammered a little as she explained, obviously worried that I would object to her hedge medicines.

"Oh no, quite the opposite—I am very pleased to see that someone is left in this kingdom who knows a bit of herb cunning." Her shoulders dropped as she visibly relaxed.

I began to think about training the girl. Maybe if I left just one person behind who could bring the healing strength of nature to these people, my memory would be redeemed.

"You know, you can use the heather tops for many kinds of sickness. I am sure your mam probably told you all about that. The brew of the flowering tops helps the battle weary and the agitated to get to sleep. It also strengthens the heart."

"Oh yes, my mam would always stuff our mattresses with heather to help us sleep. She used it in brews to increase breast milk in sickly young mothers and to poultice wounds and for rheumatism, and she even made a tea of the tops simmered with honey for coughs. She was famous for her cures. They called her a White Lady and said she was a blessing to animals and people alike!" Her face glowed as she described the uses of the little plant called heather, relieved that her mother's teachings were finding favor in my eyes.

Listening to her speak was almost like being back at the Druid School with Niamh and Dálach-gaes and their students. We were always sharing little bits of practical knowledge that could benefit the tribes. I was enjoying the exchange.

"That is excellent. Would you like to learn of another plant that can cure as many ills as your heather?"

"Oh, yes, I would!" Her eyes shone with an eager desire for learning such as I remembered from my own days in the nemed memorizing my alphabets. I had discovered yet another calling. *Teacher.*

I took her down the road to a boggy area that I had explored many times before and pointed out a thick bed of rushes.

"Those plants are called robe of physicians by the Druid. Do you know why?"

"No, my lady."

"Every single part of those plants is useful for healing, from root to tip. They are very sacred to the Druid. The liaig would be left naked without them."

Her face blanched a little, and she crossed herself as I uttered the words. She was clearly afraid to hear the word Druid spoken out loud and so freely, but since I was her superior she held her silence and continued to listen with respect.

"If you learn the uses of just this one plant, you will be able to heal almost any illness. And you can come by here any day of the year and get the medicines at no cost, in any weather. See how they flourish even in the midst of a cold, damp summer? The roots will be there for you summer and winter, even under the ice."

I took the bronze sickle from her hand and bent down to cut one of the plants from the peaty brown water.

"I will explain the uses of this plant to you—leaf, stem, and root—and you must swear to memorize everything I say very carefully, for you will have need of this wisdom for many years to come. Do you swear it?"

I must have looked quite fierce, because she was clearly terrified. But she agreed to do exactly as I said. I drew my fingernail down the base of the thick stem until a clear sap began to flow.

"The juice is used for lung fever, to stop the pain," I said. Then I held out a leaf. "The crushed leaf treats the cough when added to a brew."

"Can I add it to my heather infusions?"

"Yes, exactly—you can combine the crushed leaves with elderberries, elderflowers, mints, or any other herb you like. And when you

66

burn the leaves to an ash, you can apply the ashes to a wound. It will stop the bleeding, and the wound will heal with no infection."

I pointed out the flowering top of the plant. "A brew of the flowers will heal the stomach when someone has been poisoned by spoiled food or drink."

I peeled away the leaves and revealed the fresh green stem.

"This part stops vomiting and lowers a fever."

By now the girl was staring wide eyed. The many uses of this one simple plant seemed like a miracle.

"Do the Druid know this much about every plant?"

"Not all plants, but most—especially those with healing virtues."

I continued the lesson by reaching deep into the muck and pulling out the roots I had left behind when I first cut the plant from the bog.

"The roots may be the most valuable part. You should dry them for use throughout the year, but be sure to gather them at the end of summer because that is when they have collected the powers of the sun and they are most useful for medicine.

"A brew of these roots will lower a fever, stop a bloody cough, clear poisons from the blood, increase urine, remove gravel and stone, calm the emotions, help the digestion, cure diarrhea, and stop vomiting. I used them myself recently to stop a stubborn cough."

"This plant seems almost magical, it has so many uses!" Úna said, delighted.[3]

"That is why it is also known by the Druid as lúth legha, the physician's strength. It's not magic, really; it is simply the power of all that is. You will never go wrong if you study sacred creation. Everything we will ever need to live is given to us right here in these forests and bogs. It comes from the gods, or the one god, if you prefer, from the one sacred Source. That is what the Druid teach and what my old friend Father Justan also taught me.

"The sun shines on the plants all summer, and the plants store the sunlight so that it can be released in the dark times for those who have a need. There is an ancient sacred symbol that has been passed down to us from the ancestors that describes this truth. Would you like to learn it?"

I was treading on dangerous ground because if the girl was found with such a symbol, she too would be labeled a heretic. But I thought she should hear of it so she could show it to any other Druid healer she might encounter. Then they would know she was one before whom they could speak freely.

"Yes, I'd like to know the sacred symbol."

I took a section of stalk and folded it in half. Then I took another section and folded it around the first until I had a rough cross. I continued plaiting in this way, adding layer upon layer of reeds until the rough equal-armed cross was finished. Then I tied off the ends with long split sections of leaf.

"This is our symbol of the sun. Any Druid healer that you meet will recognize it. It will tell them that you are knowledgeable and to be trusted. We call it the Cross of Brighid because she is our fire goddess and the greatest goddess of healing that we know. She knows how to bring the fire and strength of the sun into a sick body or mind and make it well again.

"Take it with you and hide it somewhere safe, because if the Cristaidi find it they will ask you what it is. Just tell them it is their own cross fashioned of reeds. They won't know the difference."

The girl looked at me with worried eyes. "Father Cearbhall says that to speak of goddesses is blasphemy. He says his god, the one and only god, is male."

"Father Cearbhall is a man. He doesn't know everything," I replied.

I stood there thinking for a while, wondering if there was anything more I could tell her—anything I might have left out.

"There is yet one more secret that I have to share with you before you leave this place. Anytime you pick an herb for medicine, you must give something in exchange. It can be a gift of honey, a bit of cheese or apple cider, or even your own hair. That act keeps the balance between the worlds, and the spirit of the plant will stay in good relationship with you and be your helper and ally. When you do this long enough, you will be able to call on the plant's spirit even when you don't have the plant in your hand.

"You can also sing a song of blessing on the plants so that they will always have enough sunlight and rain and everything they need to grow. You can sing that the forces of blight and disease stay away from the plants, that they be nurtured by the fairies, and that they be blessed by the moon, sun, winds, and stars."

I began to sing to the reeds. It was an ancient lay that had been passed down to the Druid from the Eastern lands many generations before:

> *Blessings on the earth*
> *Blessings on the water*
> *Blessings on the fire*
> *Blessings on the wind*
> *Blessings on the sky*
> *Blessings on the sun*
> *Blessings on the moon*
> *Blessings on the stars*
> *Blessings on the universes*
> *Blessings on all lives*
> *Blessings on every friendship*
> *Blessings on every heart*
> *Blessings on every spirit*
> *Blessings on all plants*
> *Blessings on the one and the all*
> *So may it be*
> *So may it be*
> *So may it be.*[4]

"What is that song? It is so very beautiful!" Úna exclaimed.

"That is the 'Salutation to All Creation.' It is the song I like to sing whenever I pick plants for medicine. Now, let's gather up some of these roots, flowers, and stems to add to your heather brew for that sick mog of yours!"

As we trudged back towards the dun, I scanned my body with my inner eyes as I had been taught to do by Niamh and Dálach-gaes, and I noticed with surprise and satisfaction that my three fires were burning brightly once again.

"I have to thank you, Úna, for allowing me to share my knowledge with you. This simple act has restored my spirits more than you can imagine.

"The Druid teach that we all carry three cauldrons of fire within: one in the belly, one in the chest, and one in the head. The fire in the belly is the cauldron of warming that determines if we are healthy or sick. The cauldron of motion is in the chest, and it governs our feelings and emotions. The cauldron of wisdom is in the head. Each of these cauldrons must be fully upright and shining with bright fire in order for a person to be inspired and healthy. In death the cauldrons turn upside down and the fires go out, something a trained Drui can actually see.

"My own three fires have been dim and my cauldrons have been on their sides for so long, it is amazing to feel the sparks of life returning."

She took in the words respectfully, even if she did not fully understand them.

I was filled with gratitude to whichever deity or spirit had helped me and whispered a silent thank you to the wind.

part two

A Candle in the Wind

9

We were sitting inside by the hearth fire, and the young priestess was making me a strong elderberry brew to ward off the chill of the evening air.

"Shall I pour in some of the Waters of Life?" she asked as she swung the cauldron away from the fire. As you know, the Waters of Life are precious and not to be added until an herbal brew has done simmering.

"Yes, that would be lovely. As we sip our portions I will continue my tale exactly as it was related to me by those who were there."

The priestess settled in for the telling, her eyes round with wonder and anticipation. I could see that she was memorizing every word, which gave me hope to think that my story would be passed down to the future...

Artrach, Bárid, Amlaim, and Imar climbed to the top of the ridge so that they could see over the thick canopy of trees. After several days on the road, they were footsore.

"We still have about seven days of walking, by the looks of it," Bárid calculated, judging from the shape of the hills on the horizon, bathed in mist and slanting sunlight.

The three Druid from Irardacht were slightly more relaxed than they had been when they first arrived at the Druid Council. They definitely looked better fed. Niamh had made sure that their packs were stuffed with oats, dried apples, bread, cheese, and dried meats.

Artrach had proved his value as a woodsman time and again by gathering edible mushrooms, the unfurled tops of bracken, wild garlic, birch roots, watercress, and the roots of heather each time they stopped. In the evenings he would take a small iron skillet from his pack and braise everything he had collected over the fire, making a rich butter sauce for the fish they caught most evenings. Each night he would put his small wooden keg of butter into a stream, weighted down with rocks to keep it cool and safe from predators.

He tried to raise their spirits with spirited songs each night around the camp fire. It pained him to see the deep lines of worry on their faces and the thinness of their waists. *No Drui should have to live like this,* he thought.

When the three elder Druid were nestled in their blankets around the fire, Artrach faced the moon so that her beams fell full on his face and began to sing:

> *Never will I be removed from Inisfail*
> *By winds that strip the leaves from a tree*
> *Or bend the willow on the hill*
> *Nor by the winds of change and storm.*
> *Ever will I delight*
> *In the bounding of the deer*
> *In the badgers of the glen*
> *Far more than in the promises*
> *Of the joys of Heaven beyond.*

Imar chuckled at the last line. "You have a way with words, young man. You have certainly captured the essence of our dilemma. How do we Druid prosper in the time of the new religion?"

Artrach smiled. "There was a time in this land when there were no Druid. Then the Druid gained the ascendancy, and now we are disappearing once more. This is but a tide of nature. Every wave rises and falls back. But it always rises again.

"At the moment, we are like sparrows that flew from a freezing night into a warm feasting hall and had our fill of food and celebration. Now we are driven back out into the cold night. But like the birds of spring, we will return to the halls of power when the suntides turn. I am sure of this."

Bárid, Amlaim, and Imar hardly believed what he said, but the words gave them comfort. They were able to relax into their blankets and fall into a light sleep. Artrach sat with his back to a rock and kept vigil, singing an Ogum of protection over them each time he heard a sound in the night.

10

From the clouds over the dun of Íobar, a funnel of ravens had appeared out of nowhere, circling with purpose over a spot to the south. The king had been standing on the wall all day, trying to discern which side was winning. The ravens would not reveal which side was triumphant, but they never gathered until there was carrion for their feast.

By evening Íobar knew. A long line of warriors snaked towards the dun wearing victory wreaths on their heads, their harpers before them, singing a song of conquest. But he did not recognize them because they were not his warriors. They were carrying a body on a bier and clashing their shields in challenge, daring any soldiers left in the fort to meet them in battle. Worse, he could finally see his own men, their heads shorn in humiliation and with bound hands and chained feet, surrounded by their captors.

The battle chief of the enemy's warriors stood before the gate and bellowed for admittance. He was tall and blond, blood-spattered and grim-faced, and wore a rough victory wreath on his long yellow hair, made of wild leaves from the forest.

"I demand to see the king of Irardacht. I demand my father's honor price. I demand vengeance for my father's death!"

"Let him in," Íobar said to his guards.

Roin was the prince of a small kingdom just beyond the southern border of Irardacht. He and his father had led their warriors north to test Íobar's strength and to capture a herd of cattle if they were so lucky. They had accomplished both objectives, but at the last skirmish Roin's father, Lovic, had been killed by a spear through the heart.

Íobar could see that Roin had the battle rage still on him and, worse, that he was grieving for his own blood father. The price would be steep.

"I want a ring of gold for every finger of my father's hands!" Roin demanded. "My father, the king, will be buried with honor! I want a golden torque and robes of finest fur to cover him with glory on his last journey home. And I want golden armbands and torques for every one of my men. Give me these or your kingdom is forfeit!"

Inwardly Íobar felt deep relief. The boastful young man was only seeking marks of honor to take back with him when he returned home to his women and his tribes. He was too young and foolish to realize that the high kingship of Irardacht was his for the taking. Íobar was on his knees, with no food for his people, and the arrogant young whelp didn't even realize it. His father, that old fox Lovic, would never have been so stupid.

"Very well. You will have all you ask for. I will command that my warriors strip their torques, rings, and armbands from their own bodies and give them to you as your just prize for a great victory."

"And I am taking your best warriors back with me as hostages," Roin added, jutting his chin towards the miserable bunch of men who were bound together by chains and shorn like sheep.

"That is only just," Íobar said evenly before the assembled nobles and tribesmen.

In his mind he was thinking the loss of cattle was the greater tragedy, because now even more of his people would go without milk and meat. The warriors could fend for themselves.

"Now swear to me on cold iron that you will not invade my kingdom and seek revenge," Roin said, pulling his bright sword from its sheath. To their horror the court could see the dried blood still on it and the scabbard overflowing with clots of gore.

"I pledge not to call for revenge, or may the Daoine Sidhe take me," Íobar said, reverently touching iron as he uttered the oath.

He would keep his promise, but he knew—and somewhere in his mind Roin knew it too—that there was no way to stop the warriors of Irardacht from creeping over the border to steal back their cows. The bloody conflict would continue. But for now it was enough just to save face and distribute the gold.

There was a feast that night to seal the bargain, and Íobar was forced to slaughter even more of his own cattle, pigs, and sheep to preserve the rules of hospitality. The captured warriors were bound, wrists and ankles tied together, and flung into a corner of the mead hall like so many hogsheads of béoir. Their women and children stood outside the walls of the dun, weeping.

Conláed dutifully played his harp for Prince Roin and sang heroic songs of battle. Roin's men joined in drunken refrains, thoroughly enjoying themselves, as Íobar's people sat grim-faced. The mood in the hall was such that no one noticed my absence.

11

At the time I had no idea what had transpired, but I knew that it must have been something terrible. I knew it because there was a commotion going on in the mead hall, and there were knots of weeping women and children standing before the gate. There were lit torches everywhere as if it were a High Holy Day, and the scent of burning pine permeated the grassy sward of the dun, mixed in with the smells of roasting flesh. Strangers were milling around the central courtyard, brazenly looking into windows and doors.

Someone was being honored with a feast. Whether that person was alive or dead, I knew not. Whatever had occurred simply did not matter. I decided to take advantage of whatever was happening and use the unexpected chaos as my chance to escape.

Conláed was not in his roundhouse, so I left a note for him, scratched with a goose quill onto an old patch of vellum: *Thank you for everything. May the gods bless you always.*

He would know my handwriting. Besides me and Conláed, only the Cristaidi could write, and such a sentiment could never have come from them.

My charcoal-grey oiled-wool cloak served me well, and I managed to glide from shadow to shadow unseen. When I finally got to the gate there were no guards, and the women there were far too distraught to notice me, so I took to the stony path that led out into the starry blackness of the forests and fields.

I walked all night, afraid to stop except for a brief drink when I crossed a stream. I could hardly believe my luck; I felt the gods were at my back, urging me on. I knelt before a tiny rill and scooped the clear liquid into my fingers as the first rays of sunlight sparkled in the new dawn. I touched my mouth, my heart, and my forehead to bless myself with the sunlight captured in the water, "for where water and fire come together, there is always the greatest potential for magic," as Niamh and Dálach-gaes had often said.

I looked up and saw a clear sky and felt the wind from the south, a good omen, and continued walking until the shadows were lengthening once more. By now I had not eaten well nor slept for nearly two days, and I was thoroughly exhausted. I had to make a camp, no matter the danger.

I began by carefully setting up Ogums of protection. I painted the Ogums onto stones with my fingers using uisge beatha as I chanted the name of each Ogum out loud, until I had five enchanted stones in a ring around my campsite. Then I placed crossed twigs of rowan at each of the directions and invoked the spirit of that tree to surround me with her magical shield.

I carefully cut a circle of turf, set the grass aside, and then gathered dry, dead fallen pine needles and birch bark and started a fire on the bare earth with tinder and flint. As it burned down to hot embers, I picked some fresh nettles and made myself a clear green broth by dropping red-hot stones into a little cauldron that I had hung from a small iron tripod placed over the fire. By now I was giddy with fatigue, and my fingers were trembling as I used the edge of my cape to pull the hot cauldron from the flames. I dipped a wooden cup into the broth and drank the hot liquid gratefully, swallowing portions of bread and cheese until I finally felt warm and satisfied.

"Conláed would think me crazy if he could see what I am doing, all alone in the wilderness like this," I said out loud to the fire.

The fire answered back in its own language, singing and dancing like a living creature sent to keep me company through the might. I was certain that my magic would keep me safe and that the little fire would scare away the beasts of the forest, so at last I curled into my cape and fell into a sound sleep.

I continued this routine of existence, gathering herbs and cresses by day as I walked and making a new fire each night. Every morning I carefully covered the embers with cut turf to hide my passage. One evening there was a damp drizzle and I found a rocky overhang under which I could sleep. It was a peaceful few days.

One morning at daybreak, in the midst of a deep dream, I suddenly felt that I was suffocating. At first I thought I was having a nightmare, and I struggled hard to bring myself awake. But then I realized I was awake and that there was some kind of thick leather hood over my head.

I could hardly breathe; someone was tying my hands and feet together with rope. Suddenly I felt myself being lifted and turned upside down. Then a pole was thrust between my arms and legs, and I was swinging like a ham trussed for market.

"She looks strong; I wonder who she is?" a voice said from before me.

"Another catch to add to our store from Irardacht!" another added from behind, slapping me hard on the rear end and laughing. To him I was just a lowly peasant, no more valuable than a side of meat.

Now my hind parts were swinging madly from side to side, and it was all I could do to keep my neck from breaking as I fought to keep my head up, suspended as I was from a pole between two men. I was terrified. What were they planning? What would they do to me? How could I have been so foolish to leave the dun without a retinue and no way to defend myself?

They carried me for what felt like half a day until I was finally dropped with no warning onto a grassy patch of ground. Then they pulled my hood back far enough that my mouth was exposed and thrust a clay cup against my mouth.

"Drink!" someone ordered. I drank. It was water.

"I have to relieve myself," I said.

Surely they would let me take care of my needs behind a bush. I felt the ropes around my hands and feet being loosened.

"Stand up, woman," one of them said.

I tried to imagine how many of them there were by their voices, but it was very confusing. It seemed like every time someone spoke, there was a different voice; I had counted more than twenty individuals already. Then I felt a rough hand on my back, pushing me forward. I still had the leather hood over my face, but I could see the ground below by looking directly down.

"Go behind that rock," a voice commanded.

I crept towards the rock, trying not to fall. Looking down, I could see rows of feet. Some of them were shod and some of them were bare and bleeding from the sharp rocks of the road.

I must not be the only captive here, I thought.

There was some comfort in that because I was apparently one of many, not just a woman alone and sport for the men.

When I was done, the leather bag was tightened around my neck once more and my hands and feet were tied together again. This time I was swung up onto a cart. I could feel other breathing bodies all about me, none of whom were speaking. But they were all warm and alive.

Against my will I found myself drifting off to sleep, exhausted from the trauma of capture and lulled by the rhythm of the road and the warm bodies around me.

When the hood finally came off, it was dusk, and I was staring right into the eyes of another prisoner who was but inches away from my face. Both of us were bound and helpless, lying on our sides and unable to move one way or the other because of the crush of bodies.

"Hello," he said softly, with a smile and a wink.

"Very pleased to meet you," I responded formally.

There was something hilarious about the whole situation, and so we both giggled.

A tall, very serious-looking blond man with blood on his tunic came over. "Oy, you two. Stop it!" and he hit us both with the flat of his sword.

After that the only thing we could do was smile and crinkle our eyes at each other as if we were naughty children who had been caught in some prank at school.

Suddenly the young man's face went pale; he was straining to follow an altercation in the distance. I tried to hear what had captured his attention. Someone was claiming to be a Drui! The man, whoever he was, was loudly protesting his ill treatment.

Then there was the obscenely unmistakable splat of a thick piece of flesh and bone being thrown against a flat rock. There was a brief gurgling noise and then a sickening silence. Someone had clearly lost his head.

The man next to me went ashen, and then his face turned red with fury. I saw one tear of anguish slide down his cheek, and after that he wouldn't look at me, enveloped as he was in his own private agony.

No one spoke; a kind of shocked silence reigned over all. Maybe the slain man really had been a Drui? If so, the crime was beyond shameful. Even in these depraved times, to actually kill a Drui was unthinkable. Every Drui carried vast stores of wisdom and lore, genealogy, medicine, law, and poetry in their head. To kill a Drui was like burning down a library—a terrible loss for any kingdom.

And then the man turned his face to me again, wide eyed, crying silent tears. At that moment I realized they really had done the unthinkable evil deed. They had actually killed a Drui.

I reached out to the man with my eyes and tried to comfort him, feeling my own sense of shock and loss. He knew from my eyes that I understood what had happened and the full horror of it. Our foreheads gradually came together and we mourned, silently forging a bond of grief that went beyond mere words.

The next morning when I woke at the first bird song, I found that somehow I had curled in the night so that my body fitted closely against the man's chest and knees, and that his tall form was wrapped around me like a warm blanket. I could feel and hear his steady breathing just above my ear.

It was strange to be in such intimacy with someone I had only met the day before, yet somehow it felt completely natural. We had already shared tears, laughter, and long, uninterrupted looks into each other's eyes.

I tried to remember what color his eyes were. It seemed to me that they were the color of hazel leaves. His hair was certainly red like mine; locks of it spilled over my shoulders and mingled with my own tresses, making a cascade of fiery brightness around our two heads.

I had a strong premonition that the gods were behind this meeting somehow—that I had been led by all my sufferings to this man as surely as I had escaped Deaglán Mac Íobar and his father's dun.

"Thank you," I whispered to whichever unknown deity, spirit, or mischievous sprite was guiding my fate, feeling oddly at peace and comforted, if only for a moment.

12

Now we were being driven down a narrow road. I could tell because there were thick stands of rustling trees above and to either side of us. I could also hear a soft lowing in the distance that sounded very much like a vast herd of cattle.

I gradually realized that our little cart was part of a long train that contained cattle both ahead and behind us. At intervals one of our captors would ride up alongside the cart to commiserate with the other guards, swearing and complaining because cows were constantly drifting off into the forest. Rounding them up was becoming a huge task because of the trees, brambles, and bushes.

By simply listening to snatches of speech, I made out that the cows were booty and so were we. But I still had no idea who had taken us and where we were headed.

After another hard day of being hauled like so many sacks of meal, we were finally pulled out of the cart and deposited onto a grassy hillside. It was evening, and someone was standing over a large fire in the distance, stirring a cauldron filled with what smelled like mutton stew. My stomach growled uncontrollably in response, as did the stomachs of the other prisoners.

"Make yourselves at home. This is where you will be living for a long while," someone said.

"But not you or you." He pointed to my new friend and to another man of about the same age, height, and build. I suddenly realized that I didn't even know my new friend's name.

Black, red, and brown cows milled all around us, bawling loudly, begging to be milked.

"You two: your job will be to guard the edges of the herd and protect it from wolves. And make sure the cows stay well away from the bogs and cliffs! And don't think you can just walk off. We'll be patrolling the boundaries of these hills on our horses to make sure that doesn't happen," a man said to my red-haired friend and to the other man who was next to him.

They were each handed a staff and a sheepskin cloak against the rain, and ushered away.

I noticed then that I was the only female captive. The others were all warriors—tattooed, shorn, bleeding, and clearly defeated in battle. To be forced to tend cattle, which was usually a boy or young woman's task, was a further humiliation.

"You there, each of you, grab a calf and take it to that enclosure," the man said to the crestfallen warriors.

I knew from my forays into my father's barnyards that cows had to be kept near their calves in order to give milk, but the calves had to be prevented from suckling. There was a fenced enclosure just for the calves. They would have to be fed by hand throughout the day.

I scanned the area quickly in the fading half-light to see if there might be any medicinal worts in the vicinity. My eyes fell on wild knit-bone and slan-lus as the most likely healing agents in sight, and I mentally determined to find a way to mash them and distribute them to the men to salve their bleeding feet and other wounds. But that would have to wait. The cows were becoming more insistent by the minute, and the next thing I knew I was being handed a large wooden bucket and a milking stool.

"Twice a day, morning and evening, you will milk these cows. And when you are not milking, you will churn butter," one of our captors said.

There was a stack of butter churns waiting. Apparently the defeated warriors would be set to this humiliating task as well.

There were several shielings within sight, small round huts made of bent saplings and wattles and covered over with sods of peat. They appeared to be waterproof at least. I worked as quickly as I was able, knowing without being told that only when the milking was finished would I be allowed to eat a bowl of something hot and find my weary bed.

When I finally got my wooden bowl of stew, I plucked up the courage to ask a few questions.

"What kingdom is this? I mean, for whom am I now working?" I asked the man who had given us our tasks, as if I were just another dairy maid who had recently exchanged masters.

I knew that if they discovered my true status it would be very costly for my father or for Íobar to ransom me. I fully intended to escape on my own and deprive my captors of further booty.

"You are in Prince Roin's employ. His father, King Lovic, started this raid. When Lovic was killed, the whole thing became part of Roin's kingship plan. Now it's Roin's way of proving his worth to the people. He hopes that he will be elected to follow in his father's footsteps."

But that still didn't tell me who my red-headed friend might be.

That night I bedded down in my own little hut, falling swiftly to sleep on a loose pile of straw that was covered by rough sheepskins against the damp. The moon of Beltaine shone through my open doorway, and the soft snorting and breathing of cows mingled with the songs of night.

I had no hearth to smoor and bring safety to my hut, so I visualized my inner fires glowing and sent up a prayer of thanks to whichever gods were guiding and protecting me. Then I passed quickly into a black, dreamless sleep.

13

We soon fell into our weary routine. Milk the cows in the morning, carry the milk to a central location under the large ash tree, and churn the butter. Scrape the butter into wooden kegs and set the kegs into the stream. Milk the cows again in the evening and set the milk aside for churning, make more butter, and lay it in the stream. Day by day these tasks were repeated in the same order, in the same way.

Carts arrived each afternoon to pick up butter kegs and barrels of fresh milk for transport back to the local villages and to deliver empty casks ready to be refilled. The same carts brought bread, cheese, vegetables, and occasionally meat or fish for the workers.

But it wasn't all drudgery. It is well known that cows enjoy music while they are being milked, so we always traded songs while milking. Everyone joined in, especially in the choruses between verses.

I took the opportunity to provide a little bit of spiritual guidance to the men. I couldn't help it; it was part of my training. *Priestess* could have been my title, though I would tell no one.

"Be sure to pour out the first milk as a gift for the fairies," I would say each morning. "It's important that you do this for the health of the cattle, and if you do it faithfully, the herds will be well protected."

I knew that farmers who neglected the milk offerings invited sickness into their herds and sometimes into their own families.

I would walk over to a hollowed-out stone I had found and placed on top of a large flat rock. I always poured the first milk into the hollow as I faced the sun and sang, "A Daoine Sidhe, this is for you!"

Many of the men followed my example.

Healer was another title that I might have claimed. I had poulticed the worst-off of the wounded warriors with wild medicines from the fields.

"You look familiar to me somehow," said a scarred fighter by my side who was unhappily plunging milk in a large butter churn.

I had not yet been recognized and had worked hard to keep my identity a secret. Soiled as my face was and with a torn and filthy léine, tunic, and unkempt hair, so far I had succeeded.

"Oh, everyone says that. It's the red hair. You know, see one redhead and you have seen them all!" I shrugged off his comment as if I were used to such speculation.

"It's just a question of waiting for Íobar to send some of our warriors to steal back the cattle," another man observed as we churned butter side by side under the ash tree. "All we really have to do now is bide our time."

He was a warrior who must have been awarded many armbands and battle rings for successful campaigns. I could still see the whiteness of his skin where those ornaments had once circled his body. Shorn of his dignity, he looked thoroughly disgusted to be doing this kind of menial work.

The captive men constantly secreted away such weapons as they could devise, cudgels and staffs made from the trees of the nearby forest and slings made of old sheep hides and stones. When Íobar's troops finally appeared, they would be ready to jump into the fray immediately, to liberate each other and the cows. This was the well-understood plan.

While it was always a mark of skill and honor to capture human hostages and a herd of cows, it was an equal honor to recapture the same cows and bring them safely back home. And, if possible, Íobar would try to add more of Roin's own cows to the herd, and the round of thieving and recovery of cattle would continue.

This was how it always had been and always would be between the tribes.

One night as I lay on my little pallet of straw and sheepskins I heard a soft scratching on the leather door. I slid the door frame aside and to my amazement saw my friend. His long red hair was backlit by the moon, and he looked wider and bulkier than I remembered because of the sheepskins over his shoulders. He had also grown a stubble of beard, which I found most becoming.

"May I come inside?" he asked in a politely hushed tone.

"Of course," I whispered back. "I am sorry that I have nothing to offer in the way of hospitality," I murmured as he folded his long legs and made himself comfortable on the hard clay floor.

"I hardly expected food or drink. Your company is all I am after," he said, smiling.

In the clear moon glow there was just enough light that we didn't need a candle so long as the door was kept open. But this meant that we had to keep our voices low.

I knew he wasn't from Irardacht; I certainly would have noticed his red hair if he had been at Íobar's court.

"Who are you? What is your name? And how did you happen to be captured with Íobar's men?" My words tumbled all over themselves in haste because I was afraid that our meeting would be cut off before I could finally learn who he was.

"I am Artrach, a Drui from In Medon, on a mission to the north; I was traveling with three others. One of them was also taken and, as you know, killed."

We hung our heads for a moment, recalling the terrible shame and horror of hearing the Drui beheaded.

He said he was a Drui. Was that really possible? My thoughts tumbled in a silent storm.

Raw emotion flooded my chest, and I suddenly felt like weeping; whether it was from relief or gratitude at finding a friend I could trust with my very life, I knew not. But now I was certain that the gods were guiding me somehow, somewhere, for some purpose. But what did it all mean? This was far too much to be mere coincidence. I gathered my reeling thoughts into coherent words.

"I have to tell you something unbelievable: I too am a Drui! Well, almost a Drui. I was half trained by Dálach-gaes and Niamh in the court of Barra Mac Mel. I am almost qualified to carry the silver branch of the poets; I have half of the poetic art!"

Then he took my hands in his. I could feel the new calluses and scratches gained from his hard work with the cows. His eyes were moist and wide, and I thought he might also be on the verge of tears.

"Is this really true?" he asked. "To be trained as a Drui is so very rare. My teachers said that only one person in ten thousand is ever chosen, and yet we have found each other. Like this!"

We spoke long into the night. I learned that he was a student at the Forest School of In Medon, and he learned that I had been trained in the arts of the Drui and fili in the school of Dálach-gaes and Niamh. We said prayers together for Amlaim, the recently murdered Drui.

"Let's see him crossing the rainbow bridge to the House of Donn in the west," Artrach suggested.

We held hands in silence and visualized Amlaim's spirit crossing easily to the home of the God of Death in the Blessed Isles. We knew that his body would have been given only a hasty burial, so we visualized it melting quickly back into the sod, swiftly becoming food for the flowers, trees, and animals—a new expression of sacred life.

It was almost dawn when Artrach finally crept out of my little hut, and I was very sorry to see him go.

Things went on this way for several turnings of the moon. It was hard to stay up all night in conversation with Artrach and then perform the daily tasks of dairying, but somehow I managed it. The cows knew that something was amiss because I would suddenly stop singing and actually fall asleep while still sitting on my milking stool. One time a cow put her foot right into the leather milking bucket, crushing it, and I didn't even notice. I got a sharp rap on the head for that.

By now Artrach and I were cuddling together almost every night, dozing, wrapped in each other's arms more often than speaking. This meant that we were better equipped for the next day's work, and I was getting to know him on a whole other level: bone, sinew, muscle, moist lips, and tender touches.

I was amazed that after several years with Deaglán I had never felt the feelings I was now experiencing. A simple glance from Artrach reverberated deep into my belly, and his kisses sent me into shivers of quiet joy. I could lie entwined in his arms for hours just listening to his breathing, which was the sweetest music I had ever heard. I felt like a virgin, a woman who had never been touched or loved until that moment. It was all new for me, an endless wonder and delight.

I liked to think that it was the same for him. I could feel his insistent hardness the moment we lay down together. I would gently place my hand on his male parts and caress them, and he would cry out in delighted frustration.

But we never went further than that because our Druid training forbade it. We knew that if we joined our bodies we would be legally married, with all the attendant obligations and contractual responsibilities that went with that state. Neither of us would think of undertaking such a step without first consulting the Druid Council and the elders.

I learned that I could bring myself to ecstasy merely by pressing my body against his. It seemed like a miracle. How was it possible that I was experiencing more pleasure in that cold little hut than I had ever felt under the fine linen sheets and furs with Deaglán? It was a yearning pain, pleasure, and delight, all wrapped up together.

Sometimes we would simply kiss for half the night, never growing bored or tired with our patient explorations. It was as if we had entered a different time and space where nothing existed except each other, our own eternal fairy realm in a rough, dark little shieling where every moment together was a new gift from the gods.

Most evenings Artrach would reappear from the hillsides, looking for his supper. He would catch sight of me still at work under the ash tree and would come over, insisting on carrying the milk pails or butter kegs for me all the way to the stream. On the way we would hold hands and lock eyes.

"You are gazing at me again," he would say, teasing. But he was gazing back.

When I was with him, it was as if there were some irresistible magnetic pull between us the moment I set eyes on him or when his eyes found mine. Sometimes I knew he was behind me before I even turned around. I can honestly tell you that in those short weeks, despite the hard work and other humiliations, we were both completely happy.

One day we walked to the stream together and deposited the butter kegs and milk barrels into the cold water for safekeeping, and he took my hands in his.

"I love you, you know," he said.

"Yes, I do know," I answered quietly.

Our hands were still wet from the chilly waters. We both knew the most ancient and hallowed marriage rite where a couple would simply join hands under running water, the gateway to the ancestors and to the Daoine Sidhe realm. Such a union would be witnessed by all the inhabitants of the Otherworld, a most solemn vow.

We were still not prepared to pledge our troth in the sight of the ancestors, but our clasped wet hands foreshadowed the possibility. It was something we both wanted. We knew this without saying the words.

"One day I will make you mine. I swear it," Artrach murmured softly into my ear.

My response was to kiss him deeply on the lips, in full sight of the watching captives. I was amazed again at the perfect fit of our two bodies, as if we had been born for this union. Every crevice of my form matched some extension of his, while his hollow spaces perfectly fit my breasts, belly, and thighs.

We held each other in the gathering dusk, perfectly content to just stand there under the twinkling stars, pouring our body heat into each other. There were joyful whoops from the warriors.

"I think they're jealous," Artrach said with a smile, his long red hair warming my shoulders and tickling my cheeks.

His face was so beautiful; he appeared to me like a young god sent from the Otherworld to bring the love and affection that had always eluded me.

He reached into a little bag that hung from his belt and pulled out a small object, placing it into my hand. I peered at it closely in the dusky twilight. It was a beautiful little triskell.

"I found a bit of bronze wire and pounded it out on the rocks while I was watching the cows," he said by way of explanation. "Take the leather cord off your neck."

I pulled off the tiny cross that Father Justan had given me so many moons before.

He took it from my hand and affixed the bronze triskell, then lifted the leather cord gently over my head once more.

"I will treasure it always," I said, thinking that I was blessed by two streams of sacred wisdom, the Pagani and the Cristaidi, both at once.

But of all the jewels and finery I had ever received, that little bronze triskell was the most precious of all to my heart.

14

The chill winds of late summer were pushing hard across the land when Íobar's warriors finally appeared.

"At last!" cried one of the fighters who had been sitting next to me sulkily making butter since morning.

The burly men with their once-shaved scalps now bristled with scraggly beards and stubbles of hair on their heads. Their filthy leather breeks and shirts were torn, almost hanging off their bodies, while livid blue tattoos, battle rings, and bronze armbands still decorated their faces, fingers, and arms. They kicked aside the hated churns and ran to alert the others, quickly gathering up the fighting staves they had secreted away under bushes and stones.

My only thought was for Artrach, out there alone in the hills somewhere, tending the cows. I had to find him before he was taken hostage or hurt or lost to me forever. I ran in the direction of the scattered herds. My worn summer tunic caught on the blackberries and was torn anew, my shins were scratched and bleeding, but I hardly noticed.

Now warriors were closing in from every direction. Some were Íobar's men and others were Roin's. The battle cries of "Abu! Abu!" and the clash of sticks and blades sounded all around me.

"Artrach!" I cried loudly, scanning the hills for any sign of his beloved red head.

No response.

I stumbled on, tripping over rocks in my haste and biting the dirt more than once when my balance failed. Higher and higher I climbed, scrambling to get a better perspective on the struggle below.

Finally I saw him. He was in the distance, fighting off one of Roin's warriors with a thick staff. I dared not distract him with my voice; all I could do now was watch and wait. The two men seemed evenly matched, and neither of them was making much progress.

Suddenly something dark whizzed past the corner of my field of vision and I heard a sickening sound; a spear had been flung out of nowhere. It struck Artrach in the back, full force. The moment it hit, I heard the life breath go out of him.

I will never forget the unspeakable pain of that moment; as if the same spear had gored a hole in my own heart. My breath actually stopped, and I could no longer inhale for the searing pain in my chest.

Roin's man looked down, kicked Artrach's body a few times with his foot to see if he was still alive, and then turned back to join the larger skirmish. Ravens were already gathering, circling above and anticipating their feast.

My every instinct was to run to him, to pull out that terrible spear and to salve his wounds, but there were men fighting all around me.

I could not allow myself, a king's daughter, to be captured, for once they knew who I was, I could be carried away by any of the men to yet another kingdom and a high ransom would be demanded. That would destroy my father's kingdom. Or Íobar's.

Artrach was dead. The ravens were speaking clearly. I had to flee.

My heart was broken past all believing. *Why? Why did the gods always take from me anyone that I loved? Why was I never allowed true peace in this life? Why were the gods so very cruel?*

I ran and ran until my lungs were bursting with fire, and then I ran some more. Yellow bile spilled from my mouth and yet I did not stop. My eyes blurred with tears of anguish, grief, and exhaustion.

I fell and picked myself up again and again and thought that if I just kept running, maybe I could outrun my anguish—maybe it would numb the pain of my wrecked spirit and heart.

That night I made no fire; I had no appetite for food, and I no longer cared about warmth or light. Instead I gathered up handfuls of leaves and grasses and made myself a cold, dry nest in a hollow under the roots of an old oak tree. I appealed to its spirit: "Oak, be like a stout door for me against the darkness."

I wrote the oak Ogam in the air with my shaking finger and then surrendered to the numbing oblivion of sleep, trusting the spirit of the oak to hold me in its strong circle of light.

That night I had a dream, or maybe it was a vision. It was one of those dreams that are brighter and clearer than waking and that stay with you a long time.

A woman, an old grey-haired ban-Drui, appeared to me. She was dressed in flowing blue robes that rippled around her feet like the waves of the sea, and a massive golden torque glistened at her neck. When she spoke, her words fell upon me like a balm.

"Water is always water, if it stays still or becomes waves. You must find your true self—your still, inner nature. You must rediscover who you really are—your eternal being."

"Who are you?" I asked the apparition from within my dreaming.

"They called me Ethne, Rígain, and ard-ban-Drui. These are my lands, and I have been watching you."

And then she disappeared, but her voice still echoed in my head as I awoke with a start, striving to remember the words.

Her name was familiar to me from poems and songs. She was the old queen of In Medon, returned from the Otherworld to give me guidance. I felt humbled and awed.

In the morning I noted the direction of the sunrise and calculated the way back to In Medon. It seemed my only course. If I took the road towards Irardacht, I would surely be discovered. And besides, who would want me now? I was a disgraced and wayward wife. All the soldiers had seen me with Artrach. Artrach! The thought of him brought thick tears anew. I poured out my grief in torrents of rain from my eyes that dripped onto the moss beneath the ancient tree that had sheltered me through the night.

"Aoibhgreine, mo muirne."

"What! Who's there?" I spun around frantically to see who had called to me. But there was no one. Only Dálach-gaes and his family knew me by that name, my pet name. Artrach knew it too, because I had told him all the details of my childhood. But who was calling me that now?

I strained to hear more, but there was only the stillness of the rising sun and the crisp wind through fallen leaves. I knew I was completely and utterly alone.

15

I crawled up to the little wall surrounding Father Justan's hut on my hands and knees with my head down, staying low so as not to be seen. It was the wall built by Father Justan's saintly predecessor, Father Per. As a child I would run along the length of that wall, knowing that Father Justan was always there, waiting at the far end to catch me. Now that seemed like another lifetime, a dim memory of joy.

I could hear voices from within the hut, and I did not wish to be discovered by anyone other than the priest, so I sent up a silent prayer to the spirit of Father Per that I remain hidden until it was safe to appear.

After weeks alone in the wilderness, I must have looked like a madwoman or else a forest spirit that had taken on a flesh body. I certainly couldn't walk into the dun of my father like that, nor could I cross the grassy sward to the nemed of Dálach-gaes and Niamh. I felt like some wild animal in hiding, trying not to be eaten alive.

Father Justan was conversing with two monks, the sort who would arrive from time to time to pester him and make sure he was still following the catechism of the Romani church.

"I have learned that by living in this simple way I can be alone with my thoughts. Only then can I keep careful watch over them and train my mind to holy purpose," Father Justan was saying. "In meditation each day I notice that my thoughts will rise and fall. One moment they follow their own course, and then they decline. I ask God to clear my wandering thoughts, to bring them to silence, and then point me to a new, more virtuous path. This is my main work these days."

"No, no *no!*" One of the monks responded heatedly, pounding on a little wooden writing table for emphasis. "If you clear your mind in that very moment, you open yourself to demons!"

"Not so, my dear brother," Justan responded patiently, as if addressing a frightened child. "I find that by slowing down my body and then my mind, I become acutely aware of my thoughts and then of the luminous space between my thoughts. If any demon is going to attack me, it will be *through* my thoughts, not through the luminous space *between* my thoughts! Each time I reach that inner silence, I feel that I am at one with God, and that he can turn me to thoughts and actions that are truly worthy. If everyone turned their thoughts to the silence and then to God, wouldn't this world be a better, more loving place?"

The discussion went on like that into the gloaming. I was becoming desperate for food and drink. I had lived on hazelnuts, cresses, and stream water for days on end, and I longed for a bath, a hot meal, and a warm bed. Finally, I reluctantly took my leave, crawling back into the surrounding woodland to make yet another cocoon of dry leaves and pine branches. At least I would be tolerably dry through the night.

The next morning I crept back to the wall and listened as Father Justan served parting bowls of hot oatmeal to the brothers while offering his final observations on the nature of prayer.

"For me, prayer consists of listening to the silence of the world. In that silence I experience unity with all creation and I am one with the sacred mystery. In meditation my heart watches and listens and eventually my mind drifts away."

"You should be asking for forgiveness of your sins," said one of the monks with evident disapproval, "and urging others to do the same!"

"My prayer does not generally consist of asking for things, although I might sometimes pray for wisdom, protection, and the healing of others. For me, prayer is about paying attention to God's sacred creation and then giving praise for all that he has wrought."

It seemed the argument had come to an impasse, because after that there was only the soft scraping of horn spoons against wooden bowls as the Cristaidi finished their breakfast.

At last the two monks departed and I dared to pop my head over the little stone wall. When Father Justan saw me, his usually kindly face contorted in fear.

"It's me, Aislinn!" I said hastily as I rose to standing.

"Can it really be?" Father Justan was doubtful, as though I must be some kind of vision. He reached out gingerly to touch my arm, to see if it was actual flesh and bone.

"See this? Don't you recognize it?" I pulled out the little wooden cross that he had given me when I first left In Medon. I was still wearing it under my torn and stained shift. "It really is me, Father Justan. I have been traveling alone in the wilderness for days, and I am famished. Do you have any oatmeal left?"

The request for oatmeal was so simple and sensible that he at last accepted that I really was Aislinn, mysteriously returned from the northern kingdom.

He sat me down before the fire and insisted on covering me with blankets. I had been shivering for so long that I no longer noticed. Then he watched me drink several cups of hot elderberry tea with eyes wide and full of concern. As he prepared a bowl of hot oatmeal with butter and honey, I ventured to comment.

"I heard your discussion with those monks. I was hiding behind Father Per's wall so they wouldn't see me. I hope you aren't upset by my eavesdropping."

"Oh no, my child, you did exactly the right thing. If you had revealed yourself looking like this, they would have thought you a demon and demanded that you be stoned to death on the spot! They see demons everywhere. I am glad you waited until they were gone."

"I heard what you were saying about the silence of the world, about the silence between words and thoughts. That is very like what the Druid teach. We Druid say that there is a spark of divinity within every bit of creation. We know that there is a light within every stone and within every leaf, flower, drop of water, and crystal of ice. We find that we can best become one with the Divine when we go deeply into that inner silence.

"We cultivate our senses and refine them through meditation and spiritual exercise, until we can see with our inner eyes, hear with our inner ears, and completely lose the boundary between self and other. Only then are we sent out to serve the tribes."

"Aislinn, you amaze me. Any other woman would be crying for a bath and clean clothes, yet here you are philosophizing before you have even combed your hair or had a proper rest."

"I guess I have ignored my body for so long that I no longer notice its wants."

I smiled as he laid out a warm pile of blankets for me to sleep on. *Priestess*. I knew that was my true nature. Anyway, there was nothing else left for me in this world—nothing else that mattered.

16

"What are we going to do with you?" Father Justan asked, shaking his head.

I had just returned from scrubbing myself down in a stream with clean sand and then lavender-scented siabainn. It took a long time to scrub the dirt from between my toes and from my legs and hands. Father Justan had given me one of his woolen robes to wear, which I had belted with a soft rope. I was so thin from my wanderings that the rope went twice around my waist and yet there were still two long ends left hanging, almost touching the ground. My large feet slid easily into an old pair of his sandals. I had ruined my boots completely with running and with mud.

"If I ever return to Irardacht, I will be returning to a barren and loveless marriage. Deaglán never liked me, from the moment we were joined. By now his concubine has given him a child, and he has no real use for me anymore. And as you know, the peace that my marriage was supposed to ensure has been broken.

"If I present myself to my parents, they will tell me that I have to be married again and they will find me yet another husband. I just can't do that any more. I am finished with men. I will never join another man in matrimony, nor will I ever love another."

"But child, if all you have known of men is one very unhappy marriage, then you haven't yet known the joys of married life."

"Father, I have known all the joys I care to know. When I was captured I met a beautiful soul, one dearer to me than any other. We swore to be united before the gods one day, and then he was taken from me."

I couldn't stop the tears that welled up in my eyes. The memory of Artrach was a fresh wound, one from which I knew I would never wholly recover.

"Child, who is this man, and why was he taken from you?" Father Justan asked softly.

"He was snatched away from me by the gods. He was killed by a spear through the back, and that's why I came here. You're the only person I can think of who won't make demands. You're the only one who will simply listen.

"I am done, finished with life. I have nowhere to go. I refuse to reenter my father's dun; I want nothing more to do with life at court. I just want to disappear into the forest and live like you do, on stream water, hazelnuts, and blackberries." Tears began to course down my face.

"Child, you know not what you are saying. I am a hermit, but I am brought many gifts from the people of this tuath. I could not survive without their help. They make sure I have firewood and warm blankets and honey and wheaten flour and oats. They bring me chickens and even piglets when they can. They make shoes for me. That soft robe you are wearing was a gift that was laid on my doorstep not one moon past.

"In return, the people expect me to bless their children, anoint their marriages, and listen to their troubles. I also say Mass in your father's chapel, in case you have forgotten. There is much more to this life than simply sitting before a stone hut watching the dragonflies dance."

"I am so sorry, Father. I didn't mean to disrespect all that you do. But my heart is broken. When I found Artrach, I was like a moth that had first seen a light—a light that attracted with unbelievable power but never burned. It brought me only love and happiness. Now I live in darkness once again. I need to go somewhere, someplace, to try and forget all that I have lost."

"Be very careful, my child, that you don't make an idol of your lost love, whoever he might have been. There is grave danger in that. The wheel of life is ever turning, and none of us can know what God has in store. There may be a very good reason that you and your man had to be parted. At times like these, you must rely on faith to see you through."

We sat in silence for a while, just watching the flames of the hearth fire. I listened to the voices in the embers, hoping for guidance, for some kind of sign.

Father Justan stood up. "I need to go somewhere, and I don't want you to follow. Please just stay here and rest. I will be back in a few days."

He took a cloak from a peg beside the door and a walking stick.

"The house is yours, and all within it," he said, and then he ducked out of the door.

As I stood to watch him leave, a small flock of finches settled into the tree beside the hut, showing not the slightest fear, as if I weren't even there. I began to think that I was no longer quite human. Maybe I had already become a spirit, or maybe I was now a dweller between the worlds. I certainly did not belong anywhere that I could see.

Though I was still tired, I determined to keep myself busy and spent the rest of the day sweeping the hut, gathering sticks of firewood, and refilling Father Justan's clay water canisters. Then I set out to search for edible and medicinal plants.

I found a patch of wild thyme not far from the hut and collected a basketful; the brew was very useful for winter coughs. Then I collected a sheaf of long grasses and bound it with ivy, slung it over my shoulder, and carried it back to the house, where I spent the evening plaiting ropes, thinking that Father Justan would find them useful.

After a dinner of thyme tea with honey and a bowl of hot oatmeal, I smoored the fire, then fell into a dreamless sleep.

The next morning I slept long past sunrise; exhaustion and a pile of warm blankets had conspired to give me my first sound sleep in many weeks. When I woke it was late morning, and I was still alone. I split open a fresh wheel of cheese and cut a loaf of wheaten bread that had been left at Father Justan's door, and then I set out again to forage for mushrooms, berries, and medicinal herbs.

For a while that was how I spent my days, and the little hut was soon festooned with wreaths of fragrant herbs and strings of medicinal roots, mushrooms, and leaves left hanging to dry from the rafters. I collected a basketful of rosehips and another of rowan berries. A sack full of hazelnuts and a basketful of acorns added to the bounty. Father Justan would be well supplied.

17

Years later, I learned what had happened when Father Justan left me alone in his roundhouse.

He had walked to the nemed of Dálach-gaes and Niamh with a sense of trepidation. These were good people, loving and kind to everyone, but they were still Pagani, worshippers of strange gods, who believed in practices and rituals that were forbidden to the Cristaidi.

An old prayer from Inissi Leuca came to mind as he paused before crossing the threshold of the enclosure:

O my Lord and Master
I am your servant
You who made the moon and stars
I bow to wash your feet
Protect me.

Then he made the sign of the cross across his chest out of habit, thinking that it added an extra measure of protection.

He found Dálach-gaes in the ritual space, oiling the wood of the bíle with goose grease and bee's wax to protect its intricate carvings from the weather. There was a moment of awkward silence as the two clergymen looked each other over until Dálach-gaes broke the spell.

"Well met, Father Justan. To what do we owe the pleasure of this visit?"

Dálach-gaes was surprised to encounter the priest within the confines of the Druid ritual enclosure because he could not recall a single visit from a Cristaide clergyman in all the years that he and Niamh had lived there. As far as he knew, the Cristaidi regarded the Druid ritual space and school as a suspicious or even evil place.

He wiped his hands on his apron and motioned the priest towards a small semicircle of wooden benches arranged under an old apple tree. The students had sat there the day before, sharing and memorizing sacred stories.

Father Justan spoke. "I have a certain visitor at my house—someone you know well. I need some counsel on what to do about it."

"I can hardly believe that you are asking advice from a Drui." Dálach-gaes sounded perplexed.

"Normally I would not resort to this, but I am at a complete loss," Father Justan said.

Dálach-gaes understood his reticence but was intrigued. He knew that if the other Cristaidi learned of Father Justan's visit, they would give him a hard time; whatever had brought him to the nemed of the Druid must be something truly urgent. "If it is as serious as you say, then perhaps I should bring Niamh into the conversation. Sit here a while and enjoy the warm sun while I go inside to fetch her. I will have the students prepare us some refreshments."

Father Justan was glad of the chance to sit in the liquid sunlight of the afternoon. He kicked off his sandals and dug his feet into the mossy ground.

Dálach-gaes reappeared soon after with Niamh at his side. Moments later, a male student emerged from the largest roundhouse bearing a tray of cold elderberry and rosehip brew, bannocks, butter, and cheese. The student was quickly dismissed and the conversation resumed.

"Who is the distinguished visitor that you are keeping?" Niamh asked, fascinated. She thought it might be a foreign dignitary involved in some delicate political machination, or perhaps a high-ranking

Cristaide with whom Father Justan was quarreling. She had heard rumors over the years of Cristaidi who would come to pester the priest and try to bend him to their ways.

"My guest is a woman with whom you are both well acquainted."

"A woman?" Niamh exclaimed. This was not at all what she had expected.

"I am afraid that Princess Aislinn has appeared at my door—" Before he could finish the thought, Dálach-gaes and Niamh were both standing in shock.

"Where is her retinue?" Dálach-gaes asked.

"Has she been announced at court?" Niamh interjected impatiently, thinking they had been slighted. If Aislinn had arrived with northern warriors, they should have heard by now.

"It's a long story, one that will take a while to tell. The short version is that she and Deaglán were not suited to each other, and he now has a concubine who is with child. Also, the peace has been broken, and raiding is going on across the borders once again. The lady Aislinn could think of no reason to stay in the northern kingdom, and so she has returned here to us," Father Justan explained.

"But who is with her?" Dálach-gaes asked again.

"No one; she is quite alone." Father Justan's shoulders slumped a little; it was a sad set of circumstances, shameful even.

Dálach-gaes and Niamh both sat down hard on the little benches, hardly daring to believe what they had heard. Niamh finally found her voice. "Is it possible that Aislinn traveled all that way by herself? That girl was always headstrong, but to treat her own life so lightly is past believing. And after all the years of learning that we stuffed into her head, she should know better than to put herself in such danger!"

Father Justan assured them that this was the truth. He told them how she had arrived underweight, filthy, and famished at his door. He told them about a mysterious man that she had met and lost, and how perhaps this terrible grief had caused her to take an enormous risk, unheeding.

"Does the king know about this?" Dálach-gaes asked.

"No. No one knows about it except you and me," Father Justan said.

"He will have to be told," Niamh said flatly. She was thinking of Tuilelaith and of her likely disapproval of the girl. It would not be easy to break this to the parents.

"Well, what's to be done with her now?" Father Justan asked, raising his hands in desperation and with a hint of despair in his voice. His usually smiling features were contorted into a grey mask of concern.

After a moment's reflection Niamh spoke, picking her words with care because she did not want to cause offense to the priest's calling.

"On a weighty matter such as this, it is our custom to consult the gods. We have a number of methods for doing so—ways to access their will in the past, the present, and the future. In some cases we consult our visions and our dreams, or we listen to the swaying of the trees, the rustling of leaves, or the calling of birds. We might also cast Ogum sticks to divine the gods' purpose.

"But in this case, I think something weightier is called for. After all, she is a princess of the royal house, and she is also half trained to be a Fili. In short, she is a very valuable person in so many ways."

"Do you mean...?" Dálach-gaes asked, looking into Niamh's eyes in the way that long-married people often will, sharing an unspoken thought.

Father Justan was perplexed. Some silent plan was being hatched right before his eyes. He had no idea what it might be, but Dálach-gaes and Niamh already seemed to have an understanding. Why were these Druid always so mysterious?

"If this were a case of divination that involved the entire kingdom, we would sacrifice a white bull on the day of the full moon," Dálach-gaes began for the priest's benefit. "A Drui would fast for three days, then partake of the bull's meat and some of the broth, and then he or she would sleep wrapped in the bull's hide. Other Druid would sing the Incantation of Truth over the seer as they slept, and by morning the seer would have a vision, such as the name of the most worthy candidate for the kingship."

110

"But since this is a private matter that involves just one person and her personal fate, something less elaborate can be undertaken," Niamh continued, picking up where Dálach-gaes had left off. "On the day of the full moon, one of us can wrap ourselves in the hide of a newly sacrificed sheep. We can fast and then eat some of its flesh. The very best place to do this rite is at the source of a river, because such a place is pure in spirit. The gods, the spirits of the place, or an ancestor will bring a vision to whomever lies sleeping there."

"The full moon is in three days. I say we walk together to the river's source and bring a sheep with us," Dálach-gaes concluded.

Father Justan wondered how he had become so quickly ensnared in the mysterious rites of the Pagani Druid, but they seemed like good and sincere people, despite everything he had heard. And as he was at a loss how to proceed with Aislinn, he somewhat reluctantly agreed to their plan.

It will be an education for me to see what these Pagani actually do in their rituals, he reasoned to himself as a way of overcoming his fears.

Niamh, Dálach-gaes, and the priest took off alone the next morning after commandeering a huge ram, two oiled leather tarps, hatchets, buckets, fire tongs, and other supplies from the storehouses of the dun. Care was taken to be as inconspicuous as possible so as not to arouse suspicion. The Druid were still respected and feared by the majority of the dun's inhabitants, so their actions and requests were accepted without comment, and folk were happy to give Father Justan the few things he asked for because he was the one who blessed them with his words in the chapel.

"I haven't been there since we did the divinations for Barra Mac Mel's campaign to be king," Dálach-gaes remarked as they took to the road at first light. He had been a youngster in training at the time.

"I think that Niamh should do the honors, since she and Aislinn are both women," he added.

It seemed to make sense. Dálach-gaes and Father Justan would take turns tending the fire, sleeping under the tarp, and guarding the space to keep away any curious animal or human intruders.

111

After a full day's march they reached the intended spot. Their first task was to sling one of the oiled tarps over a rope strung between two trees and to weight down the edges with stones. Then they placed the second tarp on the ground beneath it, to keep away the damp.

The ram was tethered to a standing stone in the middle of a grassy field, where he contentedly ate his fill as Niamh worked nearby, cutting fresh green blades with her sickle. Dálach-gaes and Father Justan busied themselves with cleaning out the fire pit and the cooking pit, gathering rocks, and cutting up deadfall from the forest for firewood. A strong fire soon blazed in the twilight.

At dawn, as the sun was rising, they led the ram to a shelf of flat rock that sloped gradually towards the ground. There was an almost imperceptible notch carved into one side of the shelf of stone.

"This place has been used for sacrifice for thousands of sun-turnings," Niamh commented.

It's an almost biblical scene, Father Justan thought.

Niamh lovingly tied soft skin around the ram's feet to bind them, and Dálach-gaes and Father Justan slung the beast up onto the rock escarpment. Dálach-gaes murmured a prayer of thanksgiving and stroked the beast to gentle it, then cleanly slit its throat. Soon a bright rivulet of blood flowed down the stone, cascading softly onto the soil below—a blood offering for the spirits of the land.

As the carcass cooled and drained, Dálach-gaes cut off the head and placed it high in the fork of a tree to gaze out towards the sacred river as a mark of respect. The entrails were pulled out, and Father Justan was given the task of carrying them deep into the surrounding forest in a willow basket as an offering for the forest spirits. *It's odd to be doing this*, he thought as he poured the offal onto a stone hidden in a holly thicket, *but I can find no evil in it.*

Dálach-gaes removed the hide and used a hatchet to cut the carcass into manageable pieces. A large haunch was to be roasted over the fire for their dinner, while the other pieces were rubbed with salt and wild garlic and then wrapped tightly in the fresh grasses that Niamh had gathered. One choice piece of flesh was set aside, dedicated to the gods. As Niamh placed it directly into the flames, she and Dálach-gaes gazed upwards, their eyes following the smoke as it made its way to the sky world.

"May they be pleased with our offering today," Dálach-gaes said.

Stones had been layered amongst the logs in the fire pit to heat, and water was carried from the river in leather buckets to fill the cooking pit. Once the grass-wrapped meat was laid into the water-filled pit, red-hot rocks were gradually added in until the bubbling began. When it cooled, the cooked meat would be wrapped in fresh leaves and grasses and packed into leather bags for carrying. Then it would be distributed in the nearest village they encountered—the final phase of the ritual of sacrifice.

On the night of the full moon, Niamh chewed a bit of the roasted meat—the first food she had eaten in three days—and then bathed at the river's source. Father Justan excused himself, too squeamish to witness this part of the rite.

Emerging from the water, Niamh carefully patted herself dry. Then she gathered branch tips from the riverbank, which she wove into a wreath and placed upon her head. Now she was naked except for the crown of green herbs and the spirals and whorls she had painted on her face, breasts, and belly using the ram's blood.

Dálach-gaes approached her with the skin of the freshly slaughtered animal and Niamh rolled herself gingerly into it. Dálach-gaes sprinkled water from the river's source over her as a final blessing as she settled into a soft hollow of grass near the waterfall that fed the pool of the river's beginning. Dálach-gaes left her there and returned to the comforts of the fire.

The waterfall provided a curtain of sound that soon brought Niamh into trance.

When he got back to the tarps, Dálach-gaes saw that Father Justan was deep in prayer. Dálach-gaes took the first watch, and then they took turns sleeping and tending the fire throughout the night. A tribe of owls kept up a constant chorus of sound, conversing loudly across the woodlands along the riverbank.

"The owls know that something is happening, and they are talking about it—a good omen," Dálach-gaes commented.

In the morning Dálach-gaes walked to the river's edge with a woolen towel, some lavender-scented siabainn, and clean clothes for Niamh. He also carried a small silver ritual cup, a bowl of cracked hazelnuts, and a sliced apple.

His first action was to dip the cup into the water at the very source of the river and carry it to Niamh. She sat up as he presented it to her.

"Drink in life, and may your years on this earth plane be many," he said, a way of formally welcoming her back from the spirit world, because in her present state she was not yet fully human.

Then he handed her the bowl of apple slices and nuts. "Enjoy the food of the living, made from the fruits of the living land."

Niamh swallowed the cold spring water, savoring every drop, then she ate a few of the nuts and some apple slices. She could already feel her strength returning and her head clearing.

"Well?" Dálach-gaes asked when she had finished bathing and dressing.

"I had a visitor last night. It was a woman. Her name is Ethne, the former ard-ban-Drui," Niamh replied. "She said she was very happy that we did this at such a sacred place. She said she is glad we are keeping the old ways alive."

"But what did she say about Aislinn?" Dálach-gaes asked, a little impatiently.

"She showed me where to send her. I will explain it to you and Father Justan as we walk back to the nemed."

Dálach-gaes knew better than to demand further details. Niamh had been touched by spirit, and she was still integrating the message. All would be revealed in good time.

18

One morning I had slept long past sunrise and I rolled over, thinking to stir the hearth fire and cook some breakfast, when I noticed by the sunlight slanting through the door that it was nearly afternoon.

At that exact moment, Father Justan ducked through the doorway wearing a broad smile. I had not seen him for nearly a week.

"Get up, sleepy bones. I have a surprise for you!" He gestured that something exciting was waiting for me on the other side of the door.

I rolled out of the blankets and groped for a comb because my hair was snarled. It still smelled faintly of lavender flowers. I took a few moments to tease out the worst of the knots and then splashed cold water on my face from a bronze basin, belted my wrinkled tunic, and slipped into the pair of borrowed sandals.

I was barely presentable when I eased through the door opening to see what surprise Father Justan had wrought.

Suddenly I was engulfed in ferocious hugs and kisses. Dálach-gaes, Niamh, Caoilfhionn, Deg, and the children all wrapped themselves around me in a tight ball. Everyone was laughing, crying, and jumping up and down in excitement.

"Hold on, hold on!" I laughed. "You are like a pack of wolves greeting a lost den mate!"

I stepped back to look at them, the people I loved. Almost two sun cycles had passed. The children were taller; Dálach-gaes's beard had gone grey. Niamh looked the same as she always would—as eternal as the sea surrounding Innis nan Druidneach, her spiritual home.

It seemed that everyone I cared about in this life had come together to wish me well. Only one beloved face and form was starkly absent, and I could still feel his hazel-leaf eyes gazing upon me.

"Artrach, these are my people," I whispered silently to his spirit. My constant companion, I now felt him everywhere around and within me.

Dálach-gaes interrupted my thoughts. "Father Justan has told us of your adventures. I must say I am not surprised that the marriage was difficult. You have ever had a mind of your own. But your travels back to In Medon are worthy of an epic tale!"

"No one holds this against you," said Niamh, touching my shoulder gently and soothing my spirit as she always did. "No matter what the Cristaidi say, the ancient laws permit you to walk away from an unhappy union, and you are free to seek your happiness elsewhere, though it might have made more sense to leave Irardacht with a retinue of warriors. And now you must undertake yet another journey." She sighed as she looked at me, smiling with mingled pride at my courage and with concern for my lack of judgment.

"A journey?" I asked. "Where am I going this time?"

"Don't ask any questions. Just follow my directions, and all will be well."

"But—!"

She looked into my eyes fiercely as she fingered my face. The caress was loving, but I knew by her expression that she would brook no opposition.

"Don't ask any questions; just go," Father Justan commanded, echoing Niamh's tone.

"We have presents for you!" Caoilfhionn and Deg shouted excitedly. They each carried a leather sack, which they proceeded to empty out on the grass.

I surveyed the treasures spilled before me: woolen socks, stout boots for walking, a thick green oiled-wool cape, a beautiful blue woolen blanket, combs for my hair, a cauldron and a tripod for the fire, tinder and flint, a new léine and three tunics of different shades from pure white to green and blue, and a doeskin belt with golden knotwork embroidery.

There were fresh wheels of cheese encased in wax coatings, a bag of oats, a small bag of ground wheaten flour, dried apples, a sack of cracked hazelnuts, wooden plates and a wooden goblet, strips of dried deer meat bound in birch bark, and a bag of dried elderberries and mint leaves.

One of the children, Ergan, a boy who had miraculously sprouted from a knee-high elf to a strapping young man, shyly handed me a carved walking staff. An earnest-looking girl child named Slaine produced a small knife encased in a beautifully worked leather sheath. When I left, they had been mewling infants; now they were people.

"She worked the leather herself," Niamh announced proudly.

It was everything I could possibly want for a journey in the wilderness, and I was speechless.

Just then I heard a sob coming from under a nearby apple tree. I looked up and saw yet one more beloved figure. It was Róisín, my old nurse, who had tagged along but stayed several paces behind the august company of Druid out of respect.

"Róisín!" I ran up to her and wrapped my arms around her plump middle.

Her face went crimson with emotion and tears.

"Oh my lady!" she cried, extricating herself from my embrace and handing me a package.

She had wrapped something in one of her best woolen cloths; it was a pair of plaid trousers.

"These are for you to wear so your legs don't chafe while you are riding," she said.

"Riding?" I wondered what she meant.

Then I heard the tinkling sound of bells in the distance, bells that evidently hung from a horse's harness. We all turned and looked down the road where four riders were approaching at a stately pace, leading a beautiful white mare.

As the riders grew closer, I made out that the two on the outside were well-outfitted warriors sporting polished bronze shields, spears, and swords. One man in the middle was wearing bright red wool and silk and leading the white horse by a long tether. It was my father! My brother, Eógan, rode next to him, dressed all in blue, with bright silver embroidery on his cuffs and hems.

Incredulous, I stayed glued to the spot, my eyes brimming over with pride, love, and fear.

"Father Justan told me what you did—that you braved the wild forests alone to preserve my kingdom because you feared that your capture would spell ruin for us all," my father said when he was close enough for hearing, beaming down at me from his tall brown stallion.

He and Eógan slid from their horses, and my father solemnly pulled a package from his saddle, handing it to me with a proud smile.

"These small gifts are but a token of thanks for what you did so bravely."

I opened the wrappings carefully. Inside a green shawl of lambswool were an individually packed collection of precious objects, each within its own soft deerskin bag.

There were supple blue leather gloves embroidered with silver thread, a golden torque, a golden armband and ring, a golden fillet for my hair, a necklace of amber, and a pair of amber earrings. There was also a mysteriously heavy bag, which I reached into and found to be filled with coins.

"Those are séts; each of them is worth the value of half a cow. You should use them to pay for food, drink, and lodging for yourself and your retinue," my father said.

"Your mother sent the earrings," he added. "They are hers; they came all the way from Letha. Remember always that you are a princess and that your appearance reflects on us all."

His last statement was slightly ironic, given my state of wrinkled disreputableness.

I wondered why my mother hadn't come with him, but I knew that I was ever a disappointment to her. I guessed that it was because once again I was without cattle or dun and thus not worth knowing.

"Oh, Father, it's so good to see you!" I cried as I put my arms about his neck and kissed his bushy beard. He blushed at the unaccustomed intimacy. My brother, in the way of brothers, showed little emotion, but he did give me a stiff hug. After all, I had saved his future kingdom, too.

"These warriors and the mare are for your own use, to see you safely to your new home," my father said, still looking red-faced and flustered. "Bláth is a steady and gentle mount, and these two men have been with me for most of their lives; I trust them completely. You didn't think I would let my only daughter go alone into the wilderness again?"

"But where will they be they taking me?" I asked.

"Don't ask any questions; just go," Father Justan ordered quickly, just as he had before.

It seemed that everyone was in on the plan. Maybe they were afraid I would melt back into the forest if I knew what was in store. I held my peace.

I went back into Father Justan's hut and changed into the blue tunic and the deerskin belt, and slipped into the riding trousers, adding the amber necklace as a final adornment. Róisín happily combed and braided my hair; for once, the braids were not too tight.

After many tearful hugs and goodbyes, I finally mounted the little white mare, ready to depart with my small retinue of warriors. Niamh stepped forward and faced us with open palms to intone the ancient blessing for a safe journey:

Bless the pathways on which you go
Bless the earth beneath your soles
As you go upon the road
Against misfortune, against peril, against spells
Against wounding, against fright
Nor brand shall burn thee
Nor arrow rend thee
You shall go and return triumphant
As the sun who rises victorious
From the dark sea of night.

"How strange life can be," I mused as we took to the open road. "One moment I am a badger hiding in the wood. Now I am a princess once again. How swiftly the wheel of fate turns..."

I pulled out the little bronze triskell that hung next to my heart and remembered the hands that had made it. I could have sworn I heard a voice coming from beyond the trees, riding on the wind. *Aoibhgreine,* it sighed.

part three

The Rising Sun

19

Coreven and Alvinn were mostly silent for the first few days of our journey, under strict orders not to discuss our final destination. My father the ard-ri and Father Justan had agreed to this. I was confident that wherever I was being led, I could take care of myself; the last few years had shown me that much.

Three signs of wisdom: patience, closeness, the gift of prophecy. The old triad popped into my head and gave me the courage to stay silent.

Brown and yellow leaves crunched under the hooves of our horses. Alvinn's Caur was a broad-chested, war-scarred chestnut who plodded steadily along the road, unfazed by blowing leaves and darting rabbits, while Coreven's Lasar was a thin, wiry mount who skittled and shied at any unexpected object or sound. Coreven adored the tall red horse because he had won him many a purse of séts at the Lugnasad fairs. Alvinn thought of Caur as his second right arm. Bláth, my own mount, was a dainty creature who enjoyed the company of the other horses and delighted in the freedom of the open road.

The narrow road stretched out endlessly before us like a carpet of speckled gold; the trees along the way were already standing naked, the brisk winds having recently stripped them of their finery. Above us the skies had been clear blue for days, and flocks of birds would overtake us from time to time, honking and calling in excitement as they began their winter migrations. Frosty nights lent urgency to the air, as if the pace of life had suddenly quickened in anticipation of the coming cold.

I enjoyed the sensation of riding high on a horse; we covered ground much more quickly than I ever had on foot, and the views of the hillsides and copses were spectacular from my lofty perch. But my joints were becoming stiff and sore. Each time we dismounted I found it hard to walk until I had worked out the stiffness in my legs.

"I don't want to be outdoors on this night," Alvinn finally said, breaking his silence with a dark look.

Black haired and dour looking, he was a man without humor who hunched over the saddle as if the weight of the world lay upon his shoulders. Long dark curls obscured his features, a face growing thick with dark stubble from lack of shaving.

Coreven was his opposite, blond and blue eyed with a ready smile and an infectious laugh, his long blond tresses were held back in thick braids, lending an open expression to his face. Even when we were being silent he would turn to me for no reason other than good humor to give me a big grin and a wink.

And there I was in the middle. Protected and trapped, exposed yet well supplied.

"You mean because it's Samhain?" I asked innocently.

I was well aware of that fact but, knowing the superstitious nature of most warriors, I had said nothing. My plan was to leave a nice food offering at the next Sidhe mound we passed and hope that the spirits would be satisfied. I knew that if humans were not generous and failed to respect the Sidhe mounds at Samhain, it would only bring blight, bad weather, and disease. I had seen enough of those in Irardacht and would do my best to prevent such disasters any way that I could.

I shivered at the memory, even though I had on my oiled wool cape.

"It's no good to be outside on this night," Alvinn repeated bleakly when we were a few more paces down the road. He shook his head slowly from side to side for emphasis and hunkered even lower in the saddle, as if Caur could somehow protect him from the malevolent forces abroad.

"Well, then, let's find a hostel or a farmhouse where we can find hospitality," I suggested.

The sky was clear, and the prospect of yet another cold night sleeping on the ground was less than appealing. I had a bag full of séts, after all.

"No one will refuse us food and hospitality on this night," Coreven chimed in gaily with his usual wink while straining to keep Lasar from bolting. A squirrel had hopped right in front of us.

We continued along the road, crossing a boggy area where someone had laid out planks of alder wood to prevent carts and horses from sinking. Taking a sharp turn around a rocky outcrop, we encountered a small tribal holding, a clutch of willow-thatched roundhouses surrounded by a stout wooden palisade. Boys had been set to guard the entrance, and one of them gave out a shrill blast on a small metal horn as another ran into the settlement to alert the warriors.

Within moments three grown men emerged from the gate, each carrying a round wooden shield and a bronze-tipped lance.

"I haven't seen spears like that since I was a young colt!" Coreven exclaimed.

Bronze lances were a relic of the distant past but still favored by the country folk because they didn't rust.

One of the three men stepped forward, trying to look fierce.

"What are you doing here? What do you want?" His thick black brows beetled mightily as his blue eagle-eyes bored into us. The other two just looked scared.

"We come in peace; we are simply seeking hospitality for the night. *This* night," I added for emphasis, hoping the men would understand.

The three looked at each other and then slowly lowered their spears. They understood. No prudent person would want to be abroad on Samhain.

"Leave your weapons at the entrance and make yourselves welcome," the head man said gruffly.

We dismounted and carefully removed any sword, shield, or dirk we might possess, depositing each into a long wooden chest by the entrance; such a chest is used to store grain and weapons against the damp. I even laid in my walking staff, thinking they might consider it a danger. Alvinn and Coreven looked unhappy but resigned to giving up their weapons; it was the accepted practice, and they went along as gracefully as they were able.

The warriors of the village picked up the chest by the handles to carry it inside.

"The boys will see to your mounts," the headman declared as we untied our bundles and bags from the backs of the horses. Lasar tried to bite the boy who led him to the stable, while Caur remained unfazed. Bláth went along sweetly as ever, daintily accepting the stub of a carrot held out by a boy as a gesture of friendship.

There were urgent cow sounds coming from one side of the settlement. The herds had been newly brought in from their summer pastures and were expressing their dismay at the suddenly cramped quarters. As is usual with these habitations, a veil of smoke hung low over everything—a distinct change from our days in the clear open air.

We picked up our bundles and followed the men into what appeared to be the main house of the farmstead, where the clan was already gathered to entertain and comfort each other throughout the long night. The one-room roundhouse was dark, save for a roaring fire in the hearth, and very smoky. Swirling tendrils of wood smoke drifted towards the ceiling, but closer to the ground the air was clearer, so everyone was huddled as low as possible on the furs, blankets, and pallets spread about on the floor. At least it was warm.

The spicy-sweet tang of boiled cider wafted from the hearthstones where a large cauldron of the drink, liberally laced with uisge beatha, lay waiting to be shared after supper. A huge báirín breac, speckled with currants and shiny with a honey glaze, lay on a wooden platter by the hearth, where a small pig and a goose were being turned together on a long iron spit by one of the grandmothers, who was sitting on a stool in the place of honor closest to the fire.

She was evidently the female head of the clan, based on the Cailleach sheaf that hung from her neck; the doll made from the last sheaf to be harvested was slung around to dangle down her back and away from the embers. Any time a youngster reached for the báirín breac, she would rap their hand smartly with a wooden spoon.

The close air was thick with other smells: the meaty scent of newly stuffed sausages that garlanded the roof tree, drying in the smoke, and fresh strings of round apple slices that hung from the rafters, slowly desiccating. Drops of fat dripped and sputtered onto the fire, and one could just hear the wind howling against the willow rods of the smoke-charred roof.

"I am so glad you are warm and safe inside, *mo muirne*," a voice whispered into my ear.

I looked around to see who had spoken, but no one was speaking to me; all eyes were glued to the other side of the house, at the opposite side of the fire. I rubbed my ears, wondering.

At the start of the dark half of the year, everyone eagerly awaited the return of nightly storytelling, and a prosperous-looking shanachie was already in the midst of a ribald tale. It always amazes me how a tribe will pay almost any price for a story, even when their bellies are empty.

Alvinn, Coreven, and the three warriors stared straight ahead, straining to listen. No one seemed to have noticed our arrival as we stood quietly in the entrance.

"One Samhain night the Daghda, our good god of blessed memory, spied a woman bathing herself in the river Unius. She was naked and very beautiful. Her nine tresses of hair were shiny and black, and her skin was as pale as moonlight. Her eyes were as dark as the black door of midnight, and her lips were full red with the blush of elderberries. Her eyebrows, nails, and cheeks were stained dark crimson with the juice of crushed berries, and her teeth were as white as the pearls of the sea.

"Large she was, so large that she had one foot on the south bank of the river while her other foot rested on the northern shore. Does anyone here know her name?"

The shanachie swept his gaze regally from one side of the house to the other, scanning the crowd, waiting for an answer. The children stared, rapt, with eyes as round and wide as the apples that bobbed in a barrel near the fire.

"She was the Morrigu," one small child finally offered.

Everyone gasped because he had dared to say her name, and to say her name out loud might call the fearful Great Queen of Battle to them on this night of all nights. A pleasant shiver of fear coursed through the throng as the shanachie continued the tale.

"Yes, and the great queen is as large and powerful as three mortal queens put together. The good god spoke with the beautiful lady and found her pleasing and soon laid his huge warm hands upon her. He drew her to him and made love to her, and she did not object, for he was just as large as she was. She knew that he would satisfy her because he was filled with lust, and he always had a hard time finding a woman who could satisfy his desire."

The adults and older children giggled in appreciation, winking and elbowing each other. It was obvious that there were no Cristaidi in that room, a fact which I found refreshing.

The shanachie suddenly stopped speaking and rose slowly from his seat to greet us. He had finally noticed us across the fire. The room went silent.

"Who are the strangers that have appeared at our door on this night when the Sidhe mounds are opened?" he asked in rolling resonant tones. Evidently the man had some training as a bard.

The clan craned their necks to see, with wonder and fear playing in equal measure upon their faces.

"We are three travelers seeking shelter on this fearful night," I offered.

"We will ask you no questions, for it would be rude to pester you before you have eaten. Please be seated and enjoy what hospitality we have to offer. Make yourselves comfortable by the fire, for forever it has been said 'Often and often go the gods in the traveler's guise.'"

Heartened by his grand manner and kind invitation, we did as we were bidden, and the smells of roasting goose and pig soon made our bellies growl. A young tribeswoman filled wooden cups with the spicy cider brew and handed a steaming drink to each of us.

When we were comfortably settled on the hard clay floor with our packs as pillows, the head man who had met us at the entrance to the settlement rose and cleared his throat to speak.

"Now that we are all safely in for the night, the blessing can begin."

A woman who appeared to be his wife handed him a bowl of dark liquid. The man gestured towards the fire and spoke again.

"We have set apart this goose and pig for six moontides. They have been treated with kindness and fed everything they could want and more. Then they were sent to the Otherworld with prayers and thanks for the gifts they will bestow upon us, and now they both grace the central hearth of our clan. They will soon honor us and our unexpected guests by giving us meat, but before they go into our bellies, we must purify our home with the blood they have shed on our behalf."

He reached his fingers into the bowl and walked to the hearth, pouring a bit of blood reverently onto the embers as a gift to the gods. The drops of blood sizzled on the coals, adding a sweet metallic scent to the riot of smells already filling the air. Then he walked to each of the timber posts that circled the house, sprinkling fresh blood with his fingers to bless the farm and its people with the forces of life in the new sun cycle. Then he carefully sprinkled blood on the doorposts and across the threshold.

He poured the last of the blood into the hearth fire as a final offering to the spirits, wiped his hands on his dark tunic, and reached into a bag that was slung over his shoulder, pulling out freshly sharpened goose quills and handing one to each of the children. His wife passed around small ceramic bowls filled with another dark liquid and then scraps of snow-white birch bark.

"I want you to use this elderberry ink to paint a message to the gods onto each scrap of bark. Your parents and relations will help you do this. Then you can put your message into the fire to send it to the sky world."

While the children and their relatives busied themselves scratching images of what they wanted for the new sun cycle onto strips of white bark, the grandmother and her daughters began carving the goose and the pig on huge wooden trenchers. The scent of warm meat was over-whelming, and I thanked whichever gods or spirits had brought me to the safety of this generous hearth.

Later that evening, when songs were being sung and everyone had eaten their fill, I took the chance to sidle up to the plump shanachie, who was just finishing his supper.

"I can tell that you are Druid-trained by the timbre of your voice," I whispered.

He dropped his goose leg in shock. Only another Drui could have made such a statement. To find one in such a rustic setting, and a female to boot, was almost past believing.

"Whatever are you doing abroad on a night like this?" he wheezed, steadying his plate and spoon and working hard not to drop anything else.

"We are on the king's business," I said. I could hardly reveal that I myself had no idea where we were headed. "I need to know if anyone has put a plate of food out for the Daoine Sidhe," I continued in an urgent whisper. "I have seen the consequences when humans are no longer generous to the fairies. I have laid a geis on myself never to neglect hospitality to the spirits, especially on a night like this one."

"To my knowledge, no one has performed the office. It is no night to be outside when the black púca is galloping about and the dead are looking to revisit their homes."

"Yes, that may be true, but I need to show generosity to the spirits. It is my duty to the land and to the people."

The poor man sighed. He had counted on a warm, well-fed evening by the fire, not a dangerous expedition in the company of a strangely determined, if somewhat self-destructive, female Drui.

"All right, then; no one here will dare to go with you, but I myself will guide you to the nearest fairy fort. Will that suffice?"

I nodded my assent.

The warm cider and uisge beatha were having their effect. The singing was growing louder, and the celebrants were using plates and spoons to beat rhythms in accompaniment. A hilarious game of apple bobbing was taking place in one corner of the house, and bets were being laid. Alvinn, who had been skulking darkly in a corner, suddenly came to life when the betting started and had already tossed one of his bronze battle rings into the betting pool. A man in a huge straw mask was weaving drunkenly through the crowd, and everyone was trying to guess his identity. Added to this were the squalls of unhappy infants, ear-splitting yowls that were quickly stopped by their mother stuffing a breast into a hungry mouth.

We took advantage of the general chaos to edge our way out into the dark, cramming bread, meat, sausages, and apples into our clothing any way we could as we sidled towards the door. The moment we poked our heads outside, we were assaulted by a gust of wind.

"It's coming from the northwest," I declared after wetting my finger with saliva to test the wind's direction. "That means death, slaughter, and the fall of blossoms in the coming year!"

"What can we possibly do about it?" the shanachie asked, despairing.

"We can be as generous as we are able and hope that others all over Ériu are doing the same."

I knew that Dálach-gaes and Niamh and Druid everywhere would be testing the winds on this holy night and doing whatever they could to keep the forces in balance.

The moon was nearly full and the track through the fields and forest seemed almost as bright as day, so we had no trouble reaching an ancient ring fort that was covered over with vines. A large hawthorn tree grew at a crazy angle from one side of its wall; for generations it had stood uncut because no one would be so foolish as to harm a fairy tree.

I looked up at the branches, thinking I spied a shred of wind-blown cloth suspended in midair. Suddenly the cloth grew wings and then silently flapped away.

"An owl!" the shanachie yelped in a tone of real panic. "The dead are nearby; I can feel them!"

I instinctively drew an Ogum of protection in the air, choosing the Rowan symbol to make a protective shield. Then I sang a loud invocation:

Strength of sea, surround us
Hardness of rock, be ours
Power of lightning
Brightness of fire
Stability of earth
Be with us now!

I commanded these things while turning my body in a circle with my arm and index finger outstretched to inscribe a ring of protection. Startled by the noise, a family of rooks high above us in a tree took off as one into the night.

"Let's leave our offerings and go!" the shanachie cried. By now the man was terrified.

We laid our food under the fairy tree and murmured thanks to the spirits of that place, who were the guardians of the surrounding landscape. Then we walked briskly back to the farmstead, pausing only once when I stumbled over a root.

When we got to the door of the roundhouse, I wet my finger once more and held it above my head for a moment.

"Ah, good, a southwest wind. Its color is green, and it brings healing. It is the wind of the mothers," I declared with satisfaction, knowing I had done what I could to serve the people. Dálach-gaes and Niamh would be proud.

When we were safely back inside, the báirín breac was already being torn apart and distributed, one portion for each person in the gathering. Hidden within the large loaf were tokens: a small coin that meant prosperity in the coming year, a thimble for a spinster, a piece of wood for useful work, a golden ring for the one who would be next to marry.

I accepted my piece and held it in my hand, looking anxiously about to see if anyone had noticed our absence. No one had. I bit into the moist, sweet morsel. My tooth struck something very hard. Unbelieving, I reached into my mouth to fish out the object. It was the golden ring.

"That's…just…not possible," I said weakly, choking in disbelief.

"Never you mind, sweetie. It will all work out for the best. These predictions are never wrong. You'll see!" the grandmother stationed by the fire exclaimed with certainty and nearly toothless glee, waving her long wooden spoon at me as if it were a magical wand.

She and the other women obviously felt this was a sign of the best possible good fortune. I felt only numb horror.

Coreven came over to buck me up, seeing that my face had gone ashen.

"It's not that bad, is it?" he smiled, giving me a wink and a pat on the shoulder. As I sank to the floor to huddle miserably inside my cape, Coreven passed me another cup of hot cider. I absentmindedly slid the little ring onto a finger, trying to ignore what it presaged.

One by one, the children fell asleep until they were piled like puppies in softly snoring bundles covered by woolen blankets. The shanachie resumed his position by the fire and told another tale that lasted until sunrise. At last the adults of the community felt it was safe to venture back to their own homes.

"Don't forget to kill a cock and sprinkle its blood on your roof trees and doorposts!" the shanachie wearily called out to the departing revelers.

The headman and his family, the shanachie, and I and my warriors arranged ourselves around the fire and slept. I used my bundles of clothing and valuables as pillows and did not wake again until the late afternoon.

As we mounted to depart, I gifted the headman and the storyteller with one sét each. "Use them to help your people," I said as they turned the coins over and over in disbelief. The headman even bit his to see if it was real. I doubt that he had ever held such a coin in his hand before.

"See? That is what happens when you remember to thank the fairies properly," I told the shanachie with a grin.

We kicked our mounts and took off down the road once more, leaving the two men staring.

20

Alvinn and Coreven were delighted to have their horses and weapons back as we resumed our journey. Lasar seemed to have calmed down a bit; one night in a snug barn with other horses, and apples and carrots aplenty, had reassured him that not all the world was a fearful place. Caur was his usually stoic self, while Bláth minced about and even kicked up her heels. She had been admired, curried, and combed to perfection by the stable boys and seemed to know that she looked gorgeous.

That night, after a simple supper of sausages, apples, and oat bread, we bedded down around the fire. Almost as soon as I lay down in my blankets, I dreamed.

In my dream there was a large white bird. The bird was singing insistently, using her sweet voice to lead me ever onwards, through a thick grove of rowan trees to a little house in the wilderness. I peered inside the yellow light of the open door and saw a woman giving birth. I entered the house and found a silver basin filled with water, sitting on an oaken table. I scooped some water into my hand and placed three drops upon the child's brow to welcome it to the earth realm. Then I sang to the mother, which caused her milk to gush forth.

The bird lured me outside again with her singing, and this time she told me to go to a particular place.

"Where am I going?" I asked.

"Don't ask any questions; just go," she answered.

In the distance I could see a village or settlement of some kind, with smoke rising from every roof tree. There were flocks of sheep and enclosures for chickens and ducks fanning out from the settlement like the petals of a flower. I seemed to be seeing everything from the air.

I landed lightly on the ground, and the white bird told me to take up a holly stick and dig into the earth at a particular spot.

"If you dig here in this field, you will find holy water," she sang. And then she disappeared.

I awoke with a start, clear headed, remembering the dreams I used to have of the terrible black raven—when I would feel blood coursing down my face from the force of her talons.

That black spirit bird had pulled me forcibly away from Irardacht, a move that I had desperately needed to make. This dream was very different, yet I understood that the white bird was leading me somewhere new, just as the black crow once had. The image of the woman giving birth stayed with me. *Perhaps it means a rebirth for me?* I thought to myself.

"Thank you," I whispered out loud to whatever spirit was guiding me.

On the afternoon of the third day, we arrived at a crossroads marked by an ancient standing stone that was covered over with moss and delicate yellow and white lichens. The stone was so old that it listed slightly to one side. There was a faint triple spiral etched onto one face; someone generations before must have carved the design to communicate some deep purpose.

"The sign of the three worlds," Alvinn said to Coreven with a knowing look.

"This is where we leave you," said Alvinn, pulling up Caur's bit sharply, causing him to come to an immediate halt. Lasar was not in the mood for stopping at that moment, and Coreven was forced to walk him in tight circles before he finally stood still. Bláth came to a full stop without incident and stood calmly, waiting for further instructions.

"Aren't you coming with me?" I asked, bewildered.

"No, we don't even know where you are headed. Our instructions are to bring you to this place and then set you onto the western path. You are to continue your journey alone," Coreven said, a little sadly. It was not in his nature to leave a young woman alone and unprotected on a strange road.

"We will stay here for a day and a night to make sure no one suspicious follows you," said Alvinn. He was already rising in the saddle and scouting for danger, also slightly affronted to be leaving a woman alone on the highway.

"If that is what my father told you, then I must obey."

I reached into my cloak and pulled out the leather bag of séts and gave three to each of them.

"Take these for your return journey, to buy food and drink and anything else you might want."

I knew that it was a huge sum and far too generous, but I was grateful for their protection and companionship.

All three of us felt a little sad as we said our goodbyes beside the ancient stone, which I noted with interest was listing towards the west, the exact direction I was taking. I hoped it was a good omen.

Bláth picked her way gingerly between the piles of fallen leaves and branches that lay on the road. It was apparent that it was a path rarely traveled and that no one had yet found the time to clean up after the brisk autumn winds. The road grew gradually darker and narrower, with ever-thicker hedges of hawthorn and blackberry closing in on both sides. I was just starting to feel trapped by the oppressive vegetation when yet another large standing stone appeared. This one was also listing slightly and bore the same triple spiral design; it tilted towards a tiny mud path between an even thicker tunnel of thorn bushes.

By now my legs, léine, and tunic were becoming scratched and snagged on the surrounding hedges, so I dismounted and led Bláth down the muddy path by the reins for a while. By turning my body sideways, I was mostly able to avoid being caught by thorns. Then the vegetation abruptly ended and a wide expanse of grassy hillside opened up before me, dotted here and there with black, brown, and white sheep and the occasional white goat.

There were people digging in the ground for roots of some kind. They stood up at my approach and *hallooed* a welcome.

"Have you come to join us?" someone asked.

"I don't know. What is this place?" I inquired.

"Tempul Dair," someone said. "Though these days some have taken to calling it Cell Daro, the Church of the Oak."

"Do you see that large oak tree over there?" A man gestured towards an imposing tree that looked to be a thousand sun cycles or more in age.

I studied the tree. It seemed to me that it must have been the bíle of some ancient tribe, still being honored as a protector of the landscape.

"That oak is so sacred that no one is allowed to wear a weapon or place a weapon anywhere near it. Are you carrying any?" a woman asked, peering intently as if daring me to lie.

I thought for a moment, wondering if I should disarm myself so quickly just to please a group of complete strangers. But I could tell that they were holy people by their clothing and trusting manner. They each wore a simple yet well-constructed tunic of brown, black, or white, evidently woven from the wool of the sheep in the meadow, with a simple rope for a belt. The men's hair was cut in the old Druid tonsure, from ear to ear across the brow, and they were all wearing the same triple spiral symbol, a triskell of bronze or silver that hung from a leather thong around each of their necks.

I suddenly realized that despite the grime of the road I must look like a princess to their eyes, with my amber beads, sky-blue tunic, colorful plaid trousers, pea-green cape, and snowy white mount.

Throwing caution aside, I forfeited my only weapons to them: the small dirk that I always kept hidden in my boot and my walking staff. A man took the dirk and dropped it into a leather purse hanging from his belt.

"I swear to you that when you leave us, you will have it back," he said. His expression was so open and guileless that I could not help believing him.

"The staff you can keep," he added.

I slid off of Bláth and reached for her halter. As usual, my knees buckled slightly when I touched the ground, and I took a moment to shake the stiffness from my legs. *What have I gotten into now?* I thought as I was pushed by the throng towards the main house.

"We are taking you to meet the Bríg Brigu," said the woman who had asked for my weapons.

"Who is the Bríg Brigu? Is that her title?" I asked.

"She is the chief of hospitality for our community. She is the living representative of the goddess Brighid and the one who leads us. She is a Drui of the highest rank, and we call her by no other name.

"Here we serve travelers, the sick, laborers and nobles alike, and everyone is treated the same. Some come for food and drink, some just for companionship, and some come to the Fire Temple to have their deepest questions answered."

Now my curiosity was thoroughly piqued. Surely this was the place that Father Justan and my father had intended that I must go. They must have thought I would receive some kind of training here. Even Dálach-gaes and Niamh seemed to approve of the plan.

As I surveyed the roundhouses, fowl enclosures, gardens, and out-buildings, it became apparent to me that this was the village I had seen in my dream from the air. I knew that the spirits were guiding me, and I was grateful but still cautious. Who was this Bríg Brigu, and what would she think of me? Could I really have a place here? It was all so mysterious.

We walked towards a large roundhouse that sat on a low hill at the epicenter of the community. The house on the hill was whitewashed, and I could just make out large sepia-colored triskells, painted at intervals along the white walls. With its yellow roof of fresh golden thatching, the building glowed in the sunlight.

At the base of the hill was a dark slit, an opening into the earth.

"What is in there?" I asked the woman at my side, who seemed to have taken me under her charge. Her long flaxen hair was starting to turn grey, and her blue eyes radiated a calm assurance. Her white tunic was mud-stained to the knees, and she carried a large round willow basket filled with freshly unearthed carrots and other roots.

"We call that the Womb of the Goddess. There is a sacred spring under the hill, and what you are seeing is the entrance to its waters. We only ever use that water for healing and for rituals. Actually, since tonight is the full moon, you will be able to take part in one of our rites this evening. We have five of these sacred wells in different locations; they form our neimheadh."

Now I was really interested. "Your what? Where I come from, we have something called a nemed. It's a ritual enclosure."

"We have something similar, only it's much larger. Ours is a landscape temple that covers the whole of this tuath. We have a secret track that is only known to those who live here and to those who come to visit us on holy days. We call it our hidden sanctuary because our ways are invisible to those who don't know us. We have a ritual calendar that is acted out in the landscape, season by season, every sun cycle. I hope that you will walk this land and learn its secrets; we need the patronage of the powerful families to keep our ways alive.

"To unknowing eyes, there is nothing here but a collection of fields and sheep pastures around this hill, but scattered around the tuath there is one well that we circumambulate at Imbolc, another that we circle at Beltaine, another at Lugnasad, and another at Samhain. We know that the spirits move from well to well and that they stay underground at each location until the appropriate time of year, on the exact day when the rising sun enters the well and strikes the waters. We wait for that day, and that's when we come to sing to the spirits, drink the waters, and make our offerings.

"The Womb of the Goddess is the central well, and it is always most active at the full moon."

"Why is that one well different from the others?" I asked.

"Do you see that hollowed-out stone in front of the mouth of the well?"

I did see it. It appeared to be an ancient rock with a wide and smooth depression on the top.

"That stone receives water from the sky, and we also pour in waters from the Womb of the Goddess. The water absorbs the light of the sun by day and reflects the light of the full moon every moontide. That is when it becomes fully energized."

"Ah, I see. That stone is an intermediary between the waters from the underworld and the waters from the upper world, between the realms of earth and sky. In that basin of stone, the three worlds are present."

"Even so," she replied, looking me up and down with renewed interest. Apparently she approved of my observation.

At the base of the hill to either side of the Womb of the Goddess there were herb and vegetable gardens, and at the base of each garden were strange structures—rows of hollow trees that stood like so many wooden flutes stuck into the ground.

"Those are our hives. Honey and beeswax candles are an important part of our work here. We use honey for healing wounds to the body and also wounds of the spirit. The bees have a special relationship with the sun, which makes them sacred to us. If you walk the land around this tuath, you will find many bee trees."

As we climbed a spiral path up the central hill I became aware of a low, round enclosure of yew hedge that reminded me with a pang of Dálach-gaes and Niamh's nemed. As we spiraled around it I noticed that it had an opening on just one side. Passing the opening I caught a glimpse of a large, round fire. It was a Fire Altar in the ancient style! I was very excited to see that; I had never witnessed a perpetual fire before, though I knew that there was one in each of the provinces, safely hidden away from the prying eyes of the Cristaidi and other nonbelievers.

"What direction does the hedge open to?" I inquired.

141

"Every Fire Altar of this kind is oriented to sunrise on the day of its founding. Our holy wells are chosen the same way—one faces the rising sun of Imbolc, another faces the rising sun at Beltaine, and so on. The house above them all, at the top of this hill, is our Fire Temple, and that is where the Bríg Brigu lives. Its door also faces the rising sun on the day of its founding. That day was Imbolc, the day sacred to the fire goddess Brighid, our patroness."

"So you are sun worshippers?" I asked, remembering all my fervent prayers to Áine Clí sung atop the lonely walls of Irardacht; *mother of the stars, eye of the gods, queen of the heavens, sister of the moon...* Apparently my prayers had been answered in a way that I could never have expected.

"Oh, yes. For us, the three fires—that is, the celestial fire, the fire on the land, and the fire in the earth—are three sacred manifestations of the forces of Áine Clí. Brighid is our own beloved goddess who brings the fire and light into our human hands and minds. She is like a mother to us—our intermediary between us humans and the forces of the divine."

"You sound very much like a Drui when you speak."

She gathered up the hem of her white tunic in a futile effort to protect it from further encrustations of mud while simultaneously twisting her body to shield the basket of carrots into which Bláth was endeavoring to stick her nose.

"We are all Druid here," she said simply.

21

I am so sorry about the behavior of my horse!" I said to the ban-Drui who was leading me to the main house. I was struggling mightily with Bláth's halter; a passion for carrots was the one blight I had discovered in her otherwise faultless manners.

"No worries. We think of all animals as individual sacred beings in their own right—especially the white ones, whom we regard as messengers from the Otherworld. Your arrival on a white mare has caused quite a stir, because for us the white mare represents the Goddess of Sovereignty. My name is Nessa, by the way; I came here from Albu."

"I am Aislinn, from…" I paused for a moment to think what to say. It would have been far too complicated to explain my flight from Irardacht, so I finished the sentence with "In Medon." I was impressed that Nessa had come so close to deducing my true status; sovereignty and being born a king's daughter were almost one and the same thing.

"Oh, so you are a local then? The Bríg Brigu will be very interested to meet you; she believes strongly in forging ties with the local tuaths. She says that those of us who are of a like mind should get to know each other well, to be able to help each other in the difficult times. She has often said that there will be hard times ahead for those of us who treasure the Old Religion of Ériu."

The other Druid trailed behind us in a snaking line around the hill; apparently my arrival was a welcome diversion and not to be missed.

As we rounded the final loop to the crest of the hill, I saw the carved golden oak doors in the center of the building and a tall, carved oak pole to one side of the entrance, both of which bore complicated designs of interlaced knotwork, spirals, and animal motifs. A clutch of long white feathers dangled from strings tied to the top of the pole, a familiar sight that caused another pang as I recalled the days of my childhood in the nemed of Dálach-gaes and Niamh. Many were the times we had studied the fluttering feathers that hung from our bíle to divine the will of the gods.

The golden oak doors were wide open, and whoever was inside must have seen or heard us coming because a male Drui dressed in a black lambswool tunic with a silver triskell around his neck stepped out into the sunlight, carrying a thick fighting staff. He stood before the entrance as if guarding it and formally asked my name. Then he disappeared inside for a moment, reappeared once more, and bid me welcome.

"Please tie your mount to the bíle before you enter," he said.

Bláth had already attracted her share of admirers, so I left her to the attentions of the crowd.

Nessa took me by the hand and guided me through the doorway. I was momentarily blinded as we made the transition from the bright sunlight to the windowless interior, but my eyes quickly adjusted as I took in the details of the space. A shaft of sunlight shone from the doorway onto the smooth clay floor at a precise angle. I noticed that there was a stick set into the ground and grooves cut in a fanlike shape into the floor of the entrance. Nessa watched me as I stared at the marks on the ground.

"What is that for?" I asked.

"It's a time-keeping device. We call it Brighid's Fiery Arrow. We can tell the time of day by the angle of the shadow cast by that stick. You will find similar devices scattered all around our tuath. We have another kind, which is a standing stone into which a hole has been drilled near the top and a stick inserted. The same rays you see on the floor are carved into the stone, and the shadow of the stick falls on the

144

carved rays and tells us the time of day. Of course it only works when the sun is shining."

I marveled at the ingeniousness of these inventions and determined to tell Dálach-gaes and Niamh about them if ever I saw their nemed again.

The hearth at the center of the roundhouse was wide and generous; there were flat, shiny cooking stones in a ring all around it, enough to bake bread for the entire community. A magnificent cauldron hung over the flames; evidently some kind of stew was in progress.

Then I looked up and was fascinated by yet another detail. A hanging bowl of fire dangled down from the roof, positioned over the exact center of the hearth. The fire bowl was made of bronze and suspended by three thick metal chains.

Nessa followed my wondering gaze.

"That's an oil light; you've never seen one? Everything in this house is filled with symbolic meaning. The hanging bowl of fire represents the fire of inspiration and also the fires in the sky—the sun, moon, and stars. It is symbolic of the sky world and the cauldron of wisdom in the head.

"Below it is the sacred hearth that represents the fire in the land, the fire that causes life to grow, and the cauldron of motion within all beings—the spark of change and transformation that causes all plants and animals to wax and grow strong.

"Below the hearth—and invisible to your eyes—is yet another large iron cauldron, buried deep under the ground. It represents Brighid as smith, the goddess who takes the essential energies of rivers, rocks, and the land and pours them out to the people from the deepest recesses of the earth. She helps us shape those energies to make them available for our use. It also represents the cauldron of warming deep within the land and within all beings who dwell on the sacred land.

"We have smaller versions of the same things in all our houses. No matter how mean and drafty a house might be, every house here is a true Fire Temple."

Trained in filidecht as I was, I marveled at the poetry of her words and at the mystical design of the Fire Temple that we were standing in. Encoded within the details of the building was a sermon dedicated to sacred fire, the earthly counterpart of the sun, supreme nourisher and protector of human life, the greatest healer and the strongest protective magic against ill-intentioned fairies and people.

Then I studied the walls. And such walls they were! Red yew overlaid with beaten silver, gold, and bronze, they mirrored back the light of the hearth. It was so bright inside that room that it was almost as if it were daylight.

I could not see the far end of the building, the side opposite the door, because there were carved oaken screens inlaid with silver and bronze that blocked my view of the other half of the house.

"These walls and partitions are as lovely as anything in my father's house," I said. "How did you manage to commission such impressive works of art?"

"We have our patrons. Much of what you see here was brought to us as thanks offerings from those who were helped by our prayers. Our personal quarters are much simpler.

"Just as every sun cycle has a dark half and a bright half, and just as every moontide has the same, this temple has a light half that is open to the sun and the public, and a dark half hidden behind the screens. The dark half is the space where the Bríg Brigu and her closest attendants have their beds and their privacy," Nessa explained. "The rest of us sleep in our own roundhouses. You must have seen those as we climbed up the hill."

I had seen them; they were the usual grey stone or wattle-and-daub constructions with their conical willow roofs.

The gatekeeper dressed in black reappeared from within the dark recesses of the house.

"You may enter now," he said, waving his arm in a formal gesture of welcome towards the inner sanctuary.

Once again Nessa took my hand. We circled formally around the fire in a sunwise direction and went in between the two oak screens.

The first thing I noticed was the warm and inviting smell of honey and beeswax. There were lit candles on every available surface and in high niches. Fresh rushes crunched beneath my feet, and colorful tapestries graced the walls. Behind the tapestries were the same beaten-metal knotwork inlays reflecting the light of the candles. The room gleamed with a honey-rich orange glow.

The Bríg Brigu was seated on a throne made of birchwood covered lavishly with white animal pelts. She was a middle-aged woman with long blond hair that cascaded down her shoulders and well past her knees. She wore a long white wool tunic with golden knotwork embroidery along the hem and along the edges of the sleeves. I assumed that her expression of dispassionate objectivity was the result of many years of solitary meditation, fasting, and other rigorous spiritual exercises.

Around her neck was a golden torque, which sparkled in the light of the beeswax candles, and a strand of large, glass-clear amber beads. Upon her feet were leather sandals covered with strips of pure gold. Two female attendants dressed in brown wool and wearing bronze triskells and amber beads sat beside her on the floor and seemed ready to fulfill her slightest wish.

The impression was of a sunlike orb surrounded by lesser planets such as myself and the other mere Drui in the room.

"I have been expecting you for a long time," the Bríg Brigu finally said in calm, melodious tones.

"What? I mean, how is that possible?" I stammered, feeling that I was somehow being rude by questioning her statement.

"I have seen you in the flames. I have been watching your progress." She stated this simply, as if it were a full explanation.

Not quite knowing how to reply, I held my peace. One of the female attendants handed me the customary cup of joy. I waited until everyone present had been given their own small wooden cup of mid and then sipped my own portion slowly, keeping pace with the rest.

"You are so very like your mother," the Bríg Brigu observed after we had all handed our empty cups back to the female attendant.

147

I could not imagine what she meant. How did she know my mother? And in what way was I the least bit like her? I grew up roaming the woods and barns; my mother was a legendary hostess and lover of fine clothes and jewels. I didn't even look like my mother; my hair was an unruly river of flame, hers a perfectly tended golden waterfall.

The Bríg Brigu read my thoughts.

"Not that mother—I mean your birth mother. I knew her well."

This was yet another shock. My birth mother? I suddenly felt the floor rising to meet me as my knees conspired to buckle despite my best attempt at composure.

Nessa moved in quickly to console me as the male Drui and the other attendants brought pillows for my head and feet. The Bríg Brigu went on with her tale without a pause.

"Yes, I knew her when she lived here many sun cycles ago. We trained together and were as sisters. I would know you anywhere. You have her eyes and her hair."

My lower lip began to tremble, and I fought to hold back tears.

"I have no idea what you are talking about. This is scaring me, and I wish you would just tell me what it is that you know about me that I don't."

"Very well, then," the Bríg Brigu continued in her peaceful, even-toned manner. "Your birth mother was named Ana. She was born the daughter of a mog and a cattle lord and was brought here as a baby to be raised by our community. The chief wife of the house of her birth had her sent away rather than allow her to grow up in her father's household, where she would be legally entitled to an inheritance. She was left beside the Fire Altar with a small bag of séts to provide for her future dowry.

"I was also sent here as a girl by my clan because both of my parents had died of the flux, and I had no other kin to keep me. That was how I met her. Your father used to come here in his youth to study."

"My father!" I interrupted rather rudely this time, completely forgetting my manners.

The attendants gasped; they had never heard anyone talk to their priestess like that. But the Bríg Brigu was not offended; she seemed to have patience as wide and deep as the ocean and continued with her story as if I hadn't caused the least offense.

"As I was saying, your father used to come here in his youth. One day he saw Ana, and he was instantly smitten. He would not be satisfied until the Bríg Ambue, our teacher of judgment and law, gave her consent for them to handfast.

"Your father was obviously delighted. Even though Ana had been born to a mog, she was very beautiful and smart, a skilled healer and a scribe. But when he eventually took her back to his clan in In Medon after he was elected king, his family—your family—insisted that he find a chief wife who would bring real status and political advantage to their tribe. That was how he got your other mother.

"Your blood kin have ancient ties to Letha, so they contracted for a princess and also a dozen or so barrels of the best fíon, as I recall, as her dowry. Your father's clan sent a ship full of cow hides and two pairs of wolfhounds in exchange.

"He married Tuilelaith almost the same day that he met her. I was at the nuptials."

That last bit about the fíon certainly had the ring of truth to it. If there was one thing for which my mother was known for above all other things, it was her steady supply of fíon. Everyone marveled at how she got it; every barrel was worth a mog, yet she always seemed to get it at the lowest possible price.

The house went silent. For a while the only perceptible sounds were the popping and hissing of the fire and the soft bubblings from the huge cauldron over the hearth. Everyone could see that I was in shock from the revelations and they held back speech, waiting for me to recover my composure.

As I began to see the truth, I also began to understand my mother's strange indifference to me and her attentions to my brother. We didn't look anything alike, people always said, and now I knew why. I was my father's daughter, born of a woman of low status and sent to the nemed of Dálach-gaes and Niamh to be raised and Druid-trained, while Eógan, who was of royal blood on both sides, was raised and educated by my father and my stepmother.

Stepmother. I tasted the new word in my mind a few times to see how it felt, and now my tears did flow—whether from relief or sorrow, I knew not.

"But where is my mother now? Does she still live here in this place?" I asked, wiping my eyes with only the faintest sense of hope.

"Alas, no, your stepmother sent her away as a condition of her marriage to your father. The king was so in awe of your stepmother and of her royal ties in Letha that he agreed to this, though I have reason to think that he soon came to regret it. You see, Ana was the love of his life.

"It was because of her memory that he made sure you had a Druid education, even as he was trying hard to placate the Cristaidi with their growing power.

"Ana died on the road trying to get back here. She had been sent away with no retinue and no attendants because Tuilelaith regarded her as a mere mog who deserved no such consideration. Your stepmother told your father that everything was taken care of, and since he was very anxious to please her, he did not question her further. His family had convinced him of the need to cement strong ties to Letha for the trade it would bring; I don't think he had any real idea of royal ways in Letha, nor how far their behavior has been conditioned by exposure to Roma and its corrupt rulers. The Romani value power over honor and justice; he just didn't know that at the time.

"I thank the gods daily that the Romani have never invaded our shores. If he had known what danger Ana was in, he would surely have sent her here with an army to watch over her, but he left all of the details of her journey to Tuilelaith. It was a gesture of trust at the start of their marriage."

"But why didn't anyone tell me this before?"

"Because your father wanted you raised as a full princess, with all the advantages and dignities of your station, and because by law you were entitled to the same privileges as any child of his body. He treated you like a royal daughter, and everyone else followed his example."

I knew that the Bríg Brigu spoke the truth; I could feel it in my bones. My limbs quivered as my body sank back into the pillows. I could hardly focus my eyes any longer, much less even keep the lids open.

The Bríg Brigu peered down at me.

"Fetch her some food and a warm bath. Then she can sleep for a while until the moon rises."

part four

TENDING THE FLAME

22

After a hot bath and some lamb stew, I was escorted to a small but comfortably appointed recess of the main house that featured a fragrant, heather-stuffed mattress on a wooden platform, squeezed in between two carved oaken partitions. I slid into the linen sheets and woolen blankets in a stupor and fell gratefully into a chasm of dreamless sleep.

Upon waking, I noticed that my shock and fear had subsided a bit. Now I was consumed by curiosity as to where I had found myself. I examined my surroundings and found that my boots had been brushed clean of mud and left on the hard clay floor just outside of my small chamber. My staff was leaning against the wall by the door, and my other belongings had been neatly stacked on top of a carved wooden chest against the screen wall. My green cloak had been brushed clean and left hanging on a peg. There was barely enough room for the solitary beeswax candle in a silver dish and the basin of scented water on the small table at the foot of the bed.

I wondered how Bláth was getting along, but knowing her easy ways and beautiful white coat and tail, I felt sure that someone was already doting on her.

The floor of my little sleeping space was thickly covered with colorful rugs spread on top of clean rushes. I tiptoed a short distance across it, peered out of my enclosure, and found that the light of the full moon illuminated the house through the still-open doors. The glow of the hearth fire and candles also permeated the space, reflecting off of the silver, bronze, and gold of the walls. There was no need to light a candle.

I rummaged through my folded belongings and pulled the green tunic over my head. The blue one had disappeared, presumably taken away to be washed. I laid the rest of my clothes into the carved wooden chest, pulled on my boots, fastened my green cloak, and, not wanting to stand out too much, decided against wearing any jewelry or other outward marks of distinction. Father Justan's little cross and Artrach's triskell still hung safely hidden against my heart.

Emerging from my cubicle, I could hear a noise in the distance that resembled an approaching swarm of gigantic bees. I walked to the entrance and looked outside the oaken doors. In the bright moonlight I could see a long line of figures bearing lit torches. They were marching towards the Fire Temple, surging across the fields, singing.

As they came closer to the Womb of the Goddess, the line began to curl in a sunwise spiral around the hill, and I walked down the dirt path to join them, taking care not to stumble on the nearly invisible trail that was still unfamiliar to my feet.

Now I was able to make out the words; the crowd was singing a song to the moon:

Hail to thee
Full moon this night
The glorious lamp
Of every creature
We lift up our eyes
And sing your praise!

As I took my place in the midst of the throng, I added my own voice to the chorus.

We wound our way around the hill three times and then formed a silent circle three persons deep around the well before the Womb of the Goddess. One by one, the sick and lame were carried or helped towards the well where a Drui and a ban-Drui were doling out water using long-handled silver spoons.

The sick and wounded placed their offerings on the lip of the well—a small coin, a wheel of cheese, a loaf of bread—took a sip, and, while anointing their head, heart, belly, hands, and feet with the moon-blessed waters, murmured a prayer to Brighid:

O Brighid, goddess of healing
Guardian of the flocks and of the people
Watch over me!

Off to one side, there was a man seated on a three-legged stool plucking a harp and singing the "All-Heal," a song about this special night. I listened carefully. The song related that anyone who was not fully healed nine days after this rite would hear the "Ceol Side," the song of Áine, who sings to comfort the dying, and the harp of her red-haired brother, Fer Fí, the Spirit of the Yew, on their way to the Blessed Isles.

I shivered involuntarily, remembering the grievously wounded warriors of my father's tuath who were sometimes given a draft of yew to hasten an end to their pain and to speed their passage to the Blessed Isles. At times these things were a necessary mercy.

The Bríg Brigu stood to one side, silently watching, lending the blessing of her presence.

I was trembling inwardly. Should I step forward and make my own petition for healing? There were still grief and shock hidden deep inside me; I knew that I needed help. But I had nothing to offer in exchange, no gift to leave at the well for the spirits of the waters.

The Bríg Brigu must have read my thoughts because she stepped towards me at that moment and gently urged me forward, towards the healing well.

Before I could think, a silver spoon was thrust into my mouth and I was drinking in the moon-soaked liquid. As I swallowed, I could feel silver moonlight coating my heart like a healing balm. Then I reached for the waters of the well to anoint myself, and suddenly there were hands everywhere—Drui and ban-Drui alike were dipping their hands into the water and then placing them on my body: over my heart, on my head, and along my limbs. As they did this, they sang to me softly until I was wrapped in a cocoon of healing sounds and caresses.

Then the tears came, thick and warm and melting the frozen places in my heart, and still the Druid stayed with me, holding and healing until my sobbing stopped. The dark places within me were now filled with a glowing white light as from an inward, radiant sun that was shining brighter moment by moment. The Bríg Brigu looked on, approving. After a while the Druid retreated, and I stepped back into the crowd.

When all the sick and injured had received the waters, the people gradually dispersed. Far from being a solemn occasion, the air was filled with soft laughter and animated conversation as everyone stooped to pick a blade of grass or a green herb from the meadow surrounding the well.

"Why do you do that?" I asked an elderly gentleman who was pushing a fresh sprig into his cap.

"Don't you know? It is said that on this one night, all the green things around the well have magical healing properties. We always gather a leaf for luck after the ceremony."

I knelt down and plucked a leaf of my own. "Help me," I murmured to it as I held it next to my heart.

I found Nessa standing near the well, collecting the spoons and other offerings in a large willow basket to carry them back up to the temple. She had fresh sprigs of greenery behind her ears.

"Look up there," she said, pointing.

I followed her gaze to the top of the hill, where the white-washed stones of the Fire Temple gleamed in the moonlight. The structure glowed like a beacon of hope against a black and silver stream of stars.

"We do our private Druid ceremonies on the sixth day of the moon, of course," she said as I stood there open mouthed. "For us, the new moon is the silver salmon leaping up from the Otherworld below to the sky realm. We also call her the Ox Horn and the Lamp of Grace. The moment we see the new moon, we pray to her to protect the cattle."

"In my tradition, we call the new moon Áine of the Light, and we also call on her to bless the cattle if they are ill or suffering from scabs or sores," I answered in a tone of professional interest, priestess to priestess.

It felt good to be conversing with another ban-Drui, one who had undergone the same tests and initiations and learned the arts of healing, poetry, and wisdom that all the Druid held in common. We understood each other's thoughts with little need for explanation, and I began to feel that maybe, just maybe, I could make a life for myself in this holy place.

A warm breeze pricked my skin, and the hairs on the back of my neck rose in response. I could feel an unseen presence around me, and as I had heard so often recently, my name was whispered again by someone or something into my ear. *Aoibhgreíne*, it sighed.

"Did you hear that?" I asked, turning towards Nessa.

"No. I didn't hear anything," she said, stuffing the last bread loaf into her basket.

The next morning the Bríg Brigu appeared at the foot of my bed with two extra-large willow baskets on her arm. This time she was dressed in a simple brown wool tunic, and her hair was pulled back into one thick braid that wound around her head like a crown. There was fresh greenery from the last night's ritual woven into her braid, and she still had on her golden torque. However plainly she was dressed, there could be no mistaking her rank.

"The winter chill is coming fast, and we have to gather the roots we will need for medicine this winter before the frosts set in," she said in a tone of simple command.

"You should make a habit of wearing your torque," she added. "You were born into this life with a certain station. The gods had a reason for that, and it is not up to you to disregard it."

Then she slipped back out to see to breakfast. All of the available Druid had assembled at the temple for the yearly fall foraging expedition, and they would be sent out with warm and full bellies, as the laws of hospitality demanded.

Somewhat chastened, I pulled my torque from my pack, dressed, and joined the Bríg Brigu and the others at the hearth fire. They were already eating oatmeal porridge or sorting through tools and baskets, preparing for the day's labor.

23

"I have high hopes for you, you know," I said to the neophyte priestess who had just arrived with a bundle of sweet-smelling, freshly laundered sheets. An aroma of lavender suddenly permeated the room; the linens must have been rinsed with lavender water.

"Perhaps if you hear my life's story, you too will be inspired to become a leader in our community. Gone are the times when the Druid were a respected voice in the kingdom. These days our truths are passed down mostly in stories.

"Shall I tell you what the old Bríg Brigu thought about these matters?"

"Oh, yes, please do. But first let me change your bed."

The girl seemed genuinely interested, and when she was finished tucking in the fresh sheets, I spun out my tale…

On the morning appointed for the harvesting of medicinal roots, the Bríg Brigu gazed across the flames, addressing her attendants. "She has the same eyes and hair as her mother," she mused, absentmindedly stirring her bowl of porridge to mix in the knob of butter that had been spooned on top, "and the same inquisitive intelligence. It amazes me that Barra Mac Mel could have let the mother or the child go so easily."

Then she turned her attention towards me.

"Girl, it is obvious to me that you have suffered. Yet your suffering is carefully hidden behind a mask of courage. You are all legs and elbows—a gangly, thin creature with skin so tightly wrapped around your bones that you emanate nothing but spirit.

"Did the gods bring you to me as the next Bríg Brigu?" she wondered out loud.

I later learned that the problem of a successor weighed on her mind and that the words of her teacher came to her more and more often, growing more insistent with every moontide: *You only need to train one.*

"Aislinn, you come with me today," she finally said. "The others can pair up to dig the healing roots. They know what to get and where the plants grow most abundantly because they have done this every year for most of their lives."

The day was crisp but still warm in the sunshine, with only a faint hint of winter in the shadows—a good day for the foraging and the drying of roots. The Bríg Brigu left the washing up to the others and motioned me outside, pointing to an outlying round stone structure slightly below the main house on the hill.

"You will find the tools we need in that small roundhouse over there. Fetch two spades and bring them here to me."

I followed her orders without qualm, despite the noble gold around my neck. Druid-trained, I was not afraid of manual work like some of the princesses who had visited my father's dun. I had been taught the dignity of a job well done and did not think it a loss of face.

Carrying our spades and baskets, we followed the path to the bottom of the hill, veering towards the line of woodland at the far edge of the great meadow where the sheep, goats, and cows grazed. A troop of boys equipped with willow rods was keeping the animals from straying into the forest.

Along the way we passed roundhouses and three-sided animal barns. A clutch of old women dressed in black sat on stools at the center of a circle of houses, around a large fire. An enormous cauldron hung over the flames; it was the duty of these women to see to the feeding of the entire community, a choice job because their knees would enjoy the warmth of the fire all year. Boys came and went, carrying bundles of wood and peat for the flames.

Heaped beside the elderly women was a small mountain of peelings and discarded leaves from the vegetables and herbs they were adding to the mutton stew they were tending. A small white goat was wagging her tail with pleasure as she rummaged through the fragrant leavings.

Young girls with earnest expressions sat on old plaid blankets near the fire, grinding fresh wheat meal in their querns for the day's bannocks. The crones and the girls immediately stood up at the sight of the Bríg Brigu and bowed their heads in respect as she passed. A small red-headed boy dropped the load of peat he was carrying, so startled was he to see us.

"No need to rise," the Bríg Brigu remarked with a polite smile. "Please go back to your cooking."

My stomach rumbled in response to the scents wafting from the cauldron as we passed it by, despite my recent breakfast.

At the far end of the village was a straw-filled barn in a muddy fenced enclosure, filled with squealing piglets who were tussling over a large, battered-looking pan of oatmeal and milk. A dozen children and almost as many dogs sat guarding the side of the enclosure facing the forest, to ward away wolves both of the four-footed and human varieties.

The Bríg Brigu turned to me. "We get a donation of a full sack of grain and a calf, lamb, piglet, or kid from every chieftain in this tuath once in every year. They give us those in exchange for our moon rites and well blessings and for the healing work we do. But we have never before been gifted with a horse, and a beautiful white one at that."

The Bríg Brigu paused expectantly. I hadn't exactly said that I was donating the horse, but the Bríg Brigu saw that it would be very useful to have one. If they had a horse, the travel time to the outlying homesteads would be cut in half—a boon in the event of medical emergencies.

I thought it over carefully. It was a serious decision, because donating Bláth would be a final declaration that I was there to stay. I had a very independent spirit. Was I really ready to make their small community my home?

A few heartbeats later, I spoke. "Yes, you may have Bláth, on one condition: that she is happy and well cared for while she is here."

The Bríg Brigu smiled. "That is a wily answer. By including a condition I believe you are still leaving open the possibility of moving on. Well, if that was how it is, I will just have to use every charm at my disposal to bring you into the fold. Independence in a priestess is a trait that I admire, because any potential spiritual leader has to have a mind of her own and be able to think for herself. But she also has to show reverence and respect for herself, her community, and for the gods. That's a rare combination of traits, hard to find in one individual."

We reached the edge of the meadow just before the tree line.

"Most of the roots we use seem to grow at the very edge of the forest, between the sun and the shade," the Bríg Brigu observed. "Others grow in the bog by the pond on the other side of the hill."

The first plants we found were wild comfrey; the mashed roots and leaves would be spread on fractured and broken bones and applied as poultices to burns and wounds. Soon I was on my knees, digging eagerly into the loamy earth as the Bríg Brigu looked on with approval. It felt good to be working with the plants and the soil again. It also felt good to know that if my tunic and face became dirty, I would not be made to feel shame. I was in my element.

Next we located a patch of cowslip, whose roots were to be used to make an expectorant brew for coughs and congestion. I dug up some tough old dandelion roots hidden in the grass—used in liver and stomach tonics—and roots of docken, which would be simmered in apple vinegar to make a wash for skin eruptions and added to healing ointments made with butter and beeswax.

The Bríg Brigu took a small offering of cheese and bread from her basket, leaving it for the spirits of the place in compensation for their labor in providing the plant medicines for the tuath.

Then we took a narrow dirt path into the forest to look for ferns. The roots of male ferns were useful for deworming and as a bath for sore feet and varicose veins, while the roots of royal fern would be chopped, simmered, mashed, and applied to sore knees, bruises, and fractures, and added to butter ointments. We dug together in the loamy forest floor, and again the Bríg Brigu left cheese and bread for the spirits of the forest in thanks for their gifts.

Emerging from the woods, we stopped to harvest a patch of primrose—the root tea was brewed for headaches—and a stand of silverweed, whose roots would be eaten roasted or raw. We also found a swath of violets, whose roots were used for cough, insomnia, and nervous conditions, and a prickly stand of thistle, the roots of which made a brew for chest complaints.

More offerings were left for the land spirits, as well as prayers and well wishes for all the forces and beings that had helped the plants to grow.

I memorized the location and uses of all the herbs as the Bríg Brigu shared her knowledge. Druid-trained, I understood that such teaching would be given only once. As a ban-Druid, it was expected that my memory would be faultless.

By now our hands, feet, and tunics were caked with dirt.

"We can go down to the bog and wash our hands and faces," the Bríg Brigu declared, watching as I attempted to clean the mud from my fingernails using a dried stalk of ragweed.

We retraced our footsteps across the meadow and crossed to the opposite side of the hill, where springy mats of purple heather gave way to raised clumps of mosses and rivulets of clear water. Climbing up a steep embankment and then down again into a cauldron of rock, mosses, and boggy soil, we finally reached a little pond peacefully mirroring the sky. On its surface sunlight burnished the wavelets, giving an impression of liquid silver.

I delighted in a vast stand of yellow flag along the shore.

"We use those where I come from for coughs and sore throats, and we simmer the roots to poultice bruises," I said.

"Yes, we use the roots the same way. Let's wash up and then gather some."

The Bríg Brigu took a small knife from a bag that was hanging from her belt and handed it to me to make the cutting easier. I was startled to see that it was my own knife—the small dirk that had been taken from me on the day of my arrival.

"You may have it back," the Bríg Brigu said, smiling. "You have earned our trust."

I was moved. It was as if I had passed an initiation of sorts.

At that moment a flock of wild swans descended, dotting the surface of the water like fallen flowers.

"Oh, what beauty!" I exclaimed.

"A very good day-sign for us," the Bríg Brigu said. "White swans are messengers from the Otherworld in the sun. They are telling us that the sun has blessed us with her healing powers—a great omen on the day that we gather our medicines."

"You speak often of the sun and her cycles and healing powers," I observed. "Is this the Druid magic that your community uses? In the nemed where I was trained, we most often gave offerings to sacred fire and sacred water as our way of reaching the gods and shaping the world. We learned that if we gave those things with focused intent and emotion, our wishes were very often granted, especially if we also appealed to our own ancestors."

"Yes, we do focus on the light of the sun, and we observe her cycles in our neimheadh, our processional routes and well blessings at the various stations of our landscape temple. But we don't do this to ask for things or to bend fate. When we worship the sun and sacred fire, we do it to honor the light of nature, the light within the sky and the land. We humans are within that light and we are its children, every one of us encompassed within the bright beams of the goddess.

"Some dare to say that they control this light and fire. What folly." The Bríg Brigu snorted softly for emphasis.

The swans floating serenely on the surface of the waters reminded me of something.

"I know a story about swans."

"This would be a very auspicious time to tell it," said the Bríg Brigu.

We sat down on the green grass that sloped to the shoreline, gratefully dropping the weight of the heavy baskets and enjoying the splendor of the birds. I began the tale.

"Long, long ago, after the hero Cú Chulainn had taken the heads of the sons of Nechtan Scéne, he was making his way back to Emain Macha with the three heads hanging from his chariot when he and his charioteer spied a herd of wild deer and immediately gave them chase. But their horses' legs became mired in a bog, and Cú Chulainn had no choice but to run after the wild deer on foot. He caught two of them and harnessed them to the chariot pole with the two horses, to help pull the horses out of the bog.

"They escaped the bog, and as the deer and horses pulled the chariot towards Emain Macha, Cú Chulainn saw a flock of wild swans in the air. He brought down eight of the swans with his slingshot, taking care not to kill the birds, and attached them to the chariot. Then he brought down another sixteen swans and also attached them to his chariot.

"The horses and the deer did not pull very well together and became unruly, so Cú Chulainn enchanted them by giving them such a look of magic that the deer and horses were in awe of him and did his bidding. And that was how he arrived at Emain Macha, with the wild deer and the horses pulling his chariot and the swans flying above him."[5]

The Bríg Brigu was silent for a while.

"That is a powerful tale. It describes the way that the Shining Ones, the great gods and goddesses, pull the chariot of the sun across the sky. It also speaks of the three worlds. In this tale the deer represent the wild forces of fire within the land, while the horses represent the solar forces upon the land. The swans are the solar creatures of the sky.

"The fact that you have told me this story is significant. As you know, there is an ancient feast of the sun called Meán Geimhridh. It was once a High Holy Day of the people who lived on this land long before the Druid came to these shores. I have been wondering whether to take you with me to one of the hidden rituals, ones that we only rarely take part in. I believe that through you, the swans are trying to tell me something."

"I would very much like to learn all your rites, if you will allow it," I said. I was always eager for learning.

"I am very pleased by your eagerness to study our ways. It seems that in you I may have found my next high priestess, one of noble birth, with powerful family connections and Druid-trained."

I blushed at her words.

Then we stood up, startling the swans, who took off with a sound of whistling through their wings. The baskets had grown quite heavy, and I wondered how many more medicinals we were expected to collect.

We walked down to the lapping wavelets of the shore, hiked up our tunics by hitching the hems into our belts, and waded into the icy cold water to collect the roots of the white pond lily, so beneficial for diarrhea and to poultice cuts and bruises. And when we had collected bunches of yellow flag roots, the Bríg Brigu finally declared that we were done for the day.

We climbed out of the little valley and retraced our steps to the Fire Temple. When we reached the base of the holy hill, we stopped yet one more time to gather the roots of dew cup from the medicinal herb garden, to be used to stop internal bleeding.

"I think we have found everything we need for the winter. The others are collecting elder and rowan berries, rose hips, pine and yew tips, and alder and oak bark," the Bríg Brigu said as we retraced our steps up the hill.

There were chickens already roasting on the fire and fresh bannocks warming on the cooking stones of the hearth when we entered the welcoming warmth of the Fire Temple. The Bríg Brigu ordered hot baths for herself and for me as the attendants took away our full baskets and muddy shoes.

I had a fleeting recollection of my dream of the white bird leading me on to some unknown place. It seemed to me now that the white swans had called me to the Fire Temple.

How I would have loved to live here with Artrach, I thought, imagining myself walking hand in hand with him, collecting fresh herbs on the reedy shoreline under the gaze of the wild swans.

I felt another pang of longing as I imagined my birth mother walking along the same shoreline, collecting flag roots and cresses. Everyone said we looked exactly alike, our two heads wreathed in wild red tresses. If only I could have joined her, felt her love, and given it in return. *What would it have been like to have a mother who was really my mother? One who was my own flesh and blood? One who cared for me as her own precious child?* I was feeling two impossible longings for two departed loved ones. A deep sigh escaped my lips unbidden, and I looked up, embarrassed.

It was then that I noticed the gatekeeper, the man called Crithid, staring at me across the flames of the hearth, his eyes filled with smoky desire.

24

Sleet, freezing rain, and snow rattled against the flagstones outside of the temple doors as fierce winds penetrated the bunched willow branches of the roof. Occasional bursts of cold air swirled about the inner walls, lifting the colorful hangings and guttering the candles. Sometimes the candles went out completely, leaving only the glow of the hearth by which to see. We took advantage of the foul weather to stay indoors and study the Law of Bees.[6]

The Bríg Ambue, Cell Daro's current teacher of Brehon Law, was a dour-looking figure with a deeply lined face, a knot of braided grey hair, and a golden torque about her neck. She was always dressed in a dark blue robe with an enormous cowl; impatient with most mortals, she preferred to walk about with her hood raised to forestall silly questions.

She was highly respected by all the tribal chiefs, who would call on her to settle disputes within the clans because she had memorized so many different categories of law. She had decided that this day was a good one to illustrate the finer aspects of "bee trespass" for our benefit, but only two of the Druid were hanging on to her words, striving to memorize the legal niceties of the bee laws. These were the same ones who usually accompanied the Bríg Ambue to tribal councils and clan meetings and who hoped to follow in her footsteps one day.

"The person who finds a stray swarm of bees in a lawful green—the extent of which is as far as the sound of a bell or the crowing of a cock will reach—shall receive one quarter of the bee's produce; the other three quarters go to the owner of the land on which the swarm was found," the Bríg Ambue intoned in a stately voice.

"When a landowner begins beekeeping, he is entitled to three years of freedom in which the bees may forage on another's land with no liability. In the fourth year, the first swarm that departs from his hive goes to the nearest neighbor on whose land the bees have grazed. The next swarms to issue forth are distributed to each neighbor, depending upon their distance from the original hive and the amount of grazing the bees have done on their land."

"How can one possibly tell how far a bee has traveled to graze upon flowers?" someone asked.

"Not hard: you shake a bit of flour upon the bees and follow them to the end of their grazing."

The Bríg Ambue cast a prim look upon the questioner as if to say that this was a very simpleminded question, which had the desired effect of forestalling any future queries.

The recitation continued. "If a swarm settles temporarily on the branch of a tree or on a fence, the owner may recover the swarm; however, the landowner is entitled to one third of the bee's honey for a year. But if the bees settle in a permanent home, such as a hollow tree, and the bees cannot be removed without damaging the tree, the bees must be left in the tree, and the bee's original owner gets one third of the honey for the next three years. After that, the bees and all the honey belong exclusively to the landowner."

The Bríg Ambue droned on, providing a vocal backdrop for the day's activities. Most of us were busily making beeswax candles, the task that had inspired the legal instruction that the Bríg Ambue was bestowing so generously upon our heads. Now more than ever the Fire Temple felt like a hive. The smell of molten beeswax hung heavy and sweet upon the air, and the firelight and candles glowed like warm honey against the beaten silver, gold, and bronze of the walls.

I was surprised to be working with the hot wax, though I didn't mind the labor. As a princess I was forbidden to engage in that kind of manual work, but there were many times in the nemed of Dálach-gaes and Niamh when I had secretly put my hands to such occupation. Since we Druid no longer enjoy the almost royal status we once knew, and without mogae of our own, it is now necessary to participate in once unheard-of activities.

As you know, beeswax is a vital product for any educated household, Druid school, or temple. The Druid and nobles are entitled to beeswax candles, and if we want to spread the wax onto our writing tablets or use it to seal our documents or to glue household items together, these days we have to prepare it ourselves. And if we want to line our metal beakers and cups with beeswax to flavor the fion and protect the metal from rust, these days we are forced to melt and fashion it with our own hands.

Nessa handed me yet another stick with a line of long wicks hanging down so I could dip it repeatedly into a cauldron of hot melted wax with a little tallow mixed in for thrift. I marveled at the smoothness of her candles. No matter how hard I tried, mine always seemed to come out slightly bent and lumpy.

"He likes you, you know."

"Likes me? Who do you mean?"

"Crithid." She elbowed me slightly as she said it.

As usual, he was watching me with fascination from the other side of the hearth. His sky-blue eyes were framed by long chestnut curls. He was not hard to look at.

Her poke in my ribs had the effect of making me jiggle my wicks, and I knew that once again the result would be misshapen candles that would have to be used in the back recesses of the house to spare us all from public humiliation.

Crithid's face went red as hawthorn berries when he realized that we were talking about him.

"Poor Crithid. He is fierce as a dragon when he holds a fighting stick, but he never seems to find his voice with the ladies," Nessa said.

I looked up through downcast eyelids to find that he was still watching me.

My first instinct was to curl into myself, to hide within the brittle shell of my grief over Artrach. I wondered if I could ever let it go. But my voice of reason told me that sooner or later I would have to release his memory, his face, his smell, and the soft, warm feeling of his arms about me—arms that were the only real home I had ever found.

Why did it seem as if I had seen him only yesterday? It felt like only moments ago that I had witnessed that terrible sight—the spear that had ended my happiness on the earth plane.

"Whoa, what are you thinking about? You look so sad!" Nessa exclaimed.

"I can't really talk about it. It's just something that happened to me long ago."

The Bríg Ambue shot an angry glance down her nose. There was nothing more important to her than the Brehon Laws, and she felt that she was doing us a great honor by reciting them in our presence. It seemed that we had reaffirmed her low expectations of humanity.

We were silenced by her look and went meekly back to candle dipping, but I couldn't help glancing at Crithid again out of the corner of my eye. He was carefully spreading hot wax over old writing tablets, resurfacing them for future use.

When we at last finished our work and cleared away the detritus of our activities, it was time once again for a communal supper. Nessa and I sat cross-legged on the floor, trying to avoid the eyes of the Bríg Ambue, who was still radiating vague disapproval in our direction.

"I have to watch the Fire Altar tonight," Nessa whispered as she sopped up stew with a large chunk of bannock.

"Tonight! In this weather?"

"Oh, yes. We have to build and then watch the fire every day, day and night, no matter the season. The sacred flames must never be left unattended or be allowed to go out."

"That seems a huge task. How many of you are there who do this?"

"We have eighteen ban-Druid who take turns watching; each one of us stays with the fire for a night and a day. On the nineteenth day the Bríg Brigu herself takes over. I have the ninth watch; my night is tonight."

"Why nineteen? Is there significance to that number?"

"That is a Druidic mystery I'm not sure I can tell you just now," Nessa said, looking sheepish.

"Why don't men watch the fire? Can you at least tell me that?"

"Yes, I can. The fire is sacred to the goddess in the sun and to the light and healing that she shines upon us all. Therefore only women may tend the sacred flames.

"I've heard that there is a similar Fire Temple in the land called Roma, sacred to their goddess named Vesta. They also have fires of oak that are tended by women only. Although their goddess is supposedly only a hearth goddess, we know that she represents the same sacred fire that we make our offerings to."

For some reason I had a fleeting image of Artrach's flame-red hair. When Áine Clí shone on him, his head was always enveloped in a fiery glow, and the golden warmth of the sun had emanated from his loving heart. Surely my own mother, Ana, must have looked the same when she stood in the bright sunlight of a summer day. Suddenly the pain was too much to bear, and I knew I had to keep busy to fend off my personal darkness.

"Is anyone allowed to come with you? I mean, could I sit up with you this night and day as you keep your watch?"

"Do you really want to? Usually it is only young girls in training who pair up with someone in order to receive instruction. But since you have not been trained, perhaps the Bríg Brigu will allow it. I'll ask her."

We were quickly given permission. It seems mad looking back on it that I should have relished the idea of sitting outside in a gale. But that was the way I was: always hungry to penetrate the mysteries of the Druid path, wherever they might lead, and also needing some way to assuage the grief I still carried.

25

We spent a few tense hours feeding fresh kindling to the fire, adding logs, crumbling in the stubs of old beeswax candles, and even pouring oil onto the wood, anything to keep the fire alive in the teeth of the gale. It would be terrible luck for the tuath if the fire were quenched, and at one point we even hovered over the flames with our cloaks stretched out as a protective covering just to keep away the sleet.

Thankfully the freezing rains at last stopped, but the wind still gnawed our flesh.

"Why can't you build some kind of roof over the Fire Altar?" I asked.

"It is very important that the altar be open to the fires in the sky. They guide us and inspire us in all that we do."

"Oh," I said faintly, still not fully comprehending. I could barely imagine the years of hardship these women had endured to keep the fire alive in every season.

Now that we could relax a little in our efforts to keep the fire going, Nessa composed herself to make a formal invocation of Brighid, the goddess honored by the fire.

"We do this at least once in every shift," Nessa explained.

She raised her gloved hands to the sky in the *orans* position while facing the fire and sang:

A Brigit, a ban-dé beannachtach
Tair isna huisciu noiba
A ben inna téora tented tréna
Isin cherdchai
Isin choiriu
Ocus isin chiunn
No-don-cossain
Cossain inna túatha.

O Brighid, blessed goddess
Come into the sacred waters
O woman of the three strong fires
In the forge
In the cauldron
In the head
Protect us
Protect the people.[7]

Then she reached into a blue ceramic dish that rested on the circle of stones to one side of the fire.

"This is sky water that was blessed by the sun and the moon. Tonight it was also blessed by sleet and hail, which means it has powers to act quickly. Be very careful of your thoughts when you touch it, because whatever you think will immediately come to pass!"

Nessa anointed her forehead, hands, heart, and feet with the waters and then handed the dish over to me. I was happy to discover that the waters were slightly warm from the heat of the flames.

"We always keep a dish of water next to the fire because—"

I interrupted her explanation. "Because where fire and water come together, there is always the greatest potential for magic."

I thought of all the times I had heard that in the nemed of Dálachgaes and Niamh. Father Justan said the same thing, except he added that earth and air and ether were also involved. He said he learned that from the Greeks.

As I touched the sacred water to my skin, I felt a ripple of energy cascade down my body from somewhere above my head, all the way down to my feet. I could sense it purging away sorrow, doubt, and any illness that hid within me. The pain in my heart was noticeably lightened, and I could feel the magic coursing through me. I knew that some secret thought I was carrying would surely become manifest. But which one?

Nessa watched and smiled.

"You asked me why we have nineteen priestesses to tend the flames," she said as she pulled the hood of her oiled wool cloak lower down her forehead to protect her face from the winds still prowling through the protective yew hedge around the fire.

"Since the Bríg Brigu sent you out here with me, I have to assume that it is now safe to reveal the inner mystery of the Fire Altar to you. But you may not speak of this to anyone who is untrained in our tradition."

"I understand."

By now my teeth were chattering uncontrollably, and my body was shaking so badly that I could hardly speak the words. My feet felt like ice, which forced me to jig in place just to keep warm.

"As you know, this Fire Altar has been kept alive for all time and for all the people so that anyone may come here with a question and receive an answer from a priestess of the temple. Usually the people come here with their personal concerns—the health of a child or a cow, the need for gold, the desire for a wife or a husband.

"But occasionally someone comes here with a larger question, one that concerns the fate of an entire tuath or even the entire island. In such cases, we consult with the Druid of their kingdom before we give an answer, and we also consult the skies."

"The skies? Do you mean that you receive messages directly from the sky world of the gods?"

"Um, not exactly, though we do have priests and priestesses who can do that by going into trance. They scry into the flames or into sacred water or watch the flight of birds."

Those methods were very familiar to me, but I still wasn't sure what she was getting at.

"Our tradition has been handed down to us from the ancestors for thousands of sun cycles. The ancestors kept careful watch of the skies and passed down their knowledge until they were certain that they understood the pattern of things. Then that pattern was faithfully taught and handed down, priestess to priestess, just as I am about to give it to you today."

I had a brief vision of a line of holy women stretching back into eternity, from whose hands I was about to be blessed; it was both awesome and humbling.

Nessa paused for a moment to emphasize the sacred nature of what she was about to tell me. "We have learned to foretell the exact day when an eclipse of the sun or moon will occur. That is one of the great hidden mysteries of this Fire Temple and the secret knowledge that is encoded in the number nineteen."

It was not at all what I had expected to hear, and I still didn't know exactly what it meant.

"You see, there are eighteen priestesses who tend the fire and one high priestess who steps in on the nineteenth day. We have discovered a cycle in the sky world that lasts eighteen sun cycles and half a day. We call it the sky wheel.

"One sky-wheel cycle after an eclipse of the moon, an identical eclipse will occur at nearly the same spot in the heavens. In three sky-wheel cycles, an eclipse of the sun will repeat. If we know when an eclipse has happened and where it appeared in the sky, and if we keep very careful records, we are able to predict the exact day or night of the next eclipse."[8]

It took a moment to digest the information. It was almost beyond imagining that these priestesses had kept track of the great wheel in the sky for so many unbroken sun cycles.

"You said that you use this knowledge when the fate of a kingdom or of Ériu is at stake. How do you do that?"

"We have a conference with the local Druid, and then we use the awe and mystery of the event to shape the behavior of the tribes and even to influence the actions of an ard-ri. We can use an eclipse to say that the gods are angry or that a sacrifice is called for or to stop a conflict or a war. Or we might say that a great change is coming.

"When there is a cattle disease or a human sickness that is running rampant, we can say that the gods are changing fate and not to fear because a new day is dawning. There are many practical uses for the feelings of awe and doom that an eclipse inspires, especially if it's an eclipse of the sun.

"According to our stories, there was one total eclipse where the cattle returned to the byre to be milked because they thought it was evening, even though it was still mid-morning. The birds went to sleep in the trees, and the air grew remarkably cold as if it were the dead of night, even though it was high summer. The people were terrified."

"I can easily see how such things could be used to control the tuaths," I said.

I stayed quiet for a while, digesting the implications of this new knowledge. If Dálach-gaes and Niamh and the other Druid had only been privy to these ancient mysteries, perhaps the Cristaidi would not have gained control of the flaith so quickly. I understood how in order to be effective, this knowledge would have to be held tightly by a secret society and passed down and maintained carefully. Someone in the Fire Temple must be keeping precise records with immense dedication.

"The people who come for their monthly moon blessing have no idea at all what this temple is really for, do they?"

"No, they don't. But they are the ones who support our work by their gifts of grain and animals and firewood, and we could not survive without them.

"Perhaps you have noticed that the stone circles the ancestors erected in the countryside very often have nineteen stones? Now you know why.[9] In their time, the priests and priestesses would move a marker stone around the circle, placing it in front of one standing stone for a sun cycle and then carrying it faithfully to the next standing stone until the full eclipse cycle was complete. That was how they kept the tally.

"But now that there is a new religion in Ériu, one that seeks to undo our traditions, we have to keep our methods quiet. Now we work with a much smaller and less obvious way of keeping count. Hidden inside the Fire Temple is a rock with small depressions carved into it. We move special stones into each of the nineteen depressions, and that tells us exactly where we are in the cycle."

I began to wonder what depths of learning were being pushed into hiding by the new religion from the east. I thought of Father Justan and of his tolerance of the Druid faith, and of my father, who always sought to balance the needs of the old religion and the new. But in my own heart a conviction was growing that the ways of the ancestors had to be protected and then somehow revived.

I decided on that very day that I would dedicate my life to preserving the beauty and wisdom of the past.

It wasn't until mid-morning that a petitioner finally arrived seeking guidance from the fires. It was a woman, heavily pregnant and supported on each arm by an old crone. I thought those elderly women must be her grandmothers.

One of the old women spoke first. As toothless and bent as she was, there was a zealous fire in her eye. I studied the face of the other grandmother and found that she too burned with a bright inner purpose.

"We want to know who is in her belly," the first crone said, trembling a little as she uttered the words.

Nessa seemed to know exactly what they meant. She turned to the fire and gazed deeply into the embers.

"Who seeks to know this?" Nessa asked as if she had gone into trance.

"The clan mothers."

"And why do you seek this knowledge?"

The second grandmother stood a little straighter and answered, "We have recently lost our best tribal healer, a woman named Birog. She was always there for us, at our births and at our deaths. She was the best midwife of our village. She even took care of the sick animals. We fear that we will never find her like again."

The first crone found more words and seemed close to tears in her urgency. "Is Birog coming back to us again in Siobhan's belly? She was our friend!"

"Return here tomorrow and I will have your answer," Nessa replied, as if speaking down to us from a distant height.

The women seemed satisfied with the response. One of them reached into her cape and pulled out a stone jar of honey as a gift for the temple and handed it to me. Then they smiled and curtsied a bit as they steered the very pregnant Siobhan back towards the muddy path down the hill.

"They thought I was your servant!" I said.

The jar of honey was heavy in my hands and still warm from the old crone's body heat. "I notice that Siobhan never said a word," I added.

"That's because she knows she is but a vessel," Nessa said.

"A vessel? For what?" I asked.

Nessa reached for a split oaken log to lay upon the flames. "That is another Druid mystery that I can't speak of yet, but perhaps the Bríg Brigu will give permission. We can ask her at sundown when we go back inside"

Sundown! It seemed years away. But my spirits rose considerably when the Bríg Brigu's two attendants appeared carrying trays of hot drinks, scrambled eggs, and warm buttered bannocks.

Nessa laughed. "You didn't think we were deliberately sent out here to suffer, did you? It's not always this cold. In the summer it's lovely to be out under the moon and stars. And we have food and drink brought out to us at every shift."

That evening when we were safely back indoors, Nessa went to speak with the Bríg Brigu in private. I sat before the hearth for a while, not moving, just trying to soak up as much warmth as possible.

Crithid brought me a hot drink. "It's linden flower brew with uisge beatha and a little honey added for your health," he said shyly.

I accepted the cup and held it between my hands, still feeling as if ice had penetrated into my very blood. I was grateful for the steaming liquid, but I wondered if I would ever be truly warm again.

"I can rub your feet if you like," he offered shyly.

His face was filled with such gentle sincerity that it seemed a pity to refuse him. I let him remove my woolen stockings and work the icicles from my toes.

Sipping the linden flower brew, I noticed that Nessa and the Bríg Brigu were watching us from the opposite side of the hearth. The Bríg Brigu did not look displeased.

Nessa walked over carrying yet another thick woolen blanket to wrap around my shoulders.

"The Bríg Brigu has given her answer, and yes, I may reveal to you everything about the woman named Siobhan and her two grandmothers. But that will wait. Tonight you need to get your rest, because tomorrow we are going on a long journey." And then she walked away, offering no further explanation.

"I'll be coming with you as your protector," Crithid added, puffing out his chest a bit.

In his eyes I was a weak woman, I suppose. If only he could have seen me sleeping half-naked in a pile of leaves as I walked all the way back from Irardacht to In Medon.

Then I realized that everyone was in on the secret except me. Once again, Father Justan's words echoed in my inner ear: "Don't ask questions; just go."

I thanked Crithid for his kind attention to my poor frozen feet and gave him a little hug. But I still carried the image of Artrach within the secret chamber of my heart, a place I could not yet allow any other man to enter.

part five

The Goddess's Fiery Eye

26

I was just finishing a morning cup of tea with Nessa when I heard the scream of a horse. "My gods, it's Bláth!" I cried, and in an instant I was running down the muddy path, desperate with concern for my friend. I could hardly believe that these holy people who saw the sacred in all things would have hurt a horse. I was consumed by remorse, panic, and indignation. How could I have abandoned my poor Bláth? What was I thinking?

Careening around the side of the hill, I was met with a terrible sight: an overturned cart and flailing hooves that paddled in every direction, topped by a snorting, screaming, biting horse's head.

I ran as fast as I could and knelt down beside her, holding her bridle as firmly as I was able to avoid being bitten myself.

"Poor Bláth! What have they done to you? These horrible people!"

I looked up glaring, defying anyone to come close. A frightened-looking woman dared to address me.

"My lady, we did nothing. All we did was hitch the cart to her. She was fine at first, but as soon as she started walking, she went completely crazy!"

A small crowd had gathered to see what the commotion was about. I noticed that Siobhan and her grandmothers were among them and that each was carrying a large bundle.

"We didn't do anything to hurt your horse!" Crithid cried, appearing from somewhere behind the gawking onlookers. "She was fine with being hitched to the cart, but the moment she realized she had something behind her that she was pulling, she panicked, is all."

"All!" I yelled.

Then I remembered my Druid composure, took a few deep breaths, and blew into Bláth's nose. She quieted somewhat once she realized who I was.

"Does anyone have any carrots?" I asked in a loud voice. In my panic, I was momentarily convinced that I was surrounded by dolts, barbarians, and horse abusers.

"Here, m-m-m'lady," said a young man while gingerly proffering a bunch of carrots that he had most likely been taking to market.

I held the carrots in front of Bláth's nose. The effect was miraculous. Within moments she was showing interest only in the carrots and seemed to have forgotten completely the horror of that terrifying weight that she was dragging behind her.

I stood up and walked slowly backwards, away from her, still holding out the carrots, forcing her to right herself if she hoped to have at them. Meanwhile, Crithid supervised a small mob who worked to turn the cart upright even as Bláth rolled back on to her feet.

Soon Bláth was cheerfully pulling the cart as I continued to dangle the golden roots just inches from her nose. Not to prolong the agony, I slowly doled out the carrots, one at a time, as we made a slow circuit around the hill. By the time we came around to the same side again, she was used to the weight of the cart behind her, and I was exhausted.

"Get in!" the Bríg Brigu commanded, and I obediently climbed into the cart. Siobhan and the grandmothers followed. Crithid had to push Siobhan into the conveyance from behind as the rest of us yanked her up; her advanced state of pregnancy made it impossible for her to get in any other way.

Lastly the Bríg Brigu clambered in, and the gathered tribesfolk picked up the scattered pillows, boxes, bags, and baskets of provisions that had fallen out earlier that morning, piling them into the cart and onto our laps.

Crithid took the reins and led Bláth forward while Nessa walked beside the cart on the opposite side. Bláth knew that I still had carrots and quickly reverted to her usually polite manners, turning her head to eye me hopefully from time to time in hopes of a reward.

"Where are we going?" I asked when the Fire Temple on the hill was but a speck in the distance.

"We are going to celebrate the rites of Meán Geimhridh," the Bríg Brigu answered, gazing forward with regal calm.

The weather was chilly but clear. Extra blankets, gloves, hats, and capes had been provided for everyone, because a journey in winter is always a hazardous undertaking. Crithid and Nessa were warmed by their walking, while the rest of us piled on every available item as we strove to stay comfortable.

We traveled all day, moving along streams to rivers and ponds so we would always have water. That night we found hospitality in a small cluster of farm buildings. The folk living there seemed honored by our presence; warm broth, cooked cabbage, and roasted fowls were quickly manifested for us, along with enormous round loaves of spelt bread, jugs of béoir, and golden wheels of cheese.

After supper the Bríg Brigu, Nessa, Crithid, and I were invited to sleep by the fire, while Siobhan and the grandmothers were given dry accommodations in the straw of the cow barn. Before I went to sleep I visited Siobhan and the others in the barn to make sure of their comfort. I found the building to be warm from the body heat of the animals. Bláth spent a cozy night next to the other stock, munching hay.

We continued our journey in the morning. Every day for three days and nights it was the same routine: march from dawn to dusk; find a settlement of generous folk to provide supper and a fire; sleep; and take off again in the morning after breakfast.

The Bríg Brigu pressed a clutch of beeswax candles into the hands of the chief of each farmstead as we departed, leaving immense good will in our wake. We found that our Druid robes and symbols always gave us safe passage; only once did Crithid have to raise his staff at a belligerent bunch of tribesmen who attempted to extract a toll from us as we crossed their territory. They retreated quickly when the Bríg Brigu rose in anger from the bed of the wagon and spread out the wings of her cape like an enormous bat, uttering a loud curse using her voice of authority.

"Hear my curse on you: get out of my sight before I turn you all into rats! And then you will die!" Bláth reared up in fear, adding to the drama of the moment.

I trembled myself to hear the deep-pitched rumble from the Bríg Brigu's belly that seemed to shake the very trees. I knew she couldn't really turn them into rats, but the sound of it was very effective.

On the afternoon of the third day, we approached a hill with a huge round building upon it. It looked like a much larger version of the Fire Temple, only instead of whitewashed stones it was faced with gleaming white quartz. Round black stones were set into the quartz in the same spiral patterns that were painted onto the Fire Temple, and the sun's rays shining on the quartz front of the building made it shimmer like sunlight on waves. I had never seen anything so beautiful.

Surrounding the building was a ring of monoliths, and before the door was an elaborately carved stone lying on its side. The recumbent stone's surface was etched in deep spirals and whorls that looked like ripples upon water.

"There is a river at the bottom of the hill," explained Crithid as we clambered down from the wagon. "In ancient times, the tribes brought their dead here on barges to cremate them in the fire. Some still do, of course."

"Fire and water coming together again to make magic," I said out loud again to no one in particular.

I could see a knot of people standing around the entrance of the building; several of them were carrying funeral urns. There was a bonfire on the hill near the entrance and a small traveler's camp set up around the flames. Their tents and lean-tos were arranged in a rough circle; apparently we weren't the only ones who had journeyed far to be at that place for Meán Geimhridh.

Bundled and swaddled as the people were against the cold, I could still detect a few pregnant bellies hidden under thick capes that were flapping in the wind. It was strange to see so many gravid women clustered on a bleak hillside in winter.

"We must wait our turn," said the Bríg Brigu.

The grandmothers had been growing steadily more impatient as we neared the site; now they seemed excited, even agitated.

"Why are they so anxious?" I asked Nessa.

"They are hoping that everything will work out."

She said this as if it were adequate explanation. I held my tongue.

After we set up our camp, we shared what food we had with the other travelers, and they passed around leather bags filled with sweet béoir and fion. We squirted streams of liquid into our mouths as the bags made their circuit.

The camp grew more festive as the night wore on; at one point Crithid faced me from across the flames and sang an ancient love song. His voice was resonant and sweet, a fine tenor, and everyone stopped whatever they were doing to listen:

Sleep, my love, by the wave's side
Goat's milk I would give thee
Warm and sweet with honey
If you were but mine.

Sleep, my love, by the wave's side
Beer and wort I'd give thee
And bread of whitest barley
If you were but mine.

Sleep, my love, by the wave's side
Wine in the cup I'd give thee
And the yellow eggs of lapwings
If you were but mine.

Sleep, my love, by the wave's side
A house of thatch I'd give thee
Cherries and milk and flowers
If you were but mine.

Sleep, my love, by the wave's side
Cream and honey and dainties
Combs for your hair and ribbons
If you were but mine.[10]

More than one of the younger women stared at him with fascination. I was just grateful that the dark hid my blushes.

That night we slept in the cart together to keep warm. Each of us was under every available cape and blanket, except for Crithid, who slept under the wagon with his staff, ready to defend us.

The next morning, before dawn, the Bríg Brigu woke us from sleep.

"It's time!" she said in a loud whisper.

The grandmothers were instantly roused to action, rummaging furiously through the blankets and capes piled on the bottom of the cart. Eventually they found what they were after, which turned out to be a small urn.

The Bríg Brigu picked a burning brand out of the bonfire and used it to lead us up the hill and into the stone building.

"Follow me into the chamber," she said as we negotiated our way through the entrance and down a long stone hallway that opened into a large room. By now the torch was nearly out, and only smoke and a faint glow of ember at the tip remained. We were soon surrounded by thick, impenetrable blackness.

"Just wait," the Bríg Brigu confidently declared. There seemed nothing else to do.

After what felt like a very long time, the sun made its first appearance, looking like a thin crack of yellow light across the horizon. Gradually the line of light grew thicker, until the shape of an orb began to emerge. And then the first light of dawn penetrated the black of the chamber. I suddenly realized that it wasn't the horizon of the earth we were seeing; rather, it was the bottom edge of a window set into the stone wall high above the building's entranceway.

At that exact moment, something truly magical began to happen.

"Now!" cried the Bríg Brigu, and the grandmothers tore the lid off of the urn and quickly scattered the ashes from it onto a round, scooped-out stone with two smaller depressions in the front.

Everyone helped Siobhan to undress and then mount the stone; the two depressions were of a size that her two swollen breasts could fit into them, and the larger depression in the center was just the right size for her enormous belly. At first she kneeled on all fours.

"No! You have to lay your belly directly against the ashes!" said the Bríg Brigu.

"It's cold!" Siobhan wailed.

"Just do it!" said the Bríg Brigu.

Siobhan gingerly eased her huge belly onto the ashes scattered upon the stone's surface.

Just then a bright shaft of sunlight began to creep across the passageway until it penetrated the chamber, all the way to the back wall. For a few precious moments, Siobhan and all of us were bathed by a golden shaft of light.

"Birog! Birog!" the grandmothers wailed in unison. The Bríg Brigu began to chant:

Come to us from the shining realm
Return to us from the ancestors
Ride the golden shaft of light
Back to the world of the living!

We all took up the chant as we faced the glowing, rising orb. It seemed as if a pathway illuminated the womb of the earth and that a long, straight road had been created for the dead to walk upon.

Then, as suddenly as it had started, it stopped. The light faded away until we were in utter darkness once more.

The grandmothers were crying and still tearfully calling out Birog's name. Siobhan was distressed to be still on her belly, so we all moved to help her off of the stone and found her clothes to help her dress. Then the grandmothers groped in the dark to scoop up the remains of the ashes left in the hollow of the rock, carefully brushing them back into the little urn with their bare hands.

"Is this how the dead are brought back into this life?" I asked as we groped our way back out of the pitch-black chamber.

"Sometimes the dead come back to us on their own," said the Brígy Brigu. "But this is the ceremony that makes the passage certain. For it to succeed, everything has to be right: a woman pregnant at the time of Meán Geimhridh who is blood kin to the ancestor one is seeking to attract, strong emotional ties, and a real need. All the conditions were right today for the return of a beloved ancestor."

"Just as Meán Geimhridh brings the very first spark of light back to the world after the deepest dark of the year, our ritual brings back the spark of this life to one who has crossed to the ancestors in the sun," Nessa added. "Every year a child of light is reborn into the tribes—one who has traveled to the shining realms and back again to serve the people."

"The light returns to the chamber every day for five days," said Crithid. "That's why the others have gathered here to take their turn."

I thought of Artrach. How I wished that I had his ashes. I would have walked here alone, in the freezing cold, just to bring him back into my world. But it would have been a hopeless effort; I would be a grown woman and he just a baby. I knew that I would have to wait to see him in the next life.

"You are looking very serious again. What on earth are you thinking about?" Nessa asked.

But I was too ashamed to answer.

27

The day was raw and drizzling. The neophyte priestess had lit all of the candles available to us to make the room bright. She was busy whittling a clutch of Ogum staves for fortunetelling.

"Shall I tell you what was happening back in In Medon?" I asked, ever anxious to continue my tale and pass it down to the future.

"Oh, yes," she said simply. But her eyes were bright with curiosity.

Barra Mac Mel was sick. The Druid and the liaig conferred daily, recommending their poultices and brews, but nothing really worked. Barra Mac Mel had led his troops bravely; everyone said so. But the raiders had taken his kingdom's best cattle, and he and his warriors had come home in disgrace.

"Perhaps I am too old for this now," he said to Dálach-gaes, who had brought a fresh paste of comfrey root for his fractured and splinted leg bone and dried and powdered acorns to dust the infected wound in his side.

"It's winter yet," Dálach-gaes replied. "No one expects you to go riding out now. You should rest and see what the springtide brings."

But Dálach-gaes's face was grave, and Barra Mac Mel could read his thoughts; there was no need to hear them spoken.

Lying alone in the dark, accompanied only by his wolfhounds, Barra Mac Mel found ample time to review his life. His wife, the beautiful

Tuilelaith of Letha, had borne him a son. I, his only daughter, was safely under the tutelage of the Bríg Brigu. Dálach-gaes and Niamh said that the school at Cell Daro was one of the best, even better than the Druid colleges of Albu.

He knew that he was useless to Tuilelaith now; he could hardly rise from his bed, much less satisfy her. He knew that she had other lovers. And why not? It was her just due after years of service to what was a foreign land to her eyes. And if his wounds did not mend by spring, as a blemished man, he would be forced to vacate the kingship. The laws were iron-clad.

With no wife to share his bed and a kingdom slipping from his grasp, there was little left to live for. My birth mother, Ana, came to his mind more and more often in the dark hours. Was it true what the Druid said—would he find her again in the Blessed Isles, waiting for him, or perhaps in the shining realms of the sun? And if he did find her again, would she remember him?

He must have thought of me, who looked so much like my real mother. He realized with a guilty pang that he had avoided me as I grew up because the sight of me brought back too many memories.

And there was the shame. How could he have left Ana's fate to Tuilelaith so easily? The thought of Ana dying on the road alone, starving and in pain, tore at him like a wound. Did the wolves gnaw her bones? Did she blame him still?

For twenty sun turnings he had thought of In Medon as his family—thought of all the people as his kin. He had fought for them, lived for them, and bled for them. Only now that he was sick and alone did he realize his folly. His son rarely came to visit; he was too busy courting the blue-eyed Siofra. The only steady warmth he could count on in the bleakness of the night was from his dogs.

Barra Mac Mel summoned Dálach-gaes to his chamber.

"I am in pain," the king said.

"Let me make you a strong brew of primrose roots; they will help you sleep," the Drui replied.

"No, not that kind of pain. I see my life passing before me, and I am not happy."

"What can I do to help?"

"I dimly recall a ritual from my time at Cell Daro, a rite to appease the ancestors. The performance of it is said to remove all debts due to the dead."

"You are thinking of Ana?"

"Yes."

The answer came as no surprise. Dálach-gaes had known Ana well. The Druid had been pleased that Barra Mac Mel and his lover were schooled in the old ways, and they were happy to back Ana as ard-rígain. It had come as a shock to them all when Barra Mac Mel's powerful family edged out Ana in favor of a foreign princess. And Ana's disgraceful death was a blight on the entire tuath, so cruel that it was unspeakable.

Dálach-gaes asked the guards outside the king's chamber to fetch Niamh. When she got there the three talked until dawn, recollecting bits and pieces of the ritual until they were satisfied.

That morning Barra Mac Mel hobbled out to perform the rite. He did not mind the pain that shot up his leg with each step, nor the throbbing cramp in his side; these seemed a fitting penance. Dálach-gaes, Niamh, and two guards loaded him into and out of a wagon from the rath to the ritual site and then stayed behind at a respectful distance in case he should cry out for help.

Barra Mac Mel approached a fissure of rock, a natural tunnel known as the Airslocud Noíbu, a cleft between two enormous stones resembling a giant vagina set into a hill. He dropped the pack he was carrying and turned his body sideways, squeezing in. Then he pulled the pack in by the straps.

As he slid inside, he kept his mind on his firm intention: *Never again will I pass through the cleft of a living woman to be reborn, unless I am to spend a mortal lifetime with Ana beside me as my lover and wife.*

Now that he was alone within the bowels of the earth, he began to shake. His body and mind were finally able to disgorge the suffering that he carried. He was free at last to shed his tears.

"Please release me!" he wept aloud, not knowing if he was speaking to Ana his lover or to Anu the earth goddess whose body he had penetrated.

He left his first offering deeper inside the cleft of rock. Reaching into his pack, he pulled out a stone bottle of fíon. Dálach-gaes had suggested offering béoir, but Barra Mac Mel was familiar with the desires and wishes of great ladies. Surely Anu would prefer a drink of costly fíon from Letha.

He uncorked the bottle and poured the sweet fíon into a large, two-handled cup, wishing to be generous in case Anu had a consort to share it with. Then he unwrapped cakes flavored with honey, raisins, and costly imported cinnamon and laid them out carefully on a beautifully carved wooden platter.

"I invoke the goddess Anu to come and enjoy these offerings. I invoke the presence of my ancestors—all who have ever been born into the bloodlines of my family. I offer these gifts that they may be liberated from any debts, from any sufferings. I offer these gifts that they may be released from rebirth as humans, animals, trees, or plants, unless they choose to return. I offer these gifts that they may be elevated from the earth realm to the realm of the Shining Ones, if it is their will. I offer these in particular to my beloved Ana; may she know no suffering, and may I see her again when I make my journey to the Blessed Isles.[11]

"Ana, I have never forgotten you!"

Now he wept in earnest. Heaving sobs racked his form until he was forced to fall to the ground, not caring if he would ever rise again. It was finished. He had admitted his greatest wrong to the stones and to the goddess, and he had done everything in his power to right it.

When the wrenching grief at last subsided, he felt physically lighter, as if a great weight had been lifted. And then a strange current of energy began to course through his chest, building and building until he could hardly stand it.

"Send it to Ana!" he cried, visualizing a warm ball of love, tenderness, and well-being flying to her through the darkness. And then he fell back to the ground, his head pillowed on the sack he had carried, surrendered to the arms of sleep.

Outside the rock opening, Dálach-gaes and Niamh made no move to help the king. This was sacred work he was doing, and they knew that the gods would handle whatever was necessary. It wasn't their place to interfere.

Hours later, as the sun was setting behind the hill, a deep chill settled upon the landscape. The exhausted king emerged from the rocky crevice on all fours, dragging his wounded leg. But there was a calm expression on his face such as had not been seen in many turnings of the moon.

"Get Aislinn. Bring her back here to me!" he ordered hoarsely.

The guards ran back to the dun to carry out his wishes as Dálach-gaes and Niamh lifted the king into the wagon for the slow journey home.

28

I had been with the Bríg Brigu for two full sun cycles. I had made the neimheadh circuits, visiting each of the holy wells in the landscape at dawn on the appropriate holy day. By now the spirits knew me.

I would approach each holy well in the dark, pouring out my gifts of honey and cider at the base of the rowan trees and the hazels. Then I would circumambulate the well dessel nine times and always barefoot to better contact the earth. The people would follow me, also barefoot, in a single file.

We would take water from the well the moment the first rays of sun struck, and as we drank the fire-struck water we prayed for the children, for the barren women, for the health of the crops and the cattle, and for anyone else in need.

At Imbolc we left rings of candles burning in a circle around the well; at Beltaine we left honeyed milk and flowers. At Lugnasad we left a sheaf of the new grain and other first fruits of the harvest, and at Samhain we left apples, hazelnuts, and cheese. Often I would pour a silver cupful of uisge beatha into the waters as a blessing for the Sidhe.

Crithid followed me everywhere. "She has her own private retinue," folk would say. He tried to kiss me once, but I put my hands out to stop him.

I was growing used to the routines of gardening, harvesting, candle making, and bee tending, and I would often accompany the Bríg Brigu on her rounds, assisting women in childbirth and easing others across to the Otherworld. I was given my own shift at the Fire Altar; one of the other tenders was glad to be relieved of her duties, with young children at home to feed and care for.

It was nearly spring, and in accordance with the season, I had set out to gather peppergrass and sorrel from the fields and watercress from a nearby stream. A messenger appeared who had been sent to find me. He carried a wax-covered wooden message board, written in Dálach-gaes's hand. I recognized the script immediately: *Come home, your father needs you.*

I thanked the messenger, walked with him back to the Fire Temple, and then gave him a hot meal. I sent him back with a simple response: *I will be there as soon as possible.*

I knew that it must be very serious for them to have taken the trouble to send me a written message.

The Bríg Brigu asked for a private conference out of doors, away from the others' hearing. We took advantage of the bright morning to stroll down to the herb garden and sit on the little wooden bench that was not far from the beehives. Though it was still winter the bees were already making their first flights to test the sunny air; there were swelling red buds on the trees and moist sap flows to explore.

The Bríg Brigu was dressed in a simple grey tunic and a thick, grey lambswool shawl. Around her neck, as always, a golden torque glimmered in the sunlight.

"It's my own fault," the Bríg Brigu began, her usually impenetrable calm somehow broken. "I began to confuse you with Ana. After a while I even began to think that you were her, returned to help us. But of course you are not Ana, and you have your own life and destiny."

I waited for her to finish her thought. It was clearly costing her to speak; her composure was discomfited in a way I had not seen before.

"You see, I had thought to name you the next Bríg Brigu to come after me. That is why I took such care to teach you our secrets. I also made sure that the people of the tuath knew you well. I withheld no knowledge from you: you know where all our sacred herbs grow, and

199

you have all the secrets of the sky wheel. With your Druid-trained father and your powerful family behind you, you would have made the ideal candidate."

I held her words in silence for a moment, drinking in the heady praise. To be considered for such an honor!

"But I never said I was leaving," I said.

"When you depart from this place, there will be certain...irresistible forces that will conspire to take you away from us," she answered.

"I don't think I can shed this temple so easily as that!"

The Bríg Brigu sighed.

"I have not been completely honest with you. There is someone who has been seeking you for a very long time, and I put every obstacle in his path. I had hoped that you and Crithid would make a match, that his charms would somehow bind you to us. I urged him on—told him to court you. But he has clearly failed."

Now I was completely lost. Who was seeking me? And why in the gods' names didn't she just arrange a marriage? That was often done in Druid circles to keep our knowledge safe.

"Who is seeking me?"

"I will not say just yet. You must first go to In Medon and find out what the king and his Druid need from you, and then we will talk further. I can say no more."

"Don't ask any questions; just go," I said.

"What?"

"Oh, nothing—it's just an expression that I have become very familiar with."

That evening I made my goodbyes and gifted the Bríg Brigu with the carved staff that I had carried with me from In Medon.

I left at first light with Crithid at my side, as always, as my protector. We rode in a little cart pulled by Bláth. She shook her mane repeatedly and kicked up her feet, delighted to be going places under the bright, late-winter sun.

29

As we traveled, the air grew ever colder. By nightfall a fresh rime of frost had covered the grass and trees, and the winds had picked up until our faces and hands were stiff and red with the cold.

"Don't worry about it too much," Crithid said. "We can keep each other warm in the wagon."

I knew he was right. It was the logical thing to do. I suddenly had a thought that the Bríg Brigu must have planned this forced intimacy. Maybe she was even directing the weather? I knew that her magic was powerful.

We lit a fire with tinder and flint and cooked a simple meal. Afterwards we enjoyed a hot cup of elderberry brew laced with fion, and then I carefully banked the embers for the night, saying:

> *By the sacred three*
> *Brighid of the Forge*
> *Brighid of the Cauldron*
> *Brighid of the Poetic Flame*
> *I smoor the fire*
> *This night, as every night*
> *To save and shield*
> *To surround this hearth*

This eve, this night

And every night

Until white dawn

Shall come upon the embers.[12]

By now the wind was roaring in our ears. I covered Bláth with a blanket, securing it around her girth with a stout rope. Then I curled in beside Crithid, who was waiting for me in the wagon.

"I have often imagined this," he said softly. "May I put my arms around you to keep you warm?"

I had a flash of memory of a night spent in a similar wagon on the day that Artrach and I were taken prisoner. I knew where this was leading.

"I think it will be enough to just lie close and share our body heat for now."

I supposed it was inevitable that Crithid and I would end up a pair, but my heart was still given to another. I hoped to see Artrach in the Otherworld one day, and I wanted our union to be complete, for all eternity, with no other person between us. Yet I knew that it would be impossible to resist the Bríg Brigu forever if she had other plans.

Somehow, by morning Crithid did have his arms around me, after all. And my body instinctively pressed close against him, despite my best efforts. I began to think of my body as an animal with desires of its own. But in the clear light of day, we resumed our usual collegial relationship.

Things went on like that for the three days it took to get back to In Medon.

As we approached my father's dun by the road that was so familiar to my eyes, I noticed that more woodlands had been felled and that vast stretches of land were now given over to agriculture. Everywhere rock walls, hawthorns, and blackberry hedges had sprouted up to divide the fields.

The press of progress grated on me; I feared for the wild things of the forests. Where would they find a home? I knew that the yawning lengths of field meant more food for the people, but they also meant that firewood would be ever harder to come by.

A number of water mills and grain-drying huts had also sprung up outside the walls of the rath. Progress was in evidence everywhere.

"A very forward-looking place, your father's kingdom," Crithid commented approvingly.

I uttered a prayer for all the wild creatures and for the land spirits as Bláth trotted between the neat rock fences.

> *May the land grow and prosper*
> *May it have strength and life*
> *May the people be protected*
> *May the herds flourish*
> *May the white barley grow tall*
> *May the trees drip with honey*
> *And may all the wild creatures*
> *The seen and unseen*
> *Find safety and peace.*

We approached the wooden palisade of my father's rath, with its familiar veil of smoke hanging above and the usual busy lines of merchants and craftspeople coming and going. I was not recognized. A guard ran out from the gates, sword drawn, to find out who we were.

"I am Aislinn, daughter of Barra Mac Mel," I told him, and he ran back to tell the herald to announce me properly. Carnyx players appeared on the top of the outer wall to greet me with horn blasts and to alert the people that someone noteworthy had arrived.

By the time we entered the gate there were throngs of curious onlookers who had come to see what I looked like, how I had grown and changed. I was ushered to my father's bedside immediately.

Crithid stayed outside my father's roundhouse to tend to Bláth and our belongings.

Sober-looking servants surrounded my father; they were busily applying fresh poultices to his leg and to the wound in his side. He was very thin, his face was yellow, and the skin around his eyes was brown—the "configuration of death," as I had been taught. It pulled at my heart to see it. But we had never been close; it was a grief I knew I could bear.

"Come closer, my child," he said in a weak, gravelly voice. "You look well. I am very glad you came to see me."

"How could I not have come, Father?"

"I haven't treated you fairly, I am sad to say. I should have spent more time with you when you were young and growing." His hand, yellow and frail, reached out to touch me. He seemed anxious to unburden himself, so I stayed very still and listened.

"You see, you are so much like your mother that I was afraid to even look at you…"

"Shhh…," I said soothingly, as if he were a little child. I placed my palm upon his forehead and stroked it gently. "There is no need for this. The Bríg Brigu has told me everything. I know all about Ana."

And then my father began to weep. I ordered the mogae out of the room.

"Father, you summoned me here. What is it that you wish from me?"

He turned his fevered face towards me and grasped my hand.

"I wanted to see you one more time to tell you that I am sorry for the way I treated you and your mother. And I thought that maybe you might have learned some new healing magic at the Fire Temple, something more than what Dálach-gaes, Niamh, and the liaig have been able to do."

"Father, I saw the comfrey poultices that the mogae were placing onto your body. I would have done the same. The only thing I can add to that is a healing charm that the Bríg Brigu taught me. Shall I try it?"

"Yes, you may."

His eyes shone with a desperate hope that was painful to witness.

I placed my two hands about a palm's length above his body, not touching him, and stroked the air above him in repeated motions towards his feet.

"Always stroke down, towards the legs, as if you were stroking the fur of a cat," the Bríg Brigu had said. "No cat wants its fur stroked the wrong way!"

Then I began the ancient incantation:

Brighid went out in the morning
She found the broken legs of horses
She put marrow to marrow
Pith to pith
Bone to bone
Membrane to membrane
Tendon to tendon
Blood to blood
Tallow to tallow
Flesh to flesh
Fat to fat
Sinew to sinew
Skin to skin
Hair to hair
Brighid of Healing healed that
Which is in her nature to heal
Let this body be healed
If it is her will
Through the powers of life.[13]

I saw that my father's body relaxed a little. He reached for my hand again.

"Aoibhgreíne, I know that my body is broken."

I smiled a little; no one had called me that name in years.

"I need to ask you something more," he added.

"Anything, Father. That is what I am here for."

"I recall that the Druid of the Fire Temple are trained in the uses of yew, and I assume you have that knowledge now. I am loath to ask Dálach-gaes and Niamh because it might put them and their children at risk, so that is why I am asking you. Tuilelaith will not countenance this, of course. She thinks the old ways are an embarrassment."

I knew what he was thinking; yew was the cure of last resort. In ancient times the Druid would bathe wounded warriors in vats of yew; it was also said to cure those with the wasting sickness. And if the sick and wounded were not cured, then Fer Fí—the Spirit of the Yew, brother to the goddess Áine—would take them across to the Blessed Isles.

I could see that my father no longer cared if he remained in this life. The Otherworld was already beckoning.

"Father, I can do this if you wish. I assume there are still hedges of yew around the nemed of Dálach-gaes and Niamh? "

"Yes."

I left my father's roundhouse and found Dálach-gaes and Niamh outside waiting for me. Róisín was with them too, and within moments we were embracing.

"Look at you! All grown up! And no one has offered you food or drink!" Róisín said, red faced and with tears in her eyes. I noticed with a pang that her hair was now streaked with grey. Niamh and Dálach-gaes pulled me away from her and gave me huge hugs and kisses of their own. Then all of us, Róisín and Crithid included, trooped back towards the nemed for conversation and hospitality.

All of a sudden the world was turned on its side, and everything seemed to be happening in slow motion. Standing before the thick screen of yew that surrounded the nemed was a familiar form. I thought I must be having a hallucination or a vision because the form looked so very familiar. My gaze shimmered with disbelieving tears. I rubbed my eyes to assure myself that it was real—that *he* was real. The form, the spirit, or whomever it was, looked exactly like Artrach!

As we came closer, my focus sharpened. I noticed that the yew hedge was thick with red berries. I noticed every blade of grass upon the ground. I noticed the intense blueness of the sky. I noticed the man dressed in green leather who was reaching out for me. And then I was wrapped in arms that melted my body, my mind, and my heart. And when he kissed me, I knew it really was him, in flesh and form. *Artrach!*

"My love," he said simply. And we kissed again and yet again.

He searched my face with tear-filled eyes. "I am so glad you are safe, *mo muirne*."

"What did you just say? Those were the very words I heard at Samhain, coming out of thin air!"

"At Samhain I was wounded and sick with a fever. I dreamed that I found you amongst revelers in a roundhouse that was strange to me. That dream was so very clear; it was more vivid than daylight."

"That was no dreaming, my love. That was a true vision."

I could not bear to take my hands off him, and he could not bear to separate from me either. We walked into the nemed entwined as one being, staring, disbelieving, laughing, and wild with joy. I noticed Crithid from the corner of my eye, looking lost and close to tears. Dálach-gaes, Niamh, and Róisín were ecstatic.

"How is this possible?" I asked them all.

"The Bríg Brigu forbade us from telling you," Dálach-gaes explained. "She said it would harm your concentration and your training."

"I wanted so badly to come to you, but I was prevented," Artrach added.

Now I understood what the Bríg Brigu had meant when she said "irresistible forces" would conspire to keep me from her temple. If I had known that Artrach was alive—was in my father's dun—nothing would have prevented me from leaving the Fire Temple. I saw the wisdom of her efforts, but her attempts to unite me with Crithid seemed base and somehow unworthy—poor Crithid who was suffering now, a creature caught in the Bríg Brigu's snare.

I felt an overwhelming urge to confront the Bríg Brigu, priestess to priestess. How could she claim to respect me and insist that she wanted me to take her place one day, and yet deceive me? I swallowed my indignation, pocketing it away in a secret recess of my mind. One day I would confront her.

Just then a bard appeared to sing and play harp for us, and mogae from my father's house followed, carrying trays of roasted meats and fish, parsnips and carrots, watercress, cheeses and breads, and beakers of fion from my stepmother's store. As we ate and talked and laughed and caught up on the past year's news, my anger at the Bríg Brigu began to fade.

In the midst of our feasting a visitor was announced, and my other mother, Tuilelaith, appeared with a small retinue of mogae. Her entrance caused a slight pall on the proceedings, and a sudden silence fell over us.

She looked proud and stern as ever, affronted that I had not paid respects to her first, as was her due.

"Surely my own daughter should have paid me a visit before sharing a meal with all these...people." Her eyes swept the gathering as if everyone in it was beneath her in rank, including me.

"I am sorry, Mother," I mumbled. "I will pay you a visit as soon as I have finished my business here." To save face, I tried to make it sound as if I were carrying out some important diplomatic mission.

"I will dine with you at midday tomorrow," Tuilelaith said, sweeping regally from the house with her servants behind her.

There was a pause as everyone worked to shrug off the chill that had settled. Then I told them of my father's wishes. Niamh's face grew grave, and the room fell silent once more.

"As you know, the bath of yew is a noble cure that has stood the test of time. But not everyone is helped. Many are those who cross over to the Otherworld, taken by the Spirit of the Yew," she said.

"I am aware of that. But it is what he specifically asked for."

"The Cristaidi will not like it," Dálach-gaes added. "They have a strong prohibition against herbal cures and an even stronger prohibition on helping the sick to the next life."

"Have they grown so powerful that they can even dictate to a king?" I asked.

"I am afraid so," Artrach said sadly. But when he looked at me I couldn't resist gazing into his eyes and smiling. We kissed once more, not caring at all who was watching.

"I think we should leave those two alone now," Niamh said.

Artrach stood and pulled me to my feet. The scent of him was intoxicating; it was the same woodland essence of ferns and clean water and wood smoke that I remembered.

"I have a camp outside the gates. Will you come there with me?" he whispered into my ear. A hunger that was not for food shone from his eyes.

"Of course I will. I will follow you anywhere," I murmured.

"We'll take care of Crithid..." Niamh called out. But we were already leaving and past caring about anyone else in the whole world.

30

rtrach led me out of the gates and into the starry night. As we
walked we paused from time to time, just holding each other,
pressing our two bodies together, not wanting to be separate for even
an instant. I felt that I was living a waking dream.

"How did this happen?" I asked. "I saw that spear go into you—I
was so sure you were dead!"

"Didn't you hear me calling out for you? I lay sick with a wound for
many moontides. I was taken to Irardacht for healing. They tell me
that I called your name every day!"

I remembered.

"Yes, you would call out *Aoibhgreine*, and I could hear you. It was
very mysterious. I wondered who was calling me that!"

"We were never really apart, you know. Our spirits and hearts have
always been as one," he murmured gently into my ear, finishing the
sentiment with a small nibble. I felt my knees go weak.

I replied with a slow, long kiss that shook the very earth.

When we got to his camp, it proved to be a rough but sturdy beehive
structure made of supple limbs and leaves next to a little brook. The
nearly full moon shone above, and pockets of white hoar frost glowed
in the starlight at our feet. But I no longer felt the cold in any way; it
was as if my old body had been shed, and I was suddenly reborn into a

new form. And only half of that form belonged to me—the other half was Artrach.

We ducked into the little hut, and before I knew it we were lying on his pallet, our clothes off, and he was kissing my face, my breasts, and my loins. Our desire soon warmed the air of that tiny place.

"I worship you!" he said.

"You are my god," I answered back. His body was my holiest temple, the place where I had longed to worship but had been kept away from for two long sun turnings.

He suckled my breasts and I was ready for him in an instant. When he entered me it was as if the gateway between the worlds was flung wide open and all the creatures of this world and the Otherworld were crying out in joy together. *Artrach!* And the waves of that sound pounded against my loins in sweetness and fury.

It ended with a sleepy, petal-soft embrace that lasted until dawn.

We emerged from our warm nest when the sun was already high in the trees. Artrach reached down and plucked three blades of dried grass. "Grasp them tightly with your fingers," he said.

As I held them he plaited a tiny, flat braid.

"Hold out your hand."

I held out my hand and he tied the plaited grasses around my marriage finger and bit off the ends, planting a kiss on my palm.

"Now you are mine forever. One day soon I will trade these grasses for a ring of pure gold."

This time we fell onto the bare earth and he entered me again and again, and the ancient oak trees were a solemn witness to our joining.

31

I dined with my stepmother as she had requested; it was a sober and cold meal. I could not share the details of my life at the Fire Temple with her because she felt that such things were a waste of time, a silly superstition fit only for peasants. She was concerned with more practical matters.

"It is time you were married again. You are not that old; perhaps a widower will still take you. After all, you do come from a good family," she speculated.

"Of course we will have to do something about your hair. As ever, it looks like a rat's nest. And your clothing is disgraceful. You are an embarrassment to me when you go about like that. We will have to have fresh outfits made for you and burn what you are wearing now.

"Your brother has made a very advantageous union; he is now joined to the wealthiest family in our district. Maybe he can help you find someone from among his new relations." She went on to describe in detail the clothing, hairstyles, and jewelry of the women in that clan, by way of inspiring me to live up to their splendor.

I hid my feelings and finished the meal in silence.

I visited my father every day. As far as he and Tuilelaith knew, I was living in the nemed with Dálach-gaes and Niamh, with Róisín as my nurse and guardian of my virtue. But Artrach and I would slip away to his camp each night to live as a handfast couple under the oaks.

"We had better do the yew ritual here, in secret," I said to him after a few days had passed. "I have spoken to Father Justan about it, and he says that as far as he is concerned, we should do what my father wishes. However, if the abbott, Father Cassius, hears about it, there will be trouble."

"Trouble? What exactly does he mean?"

"I don't know, but I can tell that Father Justan is scared of something very bad happening—so bad that he says he can have no part in this, and that any consequences will be mine alone if I choose to proceed."

"Your father is dying; I think we should fulfill his last wish. It's the honorable thing to do."

And so we agreed. Artrach and I carried a wooden bathtub to the little clearing that we called home, and Dálach-gaes and Niamh helped us to cut yew branches from the inside of the nemed enclosure. We did not involve anyone else.

Niamh had a huge cauldron that she used for making siabainn, which Artrach shouldered into the forest. He hung it on a metal rod suspended across two stout Y-shaped tree limbs at either side of a newly dug fire pit, while I broke yew branches into small pieces and placed them into the cauldron to be simmered. Another large cauldron hung suspended over Artrach's cooking fire, ready to be filled with water for a hot bath.

When everything was prepared, Artrach and Dálach-gaes carried my father into the woods on a stretcher. They convinced the guards that it was for a religious rite and that absolute privacy was needed. When my father was safely in the clearing, Dálach-gaes went back to the nemed and pointedly told the guards that I was a trained priestess and that I was operating on my own.

We first filled the wooden tub with boiling hot water and then added cold water from the stream until the bath was a comfortable temperature. Artrach helped my father to undress. When he was settled into the bath, we gradually poured in the simmered yew, straining the brew through a willow basket.

"Aoibhgreíne."

"Yes, Father?"

"If I should pass over, I want to be buried at the Fire Temple, with all the proper Druid rites."

I swallowed hard. This would be a difficult request to honor; the flaith would be scandalized.

"I'll do my best, Father."

"I know you will."

Artrach placed an oiled leather tarp over the wooden tub to hold in the heat, and I raised my hands to the sky, singing a magical incantation for healing:

> *As you make your circuit of the plain of life*
> *May the seven daughters of the sea*
> *And the seven daughters of the sky*
> *Who shape the threads of long life*
> *Take three deaths from thee*
> *Give three lives to thee*
> *May no ghosts injure you*
> *May death not come to you*
> *May your time on earth*
> *Be bright as silver*
> *May your form be whole*
> *May your strength increase*
> *May your grave not be readied*
> *May you not die on your journey*
> *May your return be ensured*
> *May worm not attack you*
> *Nor dark elf, nor fairy host*
> *Nor thief, nor hard black beetle*
> *May no warriors rend you*
> *May you have an increase of time*
> *From the source of all*

May you be an invincible fortress
May you be an unshakable cliff
May you be a precious stone for the people
May the grace of the gods be upon you.[14]

My father seemed eased by the warmth of the bath, and he gradually began to yawn. We took this as a good sign that he was relaxing into the treatment. But when he opened his eyes I saw that the pupils were dilated and that he was becoming flushed. I had never seen a person in a yew bath before, and I had no way of knowing if this was the standard occurrence.

Artrach had a small harp from Irardacht that the bard Conláed had made with his own hand and gifted to him. He strummed the strings and sang a mystical song about yew trees:

A wheel for a king
A prince's right
Straight firm tree
Firm-strong god
Door of the sky world
Noblest of trees
Vigor of life
A bear's defense
Spell of the wise—[15]

But before he could finish, my father began to vomit and then to convulse violently. I rushed to lift off the blanket and pull his frail form out of the yew bath. I found that despite the hot water, his limbs had grown very cold. Then his head lolled back in a way that told me the end was near.

We worked together to lift his near-lifeless body from the water and to carry it to the base of an old oak, thinking that the oak's spirit might somehow revive him and, if not, provide him a strong gateway to the Otherworld.

We propped him up against the oak and tucked a blanket around him for warmth and dignity. Behind the oak the western sky glowed royal purple, red, and orange as the sun set behind the stark black lines of the late winter trees. Steam still rose from my father's form, though his skin was already cool to the touch.

I straightened my father's damp grey locks around his shoulders, using my fingers as a comb, and then centered the golden torque that still circled his thin, yellow-skinned neck. The light of the fire and the glowing sunset were reflected in the golden circlet, brightening his face.

But soon his lips were blue and his body as cold as death.

"He has made a noble ending, despite everything," I said. "For a Drui, to die at the base of an ancient oak is a very good passing, because the oak is a doorway to the sky world of the gods through its branches and a passageway to the Sidhe realms of the ancestors through its roots."

"And now at last he can join his beloved Ana; there is some comfort in that," Artrach added.

We stood together before him in respect, contemplating his life, thinking of his triumphs and sorrows.

"His breath has gone to the gods. Now he can cross the river of forgetfulness, where the waters will carry away all memory of sorrow. Only his wisdom will be left behind, joined into that great stream from which all people may draw, from which the wise ones may learn from the past," I said.

"Yes, now we can begin to make offerings to him and call on him as a beloved ancestor—" Artrach did not finish the thought because just then we heard a rustling of leaves on the forest floor and the sound of voices—sounds that told us a large group of people was fast approaching through the brush.

And suddenly there were torches everywhere. Warriors, village folk, and the Druid—even my father's wolfhounds—surrounded us in the gloaming. Father Justan was among them. I looked towards him and he shook his head silently, shrugging his shoulders as if to say that he was helpless, there was nothing he could do. Dálach-gaes, Niamh, Róisín, and Crithid looked terrified.

A Cristaide priest stepped forward out of the circling crowd. "Shame! Shame on you! You dare to come back to this kingdom, you child of a sorceress, you offspring of a prostitute! I am well aware of the truth of your birth. Your stepmother has told me you are no spawn of hers.

"You mock us and all the good people of this kingdom. At whom do you sneer and stick out your tongue? You are a rebel, the offspring of a liar! You burn with lust among the oaks and every tree of the forest!

"You have made your bed here like an animal! You have hidden your Pagani ways behind your filthy doorpost. You climb into your brazen bed hidden amongst the trees. We have seen you in your nakedness, rutting like an animal!

"Acknowledge your guilt; you have rebelled against the Lord. You have scattered your favors to false gods under every spreading tree! And you have committed the most unspeakable sin: *you have killed your own father!*"

The crowd gasped. At that, the warriors lurched forward, grabbing me and Artrach, binding our hands before us and twisting the cloth bindings with a stick to make them tighter, so tight that my hands went numb.

"He is not to blame!" I cried. "He was only serving me!"

They seemed to see the logic in that. How could a rustic woodsman with wild russet hair, clad in a green leather tunic and leggings, be the equal of a princess of the royal house? The priest walked over to Artrach and put his hand upon his head as if to bless him, as if he were a wayward child, and said, "My son, why do you consort with witches? The Lord, your god, has forbidden you to do so! These are rebellious people, deceitful as children, who refuse to listen to the Lord's instruction."

Then the priest turned back to the crowd.

"Let no one be found among you here who practices divination, engages in sorcery, interprets omens, engages in witchcraft, or casts spells! This woman belongs to Satan. She carries out Satan's plan! She and those of her kind are murderers! They have rebelled against the one true god!"

Attendants were slapping the king's face, trying to bring him back to life, but it was no use. I could have told them that.

Then a leather hood was pulled over my face and a rope tied to my bound hands. There was the sound of wailing and screaming as everyone realized that the king was truly dead.

"Don't be afraid! I will never leave you!" I heard Artrach call out from somewhere in the distance.

Then there was the vivid pain of being pulled through the forest as I stumbled and fell, pushed and shoved relentlessly up the path to the dun. Finally I was thrown onto my knees on the cold floor of the prisoner's mound, where they pulled off my hood, unbound my hands, and left me alone on the cold cobbles of the floor.

That night the priest came to see me, carrying my cape that had been retrieved from the forest, a measure of decency so I would not perish in the cold. I pulled out the little wooden cross that I still wore hidden under my clothing.

"See this?" I asked. "It was given to me when I was a child, and I have worn it faithfully. Father Justan says it is the symbol of one who gave his life for the people, who redeemed the land and the tribes out of love. He was a great Drui, a sun king who sacrificed himself for the good of all!"

"You dare to compare the Cristos to a Drui? Get away from me, Satan."

He walked away, leaving me to the cold, dark, and lonely starlight.

I had one visitor that night. It was Crithid, who appeared looking shocked and sad.

"I swore to protect you, and I will do what I can. I bribed the guards with a sét, and they let me come see you just for a moment."

I was glad of a friend, but looking at Crithid, I felt ashamed.

"I am so sorry. You need to understand that it was not my doing. The Bríg Brigu wanted us to be a pair, but my heart was already given to another."

"I know that the Bríg Brigu can be hard to resist once she has made her plans," he replied. We held hands briefly through the bars, and then a guard came to lead Crithid away.

My stepmother, Tuilelaith, arrived at dawn, with my brother, Eógan, in tow. She looked older and greyer than I remembered; her lips were pinched, and her face was white and hard as stone.

"I have nothing to offer you," she said. "We have simply come here to say goodbye. We would not have come at all except Father Justan insisted. We are only here out of charity."

Eógan looked taller and burlier than he ever had before; he had obviously been practicing battle skills with the warriors. He carried a large basket of food and drink that weighed over a very muscular arm and began pulling wrapped items from the basket one by one, shoving them under the iron grill. Then he pushed a corked stone bottle between the bars.

"It's your own fault, you know. Whatever happens to you now is your own doing," he said. His face was sad, weighed with the grief of my father's passing.

My stepmother took Eógan's arm, holding him close as if defending him from a monster. She pointed her finger at me.

"You have probably ruined your brother's chance of ever taking the throne. You are just like your mother was: willful, brazen, and selfish."

Then they swept away from my cell, their duty to me completed.

Now my world was a frozen wasteland. The warmth and comfort of the Fire Temple with its glowing walls and friendly hearth were but a distant dream, and Artrach's love seemed just a young girl's fancy, a momentary respite in the midst of cruel reality. I had awakened into the real world, a harsh and cruel place. I felt the cold fingers of death reaching for my blood and my life, and a strange numbness began to settle on me. I struggled to settle my thoughts, focusing on my third eye as I had been taught by the Druid. I was preparing to die.

That night Father Justan appeared at my door, squeezing a thick woolen blanket to me through the iron bars.

"Your father was given a Cristaide burial."

"That's not at all what he wanted!"

"I know, but none of us was in a position to argue. Father Cassius has many followers amongst the flaith. Since he got here, he has been preaching day and night against the evils of the Druid. Your actions have only provided proof of his claims."

"My actions? He is a newcomer to Ériu—he knows nothing about Druid philosophy!"

"I know, but if he repeats his message often enough, eventually the people will come to believe it, no matter how twisted it might be. He is telling everyone that you are a murderer and a witch. But he has forgiven Artrach, saying that he was bewitched by you."

"I am glad of that. At least he will be safe."

"All I can offer you now is my blessing. I know that you are innocent and that you acted only from the goodness of your heart."

Sweet Father Justan; as he made the sign of the cross in the air to bless me, there were actually tears in his eyes. He turned his back on me and disappeared into the night.

Before dawn I had yet another visitor. The two guards who were watching my cell had fallen asleep on the grass, wrapped in their capes against the cold. Artrach was able to creep right up to the cell door and whisper into my ear.

"I love you, you know that."

"Yes, I do. I love you too."

His words were like warm spring rain on frozen earth. We kissed through the bars.

"Crithid has gone back to the Fire Temple to alert the Bríg Brigu."

"Oh, thank the gods! She is the only one who can extricate me from this mess."

For the first time, I began to feel a glimmer of hope.

32

I hoarded my little cache of bread, cheese, apples, and dried meat carefully, grateful to my brother for his kindness. I had no visitors for a week. Then one morning a crowd arrived with Father Cassius at the head to judge me.

"Here before you stands a ban-Drui," Father Cassius pointed to me. By now my hair was matted and my clothes were smelly, filthy, and wrinkled. I was sure I looked like any common criminal.

"These Druid are the most wretched, barbarous, and degraded people on the island. They are without justice, without mercy. As you have seen, they will even kill their parents just to please the Pagani gods they serve.

"They perform their idolatrous rites in groves of oak trees. They strip their victims naked, tie them to a tree, and then disembowel them. Then they dance in their victim's blood and pretend to tell the future from the blood flow! This is what the Princess Aislinn was attempting to do when I stopped her. If I had not arrived in time, she would have split the king open and pulled out his entrails!"

There was a wail of horror from the crowd. Several of the women began weeping. One of them called out, "In Albu it is said that the Druid burn their prisoners in large wicker cages!"

The crowd inhaled as one, shocked at the horrible allegation.

The priest confirmed her statement. "They will burn hundreds of victims in a day, all the while singing hymns to their false, cruel gods and dancing around the burning bodies. In this way they breed all tenderness and mercy out of the people, leaving only soulless cruelty in their wake!"

Dálach-gaes and Niamh were crying now, but for a different reason. They had never heard such false and outlandish lies spoken about their ancient spiritual path; it was almost too much to bear. But they stayed put, doggedly taking in the angry rhetoric spewing from the priest's mouth.

They did it for me.

"What shall we do with this disgusting creature that fouls the very air she breathes?"

The priest swept the crowd with his glance. A man stepped forward.

"Kill her, I say."

Emboldened by the man's speech, others began adding their voices:

"Burn her, just like those Druid burn *their* prisoners!"

"Tear out her bowels!"

"Whip her until she dies!"

I could see Artrach in the crowd. White-faced, he leaned heavily on Dálach-gaes. Tears of sadness and rage were streaming from his eyes.

"Open the gates!" the priest commanded, and the guards took a large iron key and turned it in the lock.

The crowd moved closer. Now I could see the bloodlust in their eyes, something I had never witnessed before. It had a distinct smell, like a pack of hungry animals. I had a brief memory of a mob of ravens I had seen once; they had landed on a sparrow and pecked it to death, eating out its brains like a delicacy.

I instinctively moved further back into the cell in an effort to escape their wrath. I was unable to still my fear.

"Come forward, woman!" Cassius bellowed. But my legs had turned to wood, and I could not take a step. The priest came into my cell and pulled me out by the arms, then pushed me forward towards the angry crowd.

"Here she is! Will you do what you must to get rid of this stain, this blight upon the kingdom?"

"Stand down!" said a loud female voice of authority from somewhere behind the crowd.

It was the Bríg Brigu! She had appeared out of nowhere with her followers. They must have ridden day and night! She stepped forward, and the people parted like waves of the sea.

Her appearance was, to me, like the glorious sun rising up out of a cold, murky ocean. She had never looked so beautiful to my eyes, with her long hair streaming in the breeze. She carried a polished silver shield and a silver spear, like some fairy queen from the ancient tales. The white silver gleamed in the sunlight, blinding those who dared to look too long upon her. The faint smell of beeswax wafted from her snowy white robes, and as I inhaled the aroma could I feel my fear melting, liquid honey soothing my heart.

The Druid of Cell Daro were with her, gorgeously attired in their finest robes and jewelry, also carrying polished shields, burnished spears, and daggers. It was an awesome sight.

"Who is this woman?" the priest demanded.

Suddenly the people were afraid. The crowd that followed the Bríg Brigu was even larger than the assembled villagers from In Medon. And the Bríg Brigu herself had thick, ankle-length, glossy hair; terrible flashing eyes; and a massive torque around her neck. They had no idea who she was, but she was clearly very powerful.

Now the crowd stood still as sheep, mute and unsure of which way to turn or who to follow.

"Take care!" the Bríg Brigu said in a tone that cut like a sword. "If you harm one hair of this poor innocent woman's head, there will be a huge calamity upon your land."

"Don't listen to her. She is a witch!" Father Cassius cried.

The Bríg Brigu continued, ignoring the priest. "I promise that if you harm your princess, the sun goddess Áine Clí herself will blight your crops and sicken your animals!"

"She is a sorceress! Don't listen to her!" Father Cassius screamed.

The Bríg Brigu continued: "I say wait. Within three days the Goddess will pronounce her judgment. If nothing happens to hurt your fields or cattle, it will be because your new god Ísu has triumphed. But if a terrible calamity comes upon your homes and fields, it will be because the Goddess herself is seeking to defend her priestess. Will you not wait for the results of the test?"

"Don't listen to her; she is lying!" Father Cassius said.

Dálach-gaes took advantage of the frightened indecision of the crowd to step forward and attempt to sway them.

"Yes! Give her three days. Is that too much to ask when a life is at stake? Let's see whose god is most powerful!"

The people had not forgotten the exalted rank of the Druid, no matter that their holy nemed was now hidden behind screens of yew. They remembered the many sicknesses that the Druid had healed, the wounds stitched, the babies birthed. They looked from the priest to Dálach-gaes and then to the Bríg Brigu and her followers, awed and confused.

The atmosphere felt as if the air had been let out of a giant pig's bladder. Everyone seemed deflated except the Bríg Brigu and her followers, who bristled with energy and will.

I was shoved back into my cell, and the iron key was turned again in its lock. But this time I was given hot food, clean clothes, hot water, soap, and blankets, and my closest friends and Artrach stayed by the door to keep me company unimpeded. I was secure once more, safe in the midst of a great hive of love and caring.

33

The Bríg Brigu, an eminent guest, was not expected to sleep on the ground near my cell. Instead, she was settled into the round-house of Dálach-gaes and Niamh, while her highest-ranking followers went to the schoolhouse or slept in the open on the ground of the nemed. Their horses were quartered in the barns of the dun.

When he wasn't by my side, Artrach went hunting for deer. Many of the others, including the ban-Druid, went fishing and foraging for greens in the forest. We could not count on the hospitality of Tuile-laith and Eógan, who were ruling the kingdom until a formal election could be declared.

"I feel as if we are at war," Niamh confided to the Bríg Brigu.

"That's because we are," the Bríg Brigu replied. "I can foresee that this will be a very long and protracted battle, with many turnings of the tides. But surely the wisdom of the old ways will prevail. Pure water will dissolve even the hardest stone eventually."

And so we waited. One day passed, then two.

Nessa came to visit me, producing thick beeswax candles from under her cloak. "May the glow of these candles remind you of the Fire Altar. Know that prayers are being said for you at every watch, night and day."

"What do you think is going to happen?" I asked Artrach as he sat pressed close to the iron bars late one night.

"We have to have faith that the Bríg Brigu knows what she is doing," he said.

We fell asleep then, he lying on the ground next to me and the cold iron bars between our two forms. When he was near me like that, it always felt as if no evil could possibly befall us—we became home for each other, our two bodies making one complete world.

The next morning the Bríg Brigu woke everyone before sunrise and told them to sit in a large circle in the field in front of the prisoner's mound. Father Cassius was alerted by the guards and came running to see what diabolical magic was being enacted.

"Just wait and be silent," said the Bríg Brigu, "no matter what he does or says."

Everyone sat still, ignoring the priest.

"You will be lost on the Day of Judgment! The Lord is quick to testify against sorcerers, perjurers, magicians, adulterers, and whores! You are the ones who rebel against the Light. You do not know its ways or its paths!"

The priest was running around the circle now, hopping from one foot to the other in his zeal.

"You may sing now," said the Bríg Brigu to her followers.

The circle of people began to hum a little, finding a note, and then gradually a full-throated song emerged:

Hail to thee, Áine
Fiery torch of many blessings
Our faithful light in every season
Traversing the skies
On the wings of the morning!
Mother of the stars
Pour your light upon us
Glory to thee! Glory to thee! Glory to thee!

Father Cassius continued running around the circle, trying to silence the singers. My father's wolfhounds had come to investigate the commotion and were yapping and biting at the priest's heels.

I could feel great shimmering waves of power rising from the ground to the skies and I knew that magic was afoot, but I had no idea what it might be.

The Bríg Brigu motioned to Dálach-gaes and Niamh to follow her into the center of the ring. The three of them sat down, calmly holding hands in the exact center of the circle. The Druid were singing louder now, in an effort to drown out the objections of Father Cassius. This scene continued for a very long time, and every so often the Bríg Brigu or Dálach-gaes would gaze towards the heavens. I did not know why; I thought that maybe they were seeking a sign from Áine Clí.

A crowd of curious villagers and warriors had gathered and stood in clumps at intervals around the ring of singing Druid, taking in the mysterious rite.

I offered up my own prayer to Áine for protection and guidance.

The sun was halfway to noontide when it happened. The birds began to fall out of the sky in clusters, darting for the trees. Cattle that had been cutting the grass before the gates of the dun suddenly formed an orderly line and headed back to the dairy barns, even though they had been recently milked. A black veil was being drawn across the shining eye of the Goddess as all creation prepared for night—in the middle of the morning!

All except the humans, that is. Cries of fear and pleas for protection issued from the mouths of the onlookers. The Bríg Brigu raised her hands to the skies and, as if it were a planned signal, the singers went completely silent.

Now the sinister black veil completely swallowed the sun. The cries of dismay from the gathered onlookers grew even louder than before. Some fell to their knees in shock; others ran back to their homes to tend to their children and the aged.

The Bríg Brigu stood up, calmly addressing Father Cassius. "Our Goddess has made her wishes plain. She has turned her back upon this kingdom and on these people because of what you have done." She swept her arm in a circle, indicating the frightened crowds. "She will not smile upon us again until you release Princess Aislinn."

"Lies! What you see is the lord God turning his gaze away from your depraved rites! He will uncover the skies when he pleases. And he won't be pleased until all the Druid are all driven into the sea!"

But the people had their own ideas. A group of men lunged forward, assaulting the guards before my cell and pulling the iron key from the belt of one of them. Then they stormed over to let me out.

The warriors of the dun stood by watching as if they had turned to stone, making no move to aid the guards. It seemed they favored the actions of the men who sought to free me. The very moment I was liberated from my cage, the black veil started to slide away, slowly uncovering the blazing eye of the Goddess.

"I told you so! Áine is pleased! Now your grain and your herds and your lives will be safe!" said the Bríg Brigu.

"O Áine, patroness of the crops, who gives birth to the sheaves of grain, we honor you!"

The Bríg Brigu fell to her knees, and all the Druid followed suit. I shook with shock, relief, and joy. The people outside the circle were dancing, ecstatic to have regained the favor of their ancient goddess.

And then a further miracle—it still brings tears to my eyes to recount the incredible blessing we received that day. When the sun's eye was completely uncovered, a bright triple rainbow appeared, making three perfect circles around the sun.

Father Justan walked up to Abbott Cassius, and I overheard their conversation.

"See the holy sign of hope? This is one of God's miracles, is it not?"

"Miracle? I doubt it. That old sorceress somehow knew that there would be an eclipse on this day. The Druid are well known for their knowledge of the sun and the stars."

"But why do you feel compelled to spread such terrible lies about them?"

Father Cassius paused. "I would do all and anything in my power to bring them into the fold and put an end to their disgusting habits and rituals."

"Cassius, did not our Lord say 'Judge not, that ye be not judged'? We must strive to live in love with all of God's creatures, even if their ways are difficult for us to understand," said Father Justan. Then he turned towards my open cell to congratulate me and to offer his blessings.

That same day, before the townsfolk could change their minds, the Druid—including Niamh, Dálach-gaes, their students and children—took their horses, carts, and any other available conveyance and began the long journey back to the Fire Temple. It was a drastic step, but one we knew we had to take for the sake of protecting our lives and our teachings. We left my father's dun to the spiritual guidance of Father Justan and to the tender mercies of the Cristaidi missionaries to better focus our efforts on preserving the Druid path.

Artrach and I traveled in the back of a cart. He held me in a tight embrace all the way back to the Fire Temple until the warmth of his heart, blood, and bone finally penetrated every secret pocket of fear that I carried.

I was not foolish enough to think that all the effort that had gone into my rescue was for me alone. I knew that the Bríg Brigu and the Druid were working to preserve the dignity of our ancient faith. To them, I represented all that was being pushed aside in the new world that was coming.

But there was one person for whom all this effort was just for me. That was Artrach, the other half of my body and my soul.

By the time we had reached the borders of the temple lands, I was a priestess once more: proud, confident, and ready to honor my gods and the earth, moon, and sun.

Dálach-gaes, Niamh, Artrach, and I took up residence in the Fire Temple while the others melted into the surrounding tuath. From that day forth, only an eye that was schooled in the mysteries would ever be able to pick the Druid out from the farmers, beekeepers, and craftsmen of the village.

Two moontides later, we had word that my brother Eógan had been elected ard-ri. He had led a successful raid to the north and recaptured all the cattle my father had lost. He also brought back several prize breeding bulls, which cemented his reputation with the tribes.

Not long after that, I discovered that I was with child.

"It's time that we were handfast in the eyes of everyone," Artrach declared.

He secured the permission of the Bríg Brigu, my spiritual guide, and also of Dálach-gaes and Niamh, who stood in as my foster parents, and immediately began to work on a roundhouse for us and our future family. It simply would not have been practical to have a newborn infant in the Fire Temple, wailing and fussing throughout the night.

He chose a secluded location at the edge of the forest where a little stream flowed and sang merrily. With all the Druid pitching in, it took only a few days for our new hearth and home to be ready. Nessa made sure that a small bronze cauldron was buried directly under the soil of the hearth, and she also gave Artrach a bronze oil lamp to hang from the roof, directly over the hearth stones—"So that your house will be a miniature Fire Temple, just like every other roundhouse in this tuath," she explained.

The night before our handfasting, Artrach and I had separate baths in the Fire Temple, to soak in sacred herbs of purification. Vervain and juniper were chief among them, as I recall. We also trimmed our hair and offered it to the flames of the Fire Temple's hearth as a gift for the ancestors.

Dálach-gaes and Niamh offered butter to the flames of the Fire Altar and sponsored a feast of goats, sheep, and a cow. They slaughtered the animals in the ritual way, offering the parts to each of the elements and to the earth and sky before securing the animals on the roasting spits. Looking into the eyes of each beast, they first made sure it was calm, and then they cleanly slit its throat. They supervised as the skins were pulled off and the entrails removed.

As each skinned and cleaned animal was taken away for cooking in the roasting pits, Dálach-gaes and Niamh kept back a bit of its blood and a small portion of meat to place into the Fire Altar. The night before the handfasting, they joined the firekeeper at her post under the stars and placed choice bits of the animals into the flames, piece by piece, repeating by turns the ancient song of offering:

> *May your blood flow to the waters*
> *May the waters be pure*
> *May your bones feed the rocks*
> *Lending their strength*
> *May your flesh feed the soil*
> *Making it fruitful*
> *May your hair nourish the plants*
> *And cause them to flourish*
> *May your eyes join*
> *The fires in the sky*
> *May your brain join*
> *The clouds in the heavens*
> *May your skull join*
> *The great vault of the sky*
> *May your spirit run free*
> *In the sun-filled pastures*
> *Of the gods.*[16]

Then they walked together to the cow barn in the moonlight and poured a leather bucket of blood over the brownie stone, where offerings of first milk were usually made as a special gift for the land spirits.

Some of the other Druid carried the entrails deep into the forest and made an offering to the foxes, ravens, and crows, asking that they not despoil our fields.

In the morning Niamh carried a living coal from the Fire Temple to my hearth to start a new flame. Artrach and I walked alone three times sunwise around the hearth of the Fire Temple to bid it a formal farewell since it would no longer be our home. Then we and the assembled guests went outside and circled around the Fire Altar. Using a branch of oak, the presiding priestess sprinkled us with sky water from the blue ceramic bowl that was always present near the flames.

The ancestors and deities were invoked, and Dálach-gaes handed butter to Artrach three times, which he then passed to me three times. I made three offerings of butter to the Fire Altar in the name of the three worlds and then poured a cup of mid from a silver beaker into a small silver cup.

I handed the cup to Artrach and he accepted it, showing to all his willingness to marry me. He took a swallow then handed the cup back to me, and I drank the rest. Then Artrach and I walked together, hand in hand, around the fire three times.

At the last, Artrach was finally able to slip a ring of pure gold upon my finger.

"It's an extra blessing to be getting a wife of proven fertility!" he laughingly said to the assembled Druid as he placed the ring on my hand and then kissed me full on the mouth.

When the formal ceremony was done, everyone trooped down the hill to our new home and the already bright hearth where Niamh was waiting. Before any of us could enter the house, she stood in the doorway and intoned the ancient fire blessing:

> *I lit the flames as Brighid would*
> *The flames under her cauldron*
> *I lit the flames as Brighid would*
> *The flames of her forge*
> *I lit the flames as Brighid would*
> *The reddest coals of wisdom*

May she preserve this house
From foundation to roof tree
And all who dwell in it
Health, happiness, and prosperity
Be upon this house and family![17]

And then everyone was invited to enter and admire Artrach's handiwork.

"I used rowan wood wherever I could, to protect us from harm," he said proudly, pointing to the wooden spokes of the ceiling that held up the bundles of golden thatch. Everyone agreed that this was a sensible precaution. Nessa's oil lamp glowed with three oil-soaked wicks, bathing the one-room house in honey-colored light.

Bards sang and played their harps and drums for us outside on the lawn. The younger Druid danced on the grass and leapt the fires for luck, and everyone had their fill of mid, roasted meats, honey-sweetened breads and pies, and other delicacies.

Crithid, who had been moping about, looked visibly brightened at the feast. He had found a pretty flaxen-haired girl who was obviously delighted to return his attentions. I was very glad to see that.

The celebration went on for three days and nights, with guests coming and going from every corner of the tuath. Each celebrant brought us some useful tool or household item that we might need. There was a beautifully carved chest for our grain stores and another for our clothing, and piles of woven plaids and cloths were heaped on top. The Bríg Brigu gave me a quern that was handed down from her own family; I could feel the ancestral spirits that still clung to it. Before long I was appealing to them for guidance when grinding wheat or spelt. One guest even brought me a loom, which I later used outside on sunny days.

By the third day I swear I had enough baskets, pots, dishes, spoons, bowls, blankets, linens, furs, and baby clothes for three families. There was a massive pile of dry peat to one side of the house, just outside the door, and what looked like a small mountain of cut firewood neatly stacked on the other side. Everything was well covered with thick straw to keep it from the damp.

In my heart I had forgiven the Bríg Brigu for her plan to keep me and Artrach apart. I understood that everything she did was for the good of the Druid of the present and of the future.

"I am very pleased that you are bringing the next generation into this world," said the Bríg Brigu to me and Artrach when we had a moment alone, "even if it means that Aislinn won't be the next Bríg Brigu, at least for a while.

"For we are now entering the time of the dark sun, when our task is to hide and preserve our knowledge, traditions, and rituals. But one day an awakening sun will dawn, and then it will be our mission to bring our beliefs and ways back out once more, for the entire world to see.[18]

"There will come a day when all the gods will be honored. The people will finally understand that this is the way to true peace, because wherever only one god is honored and all the others dishonored, that is ever the quickest path to war."

epilogue

Spring came at last. Now the days were so warm that the Druid came to take down the sheepskin coverings from my windows so that I could see the budding trees against the clear blue sky. A yellow pool of sunlight fell across my bed, and I basked in its warm glow.

I turned to the neophyte priestess who was so important to me. "Your grandfather, Artrach, and I never found the time to tell you these tales in full, busy as we were with our students and our other obligations."

There were tears in her eyes as she met my gaze.

"Will you promise me something, my child?" I asked.

"Of course," she answered.

"Promise never to forget these things that I have told you."

"I promise," she said.

She was Druid-trained, and I knew that her word was true.

Bail, a Brighde, ar an obair.
Bless, O Brighid, the work.

hISTORICAL NOTE

According to tradition, there were once five major ritual fires in Éire. One was in County Cork, one in Sligo, one in County Offaly, and one at Cill Daire (Kildare). These fires were circular and surrounded by hedge enclosures. Women tended them, and the flames were always started by friction and fanned by bellows (never the breath). The fifth sacred fire was at Uisneach, County Meath, in the exact geographic center of the island, under the supervision of the Ard-Drui.

The most famous of these Fire Altars in modern times is the one once maintained by Saint Brighid and her nuns at Cill Daire, built on the foundations of an earlier Pagan Fire Temple. Modern nuns have symbolically re-lit the sacred flames by keeping a candle burning in Brighid's honor.

The perpetual fire of the Archdruid at Uisneach, County Meath, was the place where, according to tradition, Mide lit the first sacred fire. Flames from the central fire at Uisneach were transported by runners to every province at Beltaine (May 1) after all household fires had been put out, an act of spiritual unification in a land fractured into many small, competing kingdoms.

A bag of grain and a pig were sent to Uisneach from every chief in Éire each year in payment for the sacred flames.

Uisneach was a public park for all Irish citizens to enjoy until the government of Ireland recently sold it to a cow farmer. Now the ancient Fire Temple of the Ard-Drui rests peacefully under the cows, grass, and the hawthorns on the hill, waiting for the day when it will be brought to light and honored properly once more.

For more details on these sacred fires, please see Ó Duinn, 63–69.

NOTES

1. From *Audacht Morainn*, edited by Fergus Kelly, Dublin Institute for Advanced Studies, Dublin, 1976. Old Irish law text of advice to kings.

2. Traditional invocation attributed to Saint Patrick from the prayer known as Patrick's Breastplate.

3. For more details on the uses of heather, rowan, and reeds for healing, please see my book *A Druid's Herbal of Sacred Tree Medicine* (Destiny Books, 2008).

4. Based on the ancient Sanskrit "Salutation to All Creation": "*Bhumi-Mangalam, Udaka-Mangalam, Agni-Mangalam, Vayu-Mangalam, Gagana-Mangalam, Surya-Mangalam, Chandra-Mangalam* (salutation to the earth, salutation to the water, salutation to the fire, salutation to the wind, salutation to the sky, salutation to the moon, salutation to the universe)…"

5. Story adapted from The Cattle-Raid of Cooley (Táin Bó Cúalnge).

6. For more on the Law of Bees, please see T. Charles-Edwards and F. Kelly, "BechBretha: An Old Irish Law Tract on Bee Keeping, Early Irish Series, Vol. 1," Dublin, 1983.

7. Invocation of the Goddess Brighid by Ellen Evert Hopman. Old Irish translation by Alexei Kondratiev.

8. For a further explanation of the eclipse cycle, please see NASA's eclipse website and the Saros Cycle at eclipse.gsfc.nasa .gov/SEsaros/SEperiodicity.html.

9. While visiting Cornwall and other once Celtic areas, I was struck by how the stone circles often had nineteen stones. I used my poetic imbas to come up with a plausible explanation. See these examples: Merry Maidens, Cornwall (www.stonepages.com/england/merrymaidens.html); Callanish, Lewis, Scotland (www.stonesofwonder.com/callanis.htm); Casterton stone circle, Cumbria, England (www.timetravel-britain.com/articles/stones/stones.shtml); Boscawen Un Circle (Nine Maidens), Cornwall (www.pznow.co.uk/historic1/stonecircles.html); Torhouse Stone Circle, Wigtown, Scotland (www.ancient-stones.co.uk/dumfries/011/017/details.htm); White Moor Down, Devon, England (www.megalithics.com/england/whitmoor/whitmain.htm).

10. Loosely inspired by Carmina Gadelica 533.

11. This ritual is based on a Vedic rite performed in the holy city of Gaya, where a person passes through the natural tunnel called the Brahma-Yoni to make offerings that absolve him or her of all debts due to their ancestors and also liberates their ancestors from the horrors of the netherworld.

12. Loosely based on Carmina Gadelica 84.

13. Inspired by Carmina Gadelica 132, "Charm for a Broken Bone," and similar Anglo-Saxon and Celtic healing charms.

14. Loosely based on the ancient Irish poem called "Fer Fio's Cry."

15. Based on a *Rennes Dindsenechas* poem on the Yew of Ross, one of the five magical trees of Ireland.

16. Inspired by rituals found in the Rig Veda such as "the sacrifice of the horse" (fn p. 92), where thirty-four of the horse's ribs (he has thirty-six) are distributed, one to the sun, one to the moon, five to the planets, and twenty-seven to the constellations.

17. Loosely inspired by hymns in the Carmina Gadelica such as 339, Blessing of the House.

18. This is actually a prophecy from the indigenous elders of Mexico, who said seven hundred years ago that the world was about to enter the time of the "Dark Sun" and that the knowledge kept by traditional religions had to be held and protected. The prophecy states that we who are alive today are about to enter the time of the "Awakening Sun," and we must send out messages of healing to the world and seek true oneness with all people, not just tolerance. The prophecy seems fitting for all indigenous paths and religions, and so I have included it here.

- For more information on filidecht, the grades of poets, and laws pertaining to poets, see Liam Breatnach, editor, "Uraicecht na Ríar—The Poetic Grades in Early Irish Law" (Dublin Institute for Advanced Studies, Dublin, 1987).
- For more information on Celtic uses of plants, please see my books *A Druid's Herbal for the Sacred Earth Year*, *A Druid's Herbal of Sacred Tree Medicine*, and *Scottish Herbs and Fairy Lore*.

bibliography and sources

Bamford, Christopher, and William Parker Marsh, editors. *Celtic Christianity: Ecology and Holiness.* Great Barrington, MA: Lindisfarne Press, 1987.

Bitel, Lisa M., and Felice Lifshitz, editors. *Gender and Christianity in Medieval Europe: New Perspectives.* Philadelphia: University of Pennsylvania Press, 2008.

Campbell, John Gregorson. *The Fians; or, Stories, Poems & Traditions of Fionn and His Warrior Band: Collected Entirely from Oral Sources.* Elibron Classics (a facsimile of the 1891 edition published by David Nutt, London), 2005.

Dames, Michael. *Mythic Ireland.* London: Thames and Hudson Ltd., 1992.

Elder, Isabel Hill. *Celt, Druid and Culdee.* Thousand Oaks, CA: Artisan, 1990.

Green, Miranda. *Celtic Goddesses: Warriors, Virgins and Mothers.* New York: George Braziller, 1996.

Henderson, George. *Survivals in Belief Among the Celts.* London: MacMillan and Co. Ltd., 1911.

Hopman, Ellen Evert. *A Druid's Herbal for the Sacred Earth Year.* Rochester, VT: Destiny Books, 1994.

———. *A Druid's Herbal of Sacred Tree Medicine.* Rochester, VT: Destiny Books, 2008.

———. *Scottish Herbs and Fairy Lore.* Sunland, CA: Pendraig Publishing, 2011.

Hutton, Ronald. *The Pagan Religions of the Ancient British Isles*. Oxford, England: Blackwell Publishers, 1992.

Mackillop, James. *Dictionary of Celtic Mythology*. New York: Oxford University Press, 1998.

Ó Duinn, Seán. *The Rites of Brigid: Goddess and Saint*. Blackrock, Ireland: Columba Press, 2005.

O'Flaherty, Wendy Doniger, translator. *The Rig Veda*. London: Penguin, 1981.

O'Kelly, Claire. *Illustrated Guide to Newgrange and the Other Boyne Monuments*. Blackrock, Ireland: Ardnalee, 1978.

Web Resources

www.libraryireland.com/Social-History.php

Appendix

The Evidence for Female Druids

Gaine daughter of pure Gumor,
Nurse of mead-loving Mide,
Surpassed all women though she was silent;
She was learned and a seer and a Druid.

—from "The Metrical Dinsenchas," a history of the places of
Ireland, compiled by medieval monks

Most modern Pagans are Wiccans or Witches, according to the few
surveys that have been done; we Druids are still a tiny minority.
Women of Celtic heritage have told me that they did not pursue the
Druid path because "the Druids were all men"—but as more and more
women study Celtic history, get degrees, do research, write books, and
teach in the colleges, the word is finally getting out that this is not so.
But for millennia it has been a well-kept secret.

Some of the blame for this misconception can be placed on the
Roman historians who reported on Celtic culture, even as they deci-
mated the Druids, who were the intelligentsia of the tribes. The
Romans tended to ignore, downplay, or overlook the true status of
Celtic women.

This article originally appeared in *The Magical Buffet*, February 2008
(http://themagicalbuffet.com/blog1/2008/02/29/female-Druids/).

The next groups to document Celtic society were male Christian monks, who also tended to ignore and downplay the status of Celtic women while capturing the tales and oral histories in their scriptoria. Finally, as modern archaeology and scholarship focused on Celtic artifacts and history, scholars until very recently were almost all men, who downplayed or ignored the role of powerful women in ancient Celtic times. But the evidence was always there for those who cared to find it.

The word *Druid* derives from the Indo-European *deru*, which carries meanings such as "truth," "true," "hard," "enduring," "resistant," and "tree." *Deru* evolved into the Greek word *drus* ("oak") and referred over time to all trees as well as the words *truth* and *true*. *Id* comes from *wid*, "to know", related to both *wisdom* and *vision*. A *Dru-id* is a truth-knower and a true-knower, one with solid and enduring wisdom, a tree-knower, and an expert.

The Proto-Indo-European word *dru* meant "oak" and is related to *Druid*, so *Druid* also means "oak-knower." Oaks are the most balanced of trees; their roots grow as deep as the tree is high. They give the hottest fire (excepting the ash tree) and provide medicine via their leaves and bark as well as food (acorns) for humans, pigs, and deer. They attract the attention of the gods (via lightning) and survive to live up to a thousand years.

To be a Druid was and is to perform a tribal function. No king or queen could function without a Druid at their side; the ruler and Druid were described as "two kidneys" of a kingdom. It was the Druid who knew the laws and precedents necessary for a ruler to pass judgment.

The Druids were poets and prophets, astrologers and astronomers, seers, magicians, and diviners. They memorized the laws and kept the tribal histories and genealogies in their heads. They were ambassadors, lawyers, judges, herbalists, healers, and practitioners of battle magic. They were sacrificers, satirists, sacred singers, storytellers, teachers of the children of the nobility, ritualists, and philosophers, skilled in natural science and mathematics. They specialized in one or several of these callings and spent twenty years or more in training. We know that Druids from all areas went to Britain, specifically to present-day

Wales, for regular gatherings, and so their practices and beliefs must have been somewhat uniform. What we know of the Druids comes to us from the written accounts of eyewitnesses, from literary tradition, and from archaeology. Greek and Roman historians documented the Druids that they met; Julius Caesar, Diodorus Siculus, Strabo, Ammianus Marcellinus, Pliny, Diogenes Laertius, Suetonius, Pomponius Mela, Lucan, Tacitus, Dion Chrysostum, Lampridius, Vopiscus, Decimus Magnus, Ausonius, Hippolytus, and others wrote their versions of Druid history.

Pliny gives us the only description of a Druid ritual that we have (the Druids preferred to keep their teachings in oral form, feeling they were too sacred to write down). He describes a white-clad Druid climbing an oak tree on the "sixth day of the moon" to harvest mistletoe with a "golden sickle." Of course gold is too soft to cut herbs with, so any sickle would probably have been made of bronze, and we can only guess that the "sixth day of the moon" means six days after the first appearance of the new moon.

Tacitus gives us the vivid account of the slaughter of the Druids by Roman soldiers on the island of Mona (Angelsey) in Wales. He says there were cursing black-clad women there defending the island. Since the island was the most sacred stronghold of the British Druids, one can assume that these women were ban-Druid (female Druids), though since he does not say this outright, we can never be sure.

Strabo describes a group of religious women living on an island at the mouth of the Loir River, but he does not call them Druids. In the *Historia Augusta* (a late Roman collection of biographies, in Latin, of the Roman Emperors from 117 to 284 CE), we learn that Diocletian and Aurelian consulted with female Druids, as did Alexander Severus.

In Irish traditional accounts there are references to "bandruid" and "banfilid" (female poets). Fedelm is a female seer, and Accuis, Col, and Eraise are female Druids mentioned in the Tain (The Cattle Raid of Cooley). Eirge, Eang, and Banbhuana are Druidesses mentioned in the Siege of Knocklong, and Dub and Gaine are mentioned in the Dinsenchas.

Fedelma was a woman in Queen Medb of Connacht's court who was a "banfili" (female poet) trained in Alba (Britain). The death of female poet Uallach, daughter of Muinechán, who was the "woman poet of Ireland," is mentioned in the Annals of Innisfallen for the year 934 and the Brehon Laws describe heavy penalties for illegal female satirists (whom they compare to female werewolves!). It is clear from these accounts that at least some women had attained the rank of Druid.

To shore up the evidence, it is helpful to look at the status of women in Celtic society before the Roman and Christian incursions and after. The marriage laws are an interesting place to start. The ancient Brehon Laws recognized nine types of marriage. In the first degree (the most desirable), both partners came to the union with equal wealth and status. In the second degree, the husband came to the union with more wealth, so he was in charge. In the third degree, the wife came with more wealth, so she was in charge. In all cases divorce was available to wives, and in the first two degrees of marriage the husband had to pay a bride price to her father the first year, and every year after that a large portion of the coibche (dowry) went to the bride herself so that she could remain independent if the marriage failed. In the event of a divorce, each spouse could claim any property they had brought to the union, and the wife kept all the coibche she had accumulated. (Christian women would not see this kind of fair treatment again until very recent times.)

Plutarch in On the Bravery of Women states that Celtic women participated in assemblies, mediated quarrels, and negotiated treaties; for example, one between Hannibal and the Volcae (this kind of ambassadorial work is a specifically Druidic function). Strabo says that Armorican priestesses (in modern-day Brittany) were independent of their husbands.

We know that Celtic women wore trousers (the Celts invented trousers, and there is a statue of a woman so dressed in the British Museum). Gallic females went to war with their husbands, and Irish Celtic women fought alongside their men. In some Roman reports, they said the women were even fiercer than the men! (It took a series of laws issued over several centuries after the Christian missionaries arrived to wean Irish women away from weapons, indicating problems with compliance.)

In the first century CE, Tacitus wrote that "the Celts make no distinction between male and female rulers," and powerful Celtic women appear in the tales. By tradition Macha Mong Ruad (red mane) founded Emain Macha (Navan Fort) in Ulster. The two most famous warriors in Irish history—Finn MacCumhail and Cú Chulainn—were both trained by women. Finn was raised by two females, a Druidess and a warrior woman who taught him the crafts of war and of hunting, while Cú Chulainn learned the arts of war from Scáthach, who had her own martial arts school.

Boudica was a Celtic queen who led the last British uprising against the Romans in AD 60. She was a priestess of Andraste, goddess of victory. Saint Brighid of Kildare (*Kil-Dara*, Church of the Oak) had a different kind of power. She was the daughter of the Druid Dubhtach, and according to the *Rennes Dindsenchas* was a "bandrui" (female Druid) before she converted to Christianity. She had both men and women in her religious community, and she and her nuns kept a Fire Altar, which was tended continuously until 1220, when an archbishop ordered it quenched. This Fire Altar mirrored the perpetual fire of the Ard-Drui (Arch-Druid) that had burned at Uisneach for centuries. Thankfully, the fire has been re-lit in modern times and is now being tended once again by nuns and lay folk in Kildare and all over the world.

Archaeology gives us more evidence for female Druids. An inscription was found in Metz, France, that was set up by a Druid priestess to honor the god Sylvanus and the local nymphs of the area. It was found on the Rue de Récollets: "*Silvano sacr(um) et Nymphis loci Arete Druis antistita somnio monita d(edit)* Arete the Druidess, high priestess, guided by her dreams, offered a sacrifice to Silvanus and the local nymphs" (*Année Épigraphique* 1983, 711).

Two famous burials, the Vix Burial and the Reinham Burial, point to very powerful women of their time. The Princess of Vix (who may have been a priestess) dates from the late sixth to fifth centuries BCE in present-day Burgundy, France. She was a woman of wealth and authority, whose rich grave goods came from as far away as the Mediterranean Sea. Her wood-paneled, chambered grave held a huge bronze "krater" (a large ornamental urn used to mix wine and water for banquets), elaborate jewelry of bronze, amber, diorite, and serpentine, and a golden torque (a neck ring), symbol of noble status. She also had fibulae (brooches) inset with Italian coral.

Many other female burials have been discovered between the Rhine and the Moselle Rivers, where the women are laid out on wagons with rich jewelry and more impressive grave goods than some of the warrior chieftains of the time. The Reinham Burial dates to the fourth century BCE by the River Biles in Germany and was an oak-lined chamber filled with precious objects and jewelry. The body was laid out on a chariot, with food and drink provided for her otherworldly sojourn. She was also buried with a torque on her chest, symbolic of her noble status.

So what happened? Why did an indigenous culture that featured educated and powerful women devolve into a culture where women were demoted to the status of chattel?

By the first century CE in Britain, the Romans were actively and deliberately suppressing the Druids, who were the intellectual elite, the advisors to the nobility, and the glue that held the kingdoms together. Roman propaganda campaigns claimed that the Druids were the perpetrators of "savage superstition" and of horrific human sacrifice (at the same time that the bloody and violent Roman circuses were going on). Druidesses were described as seers who were working on their own, rather than as powerful royal advisors and clergy. A policy of deliberate extermination was carried out, brought to conclusion by the terrifying slaughter of the Druids at Angelsey.

The Romans never conquered Ireland, and the worship of the Pagan gods continued there officially until the death of King Diarmat in 565 CE. (Unofficially, it goes on to this day.) But as Christianity gained power in all areas, Roman ideals of matronly behavior and womanhood took over, though in the few centuries that it was allowed to flourish, the Celtic Church continued to exalt powerful priestesses such as Brighid of Kildare and Beaferlic of Northumbria. As the Roman Christian Church gained ascendancy, female Druids were labeled "evil witches" and "sorcerers" as a way to smear their reputations and make people fear them. Religious orders founded by women were systematically dissolved upon their founder's death, preventing continuity of female-centered orders.

The Druids were demoted in the laws to figures of ridicule—mere magicians stripped of their sacral function and status. Women in Celtic areas were forbidden to bear arms, and their status dropped in most areas of life and society.

The current Druid revival of modern times began in the early eighteenth century, first in France and then in 1717 in England, the same year that the English Masons were established. The earliest English Druids of the current revival were all Masons and all men; the poet William Blake was a prominent example. Gradually over the last few centuries, as more was understood about the actual Druids of history, the Druid orders became more egalitarian in their membership until today, when most orders are roughly half male and half female. Women in most orders (the only exceptions being the old English-based orders with roots firmly in the eighteenth century) have the same opportunities to be leaders and clergy as men. Female Druids of today most often look back to our status in ancient times. We view ourselves as the inheritors of a rich ancestral lineage going back to the Iron Age. That does not mean we have an unbroken tradition; we are actively engaged in reconstructing the ancient indigenous European tribal religion (leaving out the nasty bits such as slavery, animal sacrifice, and head hunting, of course!). I took an informal poll of the women on the Whiteoak mailing list to see why they became Druids and what, if any, problems they have faced on this path. One said that she was thrilled to find a religious tradition that worships outside in daylight!

All the women who responded said they were voracious readers who, upon learning how much of Celtic history and tradition was still out there, became absorbed in the topic. The women all reported being scholars of one degree or another; in common with the ancient Druids, modern ones tend to be intellectuals (one of the worst insults you can hurl at a Druid is to call them a "fluffy bunny").

Several of them complained that in modern times, Druids are very hard to find. Unless one lives in a large metropolitan area, this is almost always the case. To put together a gathering of modern Druids, you will have to send notice out to several states.

Some female Druids report that they are Pagans who were not attracted to Wicca, which was, after all, invented in the 1930s by Gerald Gardner (see Ronald Hutton's excellent book *The Triumph of the Moon*). They wanted something that was tied to actual Celtic tradition.

Others had problems with Wiccan theology. Wicca is duotheistic; it assumes that all the goddesses are one goddess and all the gods are one god, so it hardly matters whom you call on in a ritual. The Celts, and every other indigenous Pagan tradition that I am aware of, were and are polytheistic. They see their deities as separate personalities with different and distinct functions, though some—for example, the Hindu-Vedic religions—posit an ultimate source for all the gods and goddesses and all creation, called the Atma in Vedic scripture. (Many Druids study Vedic texts because the Vedic people were the ancestors of the proto-Celts, and Vedic ritual and Celtic ritual must have had many similarities. We know that they had many basic principles in common: triple deities, making offerings to sacred fire and sacred water, the primacy of cows, etc.)

Another problem with modern Wicca for some is the so-called Wiccan Rede ("An' it harm none, do what you will"). This tenet has been used as an excuse to behave in self-centered ways that no tribal society would tolerate. Druids study the Brehon Laws, and we know that the ancients expected strict codes of behavior from all levels of society.

Wicca was revolutionary at its founding because it emphasized the role of the priestess in a way that had not been seen since ancient times. As a result, many Wiccan and witchcraft groups are led by women and composed of mostly women (or all women). Those who became female Druids found this to be unbalanced and not much different from male-dominated patriarchal Christianity, Judaism, or Islam. They sought a Pagan path with a healthier balance of males and females. Some report that they still have problems with sexism; even after they had attained the title of Arch-Druidess of their grove (a grove is the Druid equivalent of a coven), there were male Druids who would challenge their decisions in a way that they would never challenge a male Arch-Druid. They would continue to nag the Arch-Druidess, figuring that if they did so long enough she would give in to their opinions.

None of these women came to Druidism out of rebellion against another religion. They came to it from a love for nature and the old European tribal ways. I can identify with these reasonings; they are all familiar to me and true.

Notes

Thanks to Stacey Weinberger (of RDNA), Sín Sionnach (a solitary Druid), and Athelia Nihtscada (of RDNA), for their input. For an overview of ancient reports, see John Matthews's *The Druid Source Book* (London, 1996). For Brehon Laws and the laws of marriage, see Fergus Kelly's *Guide to Early Irish Law* (Dublin Institute for Advanced Studies, Dublin, 1991).

To explore the status of ancient Celtic women, see www.unc.edu/celtic/catalogue/femDruids

For more on sex and gender in Iron Age studies, see www2.iath.virginia.edu/Barbarians/Essays /gender_main.html

For more on modern shrines dedicated to the goddess Brighid, see shrineofbrighid.com/; www.ordbrighideach.org/raven/; and treesong.org/brighid/

For information about Druids and modern Druid orders worldwide, see The Order of the White Oak, World Druid Council,
Ord na Darach Gile—Comhairle Domhanda na nDraoí,
www.whiteoakDruids.org

Ellen Evert Hopman's home page: Please visit the site to order
books and DVDs, sign my guestbook, and contact me:
www.elleneverthopman.com

Druid Groups in Ireland

Doire Lois Muileann (Lismullin Grove): A group of people who
came together out of the 2007 Direct Action protests against
the construction of the M3 Motorway through the Tara Skryne
Valley. We come from many different walks of life and from
many different faiths; Druid, Catholic, Protestant, Hindu and
others. We follow in the footsteps of our indigenous ancestors
and guardians of the Sacred Valley at Tara seeking to keep
alive the traditions and customs of our people and our deep
connection to the land. In addition, many members are active
in the preservation of the Tara Skryne Valley against further
inappropriate development.

Our Grove is named Doire Lois Muillen (Lismullin Grove) in
honor of the Lismullin Henge, a unique ceremonial enclosure
which was demolished and preserved by record during the
construction of the M3 Motorway. For more information, see
www.taraskryne.com.

Druid Clan of Dana: The Druid Clan of Dana (DCD) is a
Foundation-Center Society of the Fellowship of Isis. It was
established by Olivia and Lawrence Durdin-Robertson in 1992.
See www.fellowshipofisis.com/Druidclanofdana.html

Irish College of Druids: Northern Ireland–based Druidism. See
www.irishDruidcollege.com/

Irish Druid Network: An organization run by Luke Eastwood to facilitate Druid communications. Includes grove and organization listings for Ireland and Northern Ireland: www.irishdruidnetwork.org/

Solas Bhríde (Brighid's light/flame): A small Christian-based center that has as its focus St. Brighid and Celtic spirituality. They seek to unfold the legacy of Brighid of Kildare and its relevance for the world. Organizers of a weeklong celebration in Kildare at Imbolc, with dancing, spiritual drumming and talks on Brighid: www.solasbhride.ie/

Druidschool: Learn and live as a Celtic Druid in Ireland. Run by Con Connor and Niamh Eustace, and based in County Roscommon: www.druidschool.com/

Caveat: I do not have personal experience with these Irish groups, with the sole exception of the Druid Clan of Dana. Lady Olivia Robertson made me an Arch-Druidess, Grove of Brighid, Druid Clan of Dana, when my first book came out (*Tree Medicine Tree Magic*, Phoenix Publishing Inc., 1991, now sadly out of print). I have visited with her at her castle in Ireland and taken the waters of her holy well. My grateful thanks go to Raymond MacSuibhne and to Carmel Diviney for providing this short list of modern Druid groups in Éire.

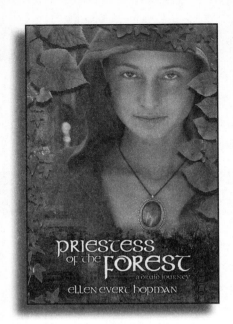

PRIESTESS
OF THE FOREST
a druid journey
ELLEN EVERT HOPMAN

Priestess of the Forest

A Druid Journey

Ellen Evert Hopman

In the tradition of Marion Zimmer Bradley's *Mists of Avalon*, Ellen Evert Hopman weaves Druid history and spirituality into an engaging love story. This Bardic teaching tale is set in a fictional third-century Ireland when Christianity is sweeping across the Celtic Isles. During this time of crisis, love blooms between Ethne, a Druid healer, and her patient, a Fennid warrior. Their passionate affair suffers a tragic blow when Ethne is called upon to become the high queen.

Told from the Druid perspective, Hopman recreates the daily life, magical practices, politics, and spiritual lives of the ancient Celts during this historic turning point. Druid holy days, rites, rituals, herbal lore, and more are brought to life in this Celtic fantasy—illuminating Druidic teachings and cultural wisdom.

978-0-7387-1262-8

$18.95

6 x 9

408 pp.

glossary; epilogue

THE
DRUID
ISLE
ELLEN EVERT HOPMAN
Author of Priestess of the Forest

The Druid Isle

Ellen Evert Hopman

The Druid Isle takes you into the world of Ethne, a Druid healer, and her warrior partner, Ruad. When their beautiful daughter Aífe undertakes training on a Druid island, she falls in love with Lucius, a handsome young man who has traded his priestly studies at a Christian monastery for the Druid life. But their love—and their beliefs—are threatened in the face of a lustful king and relentless Roman monks.

Set on a third-century island off the coast of Scotland, this instructional Celtic tale delves deeper into the spiritual mystery of the Druids and offers a fascinating look at the Romans, Gauls, and Britons.

978-0-7387-1956-6

$18.95

6 x 9

384 pp.

glossary, appendices, epilogue

To Write to the Author

If you wish to contact the author or would like more information about this book, please write to the author in care of Llewellyn Worldwide, and we will forward your request. Both the author and the publisher appreciate hearing from you and learning of your enjoyment of this book and how it has helped you. Llewellyn Worldwide cannot guarantee that every letter written to the author will be answered, but all will be forwarded. Please write to:

Ellen Evert Hopman
c/o Llewellyn Worldwide
2143 Wooddale Drive
Woodbury, MN 55125-2989

Please enclose a self-addressed stamped envelope for reply,
or $1.00 to cover costs. If outside the USA, enclose an
international postal reply coupon.

Many of Llewellyn's authors have websites with additional information and resources. For more information, please visit our website:

WWW.LLEWELLYN.COM